# the
# unchurched
# next door

## Other Books by Thom S. Rainer

Surprising Insights from the Unchurched
High Expectations
The Everychurch Guide to Growth *(coauthor)*
The Bridger Generation
Effective Evangelistic Churches
The Church Growth Encyclopedia *(coeditor)*
Experiencing Personal Revival *(coauthor)*
Giant Awakenings
Biblical Standards for Evangelists *(coauthor)*
Eating the Elephant
The Book of Church Growth
Evangelism in the Twenty-First Century *(editor)*

# the
# unchurched
# next door

### Understanding Faith Stages
### as Keys to Sharing Your Faith

# Thom S. Rainer

**ZONDERVAN™**

GRAND RAPIDS, MICHIGAN 49530 USA

**ZONDERVAN™**

*The Unchurched Next Door*
Copyright © 2003 by Thom S. Rainer

Requests for information should be addressed to:
Zondervan, *Grand Rapids, Michigan 49530*

---

Library of Congress Cataloging-in-Publication Data

Rainer, Thom S.
    The unchurched next door : understanding faith stages as keys to sharing your faith /
Thom S. Rainer.
      p. cm.
    Includes bibliographical references and indexes.
    ISBN 0-310-24860-4
    1. Non church-affiliated people.   2. Evangelistic work.   I. Title.
BV4921.3.R35  2003
269'.2—dc21

                             20030100040

---

This edition printed on acid-free paper.

Illustrations by Samuel S. Rainer III and Arthur T. Rainer. Copyright © 2003.

*Interior design by Tracey Moran*

*Printed in the United States of America*

---

03 04 05 06 07 08 09 /❖ DC/ 10 9 8 7 6 5 4 3 2 1

*To the boys of Christian Academy of Louisville,*

*who have brought so much joy and laughter to the Rainer home*

*for the past nine years.*

*And always to*

*Nellie Jo,*

*God's gift of a wife to me.*

# Contents

# Acknowledgments

As I write this, it is the week before Thanksgiving. And while I should always have a thankful heart, my sense of gratitude is especially profound at this moment. Another project is complete. Another book is done. I am relieved, grateful, and even wistful all at the same time.

The relief is for obvious reasons. Yes, I have written another book. But this book is hardly the work of one person. The research team members, whose photos you see on page 11, were incredible. Simply stated, they were the best team I have ever seen. They did not merely conduct research; they poured out their hearts to the lost and unchurched people they interviewed. "Thank you" is too small a response from me to these men and women.

Two leaders of the research team deserve special recognition. Twyla Fagan started this project as a Ph.D. student and part-time researcher. I was so impressed with her work that I hired her full time. Thank you, Twyla, for making this project one of the most fascinating and rewarding endeavors ever done. Your leadership was key.

Deborah White started this project as a student doing research. I was so impressed with her work that I hired her also. I cannot do too many research projects, because I will go broke hiring people!

Special appreciation goes to two exceptional women. Kathy Fredrick is my remarkable and accomplished secretary. She is simply the best. I cannot enumerate all that she did to make this project and book a reality. I hope Kathy will be around for many years to come.

Thanks also to Reba Pendleton, also known as "McEntire." God blessed our office when he brought your cheerful servant spirit to us.

This book is my second work with Zondervan and, like the first, it has been a joy. Paul Engle is a gentleman, a scholar, a Christlike example, and a great editor. I pray that this book will be but the second of many with Zondervan.

This book is first dedicated to a group of boys I love unashamedly. They are the friends of our three sons, who have spent literally thousands of hours at our home. The last wave of boys is now coming to an end as our youngest son, Jess, graduates from high school. The joy and laughter the boys of Christian Academy of Louisville have brought to the Rainer home is immeasurable. God knows how deeply I love these guys and how much I will miss them. They came into our home as boys, and they leave as men. Though I will miss them greatly, my life is much richer for the years I have spent with them.

The clock is ticking rapidly. In just a short while, the last of our three sons will leave the house. The day that I have dreaded in many ways is close. The empty nest is about to become a reality.

The depth of the love I have for Sam, Art, and Jess is unbelievable. Even as I type these word about my sons, I am wiping tears from my eyes. How I love you guys. You have been the greatest boys in the world. You put up with your dad's travels and writings and crazy schedule and loved me unconditionally. Yes, you have been the greatest boys in the world. But now you are men. And your dad is unbelievably proud of each of you.

But there is a positive side to the empty nest. For the years that God gives us, I will get to spend them with the love of my youth, the love of my middle years, and, God willing, the love of my senior years. Nellie Jo has been a stay-at-home mom for twenty-three years. She has held the home together while I worked, traveled, and wrote. Now I hope that most of my trips will not be alone. It is your time, Doll. Thanks for a quarter century of love, commitment, and understanding. The first twenty-five years have been great, but the best is yet to come.

# The Research Team

Jon Beck

Twyla Fagan

Travis Flemming

Guy Fredrick

Kathy Fredrick

Patrick Hanley

Bland Mason

Brad Morrow

Chris Myers

Reba Pendleton

Todd Randolph

Rusty Russell

Warner Smith

John Tolbert

Deborah White

## Introduction

# Why Justin Is Not Like Jane Is Not Like Jack

Life is what we make it, and then we die.

*—Justin M.,*
*U5 from Idaho*

Justin M. is a college-educated businessman on the ladder of success. He is also a self-professed atheist. He cannot recall a time when he believed any kind of god actually exists. Not surprisingly, Justin never attends church. He never prays, because "god is nobody to me."

This twenty-something young man has never been married. Ironically, his last roommate was a pastor. And Justin liked the pastor roommate because "he was caring and never bothered me with any talk about religion or god." In fact, Justin cannot recall any Christian sharing with him how to go to heaven. But that matters little to him, he told us, because "heaven is here on earth. It's what we want it to be. Hell is some girls I dated. I simply believe that when you die, you die."

Justin's belief about Jesus Christ is straightforward: "It's all a fabrication. I don't usually give it much thought." His few experiences with

Christians have been mostly negative. "A girl I dated has two very strong Christian parents, and they tried to derail my life because of my belief, or rather, nonbelief," he told us. "They just couldn't understand me and thought I was hurting their daughter with my beliefs. It made me sick."

Justin is a U5, an "unchurched 5" person, according to our study. As we will see shortly, a U5 is the most antagonistic to the gospel, to Christians, and to the church. As was the case with most of our interviews of U5s, we came away from the interview shaking our heads, wondering if there was any hope for the person.

> "Heaven is here on earth. It's what we want it to be. Hell is some girls I dated. I simply believe that when you die, you die."
>
> *Justin M.,*
> *U5 from Idaho*

Deborah White, one of the "stars" on the research team, interviewed Justin M. She discovered Justin through a friend at work. Listen to Deborah's comments about her encounter with Justin: "This guy is definitely a U5. He wants nothing to do with the church. Throughout the entire conversation he ranted and raved about Christians being hypocritical and negative and closed-minded to new ideas."

"Does Justin perceive any voids in his life?" we asked Deborah.

"On the surface, no," she replied. "He says 'he' is all he needs. He has what it takes to succeed and be happy. I will never forget his words, 'Life is what we make it, and then we die.'"

Like many of our researchers, Deborah could not help but get emotionally involved with these unchurched persons during the interview process. She concluded: "I don't know what would turn this guy around, besides the Holy Spirit, of course. I hope people are praying for this man every day. God *can* move mountains, and God *can* change the heart of an atheist."

## Welcome to the World of the Unchurched

Thanks for joining my research team and me on a most fascinating journey. The research team spent hundreds of hours listening to

14

unchurched people in all fifty states and Canada. We listened to the rich, the poor, and the middle class. We heard from people of many races and ethnic backgrounds. We heard from the uneducated and the highly educated. Older youth and adults of all age groups participated in our study. Indeed, the mosaic of North America was represented well in our research.

So what did we discover and why do we want you to read this book? First, we want you to know that the unchurched are not some alien creatures with whom we have nothing in common. Indeed, the story of Justin M. proved to be the exception rather than the rule. Most of the unchurched are your neighbors, your coworkers whom you know well, and even your family members. That is why we call them "the unchurched next door." They have much in common with us. Many of them have your moral values. Most are not antichurch or antireligion. They are very much like you — except that they are lost without Christ.

A second discovery we made is that reaching lost and unchurched people is not always best accomplished with some cookie-cutter strategy. The unchurched are different in how they respond to the gospel. We want you to be aware of these differences so that you can reach out to the unchurched in the most effective ways. We called these different levels of response or receptivity "faith stages." I will explain the faith stages in more detail shortly. First, I want you to hear from an unchurched person who had quite a different response from that of Justin M.

## Jane T.: Waiting on Deborah and Jesus

Since researcher Deborah White had such a difficult interview with Justin, I asked her to tell you the story of Jane T., who is on the opposite end of the response scale. We call her a U1 because she is so close to accepting Christ. Or perhaps I should say that she *was* so close to accepting Christ. Or maybe I should be quiet and let Deborah tell you the story herself.

"Jane is a thirty-seven-year-old, single mother from Kentucky," Deborah begins. "I have known her for almost two years and have never 'found the time' to share the gospel with her. You see, I am Jane's boss, and that little technicality made me very uncomfortable. I have always made it known that I was a Christian and that my life revolves around church and God, but I soon realized that I was actually hiding the gospel from some folks who may never hear about Jesus Christ otherwise. Jane, I soon discovered, was one of those persons."

Deborah continued to tell the story about how this research project led to her encounter with Jane. "When I was asked to join a group of researchers to assist Dr. Thom Rainer on an upcoming project, I considered it an honor and was excited about where it could lead. I soon discovered that, once again, God had other ideas than just working on a research project; he had kingdom plans at work.

"At the start of the project, I felt led to speak to some of my employees, a chance, I thought, to get out of my comfort zone. I prayed about it and ended up having a few impromptu conversations with Jane over the next week. When I discussed the possibility of interviewing her for this project, she quickly agreed. I made arrangements to call on her the following Thursday night. I would soon learn that it would truly be a God-inspired, divine appointment."

As Deborah continued to tell her story, we could hear the excitement in her voice increasing. "When I phoned Jane the next evening, she was very positive and upbeat. She told me that the last time she attended a church was when she was four years old, and she couldn't recall the name of the church or the denomination. Despite this fact, she claimed to have a very friendly attitude toward the church. She said she often watched a service on television, but she never really had found time to go herself. She quickly added, however, that her youngest daughter attended a Baptist church every Wednesday night with a friend. As the interview continued, Jane shared that she had a very limited knowledge of the Bible, but that she knew God was her creator and she prayed to him daily.

"I proceeded to ask her if heaven and hell existed, and she answered 'yes' to both," Deborah told us. "'If heaven exists,' I asked, 'how does someone get there?' Jane answered, 'Make peace with God and the things you've done.' When I asked if a Christian had ever shared with her how to become a Christian, she whispered, 'no.' She knew so little about someone she wanted to know so badly, and no one had ever told her. I then asked if I could share my beliefs, and she answered expectantly, 'yes.' For the next fifteen minutes, I shared with Jane who God is and what it means to have a personal relationship with him through Christ, something I should have done a long time ago.

"Jane began to open up more and shared with me details of her childhood. Her parents claimed to be Catholics, but they never attended church or discussed God. Over the next month, God continued to bring Jane to the forefront of my prayers. I began to share Christ on a daily basis, both through words and actions. I provided her with her very first Bible, encouraging her to read it, starting with the book of John. Instead of being only Jane's boss, I was becoming her friend.

> "She knew so little about someone she wanted to know so badly, and no one had ever told her."
>
> *Deborah White,
> on her interview
> with Jane T., a U1*

"Two and one-half months after my initial contact with Jane, I visited her with a couple of friends from my Sunday Bible fellowship class. When that next divine appointment came, the Holy Spirit prepared the way for us to share the plan of salvation, and this time Jane opened her heart to Christ. The God she once knew so little about is now her personal Lord and Savior. And to think, all because of a research project and an obedient student, the kingdom has increased by one."

Thank you, Deborah. Your words reflect what this book is all about.

## About the Study of the Unchurched Next Door

For two years a team of researchers entered into the world of the unchurched. The purpose of this project was to find out what is on the minds of the unchurched so that we could provide you, the

Christian, with information you can use to reach the growing unchurched population. It is my prayer that you will come away from this book inspired, motivated, and even convicted to do what it takes to reach the unchurched.

Our team conducted 306 interviews with men, women, and a few older youth across America. These unchurched persons came from all fifty states and Canada. They were split almost evenly between males and females. They represented every conceivable demographic area of America. Figure I.1 shows the areas in which they live.

**Figure I.1**

| | |
|---|---|
| Open country/rural area | 7% |
| Town (population 500 to 2,499) | 8% |
| Small city (2,500 to 9,999) | 9% |
| Medium city/downtown (10,000 to 49,999) | 8% |
| Medium city/suburbs (10,000 to 49,999) | 16% |
| Large city/downtown/inner city (50,000+) | 10% |
| Large city/suburbs (50,000+) | 42% |

Where did we find these unchurched persons? Every person on my research team, it seems, used his or her own creativity. John Tolbert spoke with fraternity brothers from his college days. Twyla Fagan simply boarded a jet and invaded the two nations of Texas and Canada (the "nation of Texas" quip is for my Texan friends who still believe there is no life outside the Lonestar State). Several of the researchers called family members for the names of unchurched neighbors and friends. And when Bland Mason was given the assignment of finding unchurched people in Oregon, he went to the websites of Oregon State University and the University of Oregon. He emailed some student leaders, administrators, and faculty and found several unchurched men and women who were happy to do the interviews. Rusty Russell found some success with the "cold call" approach of telephoning some people in the area codes of the states to which he was assigned. Jon Beck asked members of his church for names of friends and family members who are unchurched.

Throughout this process, the research team and I have attempted to discern as much information as possible about the world of the unchurched with a prayer that you, the Christian, will be better equipped to reach your friends, neighbors, coworkers, family members, and acquaintances with the gospel of Christ. We tried to connect with every major age group and ethnic group. The data below demonstrates some of the success we have had.

### Table I.2

| | | | |
|---|---|---|---|
| Anglos | 80% | Less than 18 years old | 2% |
| African American | 9% | 19 to 35 | 52% |
| Hispanic | 3% | 36 to 50 | 26% |
| Asian American | 2% | 51 to 65 | 16% |
| Other | 5% | Over 65 | 4% |

The impetus behind this project came from new Christians. In a previous book I wrote, *Surprising Insights from the Unchurched* (Zondervan, 2001), a group we called the "formerly unchurched," men and women who had recently accepted Christ and become active in the church, urged us to look at non-Christians according to their "faith stages," a term we will explore shortly. The formerly unchurched also encouraged us to look at the wide mosaic of unchurched persons, and not to accept the stereotypical picture some churches and Christians have of non-Christians. We thus looked at people in a variety of locales, a variety of ethnic groups, and a diversity of ages. And as the data below suggest, we were also successful in listening to the unchurched from a variety of educational and income levels.

### Table I.3

| | | | |
|---|---|---|---|
| High school graduate or less | 24% | Less than $20,000 income | 23% |
| Some college | 40% | $20,000 to $49,999 | 45% |
| Undergraduate degree | 22% | $50,000 to $99,999 | 24% |
| Master's degree | 10% | $100,000 and over | 7% |
| Doctoral degree | 4% | No answer | 1% |

But the primary issue we attempted to address was the faith stages of the unchurched. This distinction among the unchurched proved to be the most fascinating.

## The Faith Stage Issue

Franklin R., a formerly unchurched, forty-something African American from Ohio, gave us this insight: "You need to ask the unchurched questions that will help you know where they are spiritually. Ten years ago I claimed to be an agnostic. But just a year ago I was ready to accept Christ; I was just waiting for someone to tell me about Jesus." Franklin continued, "The best way to reach me ten years ago would have been much different from the way to reach me a year ago. Last year someone invited me to go to his church. I gladly accepted the invitation, heard the gospel, and accepted Christ — all within six weeks.

"But," Franklin continued, "I never would have accepted an invitation to go to church ten years ago. You would have needed another way to get me closer to the cross."

Franklin's request became our quest. We know intuitively that different unchurched people respond to the gospel and to Christians differently. What we have attempted to do is to identify these different levels of response and then determine the best ways for Christians to reach these unchurched persons at their different "faith stages." Years ago a missiologist named James Engel created a visual scale to identify non-Christians to determine the best ways to communicate the gospel to them.[1] We have built upon the "Engel scale" to help us see the spiritual receptivity of unchurched persons in America. We originally called this visual aid "the gospel receptivity scale," but all of the researchers simply called it "the Rainer scale." With apologies for my lack of modesty, but with a desire for clarity and simplicity, I will heretofore refer to the following as the Rainer scale.

## Figure I.4 The Rainer Scale

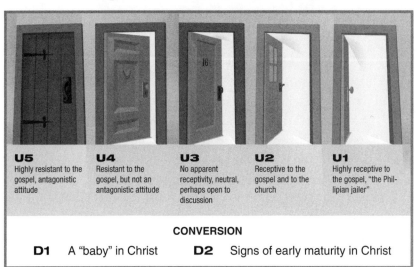

| U5 | U4 | U3 | U2 | U1 |
|---|---|---|---|---|
| Highly resistant to the gospel, antagonistic attitude | Resistant to the gospel, but not an antagonistic attitude | No apparent receptivity, neutral, perhaps open to discussion | Receptive to the gospel and to the church | Highly receptive to the gospel, "the Phillipian jailer" |

**CONVERSION**

**D1** A "baby" in Christ    **D2** Signs of early maturity in Christ

The Rainer scale became our framework for listening to the unchurched. Did he act antagonistic when we asked specific questions about Christ? Was there some openness to the gospel as she shared her religious background with us? Did she act like she was just waiting on someone to tell her how to be saved? And after we did our best to determine our participants' faith stages, to what did they indicate they would respond? An invitation to church? The development of a relationship with a caring Christian? A gospel presentation? A big Easter or Christmas event at the church?

After matching their faith stages with their openness to specific approaches by a Christian, we then asked the formerly unchurched (the new Christians) if our interpretations matched the reality of their own experiences. From this massive amount of information, we have developed for you a way to reach those unchurched people with whom you have contact every day. But before we proceed further, I would like to share with you one major finding of our research, a piece of information critical to your success in reaching the unchurched world.

*The Unchurched Next Door*

Perhaps as much as any information we gleaned throughout this process, we have been amazed at how much unchurched people look and act like us, Christian churchgoers. At first glance such a statement may seem appalling, for Christians are to be "the light of the world" and "the salt of the earth." We are supposed to be significantly different from the lost and unchurched world.

I do not mean to suggest that there are *no* differences between a lost and saved person. Obviously one has been saved by Christ and one has not. One is heavenbound and the other is hellbound. One is, it is hoped, motivated to do those things that please the Savior; the other has no such foundation.

But when I speak of common ties, I am referring to that which takes place in the everyday walks of life. Most of the unchurched are concerned for their families. Their moral values are not radically different from ours. They work alongside us, and their children and our children play together. Some of the unchurched are the teachers of our children. The unchurched live in our neighborhoods and carry on friendly conversations with us. They often carry the same financial burdens we do, and they are just as patriotic as we are. And many of the unchurched live in the same home we do; they are our family members.

Yet I have been in churches where a Christian leader has spoken of the "pagans" as if they are fire-breathing aliens from another planet. They are often stereotyped as angry at Christians, doubtful of the existence of God, and bitter toward the church. Yet the reality is that 95 percent of the unchurched would meet none of these descriptions.

> Only the U5s were antagonistic toward the gospel and angry at the church. Yet the U5 group accounted for only 5 percent of the unchurched in America.

The faith stages concept helped us immensely in our understanding of the demeanor of the unchurched world. Only the U5s were antagonistic toward the gospel and angry at the church. Yet the U5 group accounted for only 5 percent of the unchurched in America. Note the number of unchurched persons by each category according to the Rainer scale.

### Table I.5

| | | |
|---|---|---|
| **U5** | Antagonistic | 5% |
| **U4** | Resistant | 21% |
| **U3** | Neutral | 36% |
| **U2** | Friendly | 27% |
| **U1** | Very friendly | 11% |

Most of the unchurched are not antichurch or anti-Christian. Yes, some have been burned by bad experiences with churches and with Christians, but as a rule they tend to be forgiving. And they do not typically judge all Christians by one bad experience.

These non-Christians are truly the unchurched next door. They are the people we meet every day. They work alongside us, live by us, and even live with us. Though we will share with you information about U5, antagonistic Christians, please do not think that they represent most unchurched persons. We will spend most of the time in this book talking about the other 95 percent, the unchurched next door.

*Ten Surprises from the Unchurched*

Most research projects have a few surprises (things that go contrary to expectations), and this project was no exception. Below are the ten surprises, not listed in any particular order, that were contrary to the expectations of the research team.

*Surprise #1: Most of the unchurched prefer to attend church on Sunday morning if they attend.* Perhaps the unchurched responded this way because that is the time they have always heard church should be. But when we asked the formerly unchurched (new Christians attending church), they gave us the same response. A very distant second preference was a weeknight service other than Friday night.

"If I attended church, I would go the only time I could go regularly," said Al V. of Tulsa. "I work five days a week, and I like to go home to my family at night. And we almost always have some activity that one of our kids is involved in on Saturdays. I just think Sunday is the best time. And Sunday morning is best, because we get the kids to bed at a decent hour on Sunday night."

*Surprise #2: Females are likely to be either the most antagonistic or the most receptive to the gospel.* The majority of the unchurched females did not equivocate in their responses to the gospel. They were the overwhelming numbers in the U1, U2, and U5 groups, but not in the noncommittal U3 group. The women either adamantly rejected Christ or, on the other extreme, were highly receptive to becoming Christians. We will look at this issue later in a little more depth.

*Surprise #3: Most of the unchurched feel guilty about not attending church.* Though we did not ask a specific question about their feelings about not attending church, the majority of the unchurched expressed guilt in different ways. These guilty feelings were especially prevalent among adults who had children living at home. "Every Sunday morning I wake up and feel terrible about not taking Shanna and Tim to church," Mary G. of Sarasota, Florida, told us. "Mike [her husband] feels the same way. It's tough to start a habit of doing something you've never done before."

So, if they felt guilty, why did the unchurched continue to avoid church? As strange as it may seem to churchgoing Christians, the church intimidates unchurched people. They do not think they can fit in at a place they have never attended. And they are uncertain about church protocol. They just fear that they will feel out of place.

> As strange as it may seem to churchgoing Christians, the church intimidates unchurched people. They do not think they can fit in at a place they have never attended.

Is there anything that could get the unchurched to church? That answer led us to the next surprise.

*Surprise #4: 82 percent of the unchurched are at least "somewhat likely" to attend church if they are invited.* Perhaps we need to pause on this response. Perhaps we need to restate it: *More than eight out of ten of the unchurched said they would come to church if they were invited.* If you take anything from this book, please remember this point.

Eight out of ten unchurched persons said they would come to church if they were invited.

What constitutes an invitation? For many of the unchurched, it was a simple statement of invitation to come to one's church. For others, it was an invitation that included the offer to meet someone at church to show them around. In either case, the process was pretty basic. If we invite them, they will come.

The next obvious question is: Are Christians inviting non-Christians to church? The heartbreaking answer is no. Only 21 percent of active churchgoers invite *anyone* to church in the course of a year. But only 2 percent of church members invite an unchurched person to church. Perhaps the evangelistic apathy so evident in many of our churches can be explained by a simple laziness on the part of church members in inviting others to church.

> Perhaps the evangelistic apathy so evident in many of our churches can be explained by a simple laziness on the part of church members in inviting others to church.

Walk with me through a few simple calculations. Let us suppose that, instead of 82 percent, only one-half of the unchurched in America would come to church if invited. That means that out of 160 million unchurched persons, 80 million would be willing to come to church. Can you imagine how many people would be reached for Christ if that happened?

Now, may I ask you a question? When is the last time you invited an unchurched person to church? When is the last time you offered to meet someone and show him or her around the church? The answers you give could make the difference in the eternal destiny of an individual. Perhaps it is time we sounded the clarion call to invite the unchurched to church. It may be that simple, and it may be that profound.

*Surprise #5: Very few of the unchurched have had someone share with them how to become a Christian. And Christians have not been particularly influential in their lives.* This surprise is not really a surprise after hearing about the failure of churchgoers to invite the unchurched to church. If Christians do not invite non-Christians to church, we cannot be surprised if Christians do not share the gospel or influence the unchurched.

I wish you, the reader, had the same opportunity we had to listen to these unchurched persons. If you could have heard how many of the unchurched are waiting on someone to explain the way of salvation, you might have a whole new outlook on reaching these people. You might be surprised that, when we Christians think "the time is just not right," the unchurched are wondering why we are so reticent.

*Surprise #6: Most of the unchurched have a positive view about pastors, ministers, and the church.* Only a few said that ministers are hypocritical, only after money, always drive nice cars, and have a condescending view of others. The scandal of the televangelists and other Christian leaders is a faded memory for most of the unchurched. And for those who still have vivid recollections of the tainted past, most do not believe that all pastors and ministers are like their fallen brethren.

Perhaps even more surprising was the generally positive attitude the unchurched had toward the church. For the vast majority of the unchurched, the church *is* still relevant today. Indeed, many of them perceive the church as the most relevant institution in society.

This surprising response then begs another question. If the unchurched see the church in a positive light, and if they perceive the church to be relevant, why are they still unchurched? The answer seems to be twofold. First, some of the unchurched *have* visited churches, but their experiences have been negative. Unfriendliness, unkempt facilities, poor signage, and general confusion have been some of the descriptions about the church from the unchurched. What is amazing is that most of the unchurched still view the church positively after a negative experience. These men and women tend to be a forgiving lot even if they are hesitant to return to church.

But the second reason for their not attending church takes us back to the fourth surprise. Most of the unchurched have never been invited to church. And most of them would attend if invited. If you choose to close the book at this point and read no more, I pray that my point has been made. Invite an unchurched person to church!

*Surprise #7: Some types of "cold calls" are effective; many are not.* A debate persists in the Christian community about the effectiveness of cold-call evangelism. The definition of cold call is simply "uninvited." The type of cold-call evangelism most often resisted by the unchurched is an uninvited visit to their homes. "I really don't mind talking to people from churches," Roger S. of Wisconsin told us. "But please don't show up at my home without an invitation. It reminds me of a telephone solicitation, only worse!"

The formerly unchurched agreed. These new Christians said that unexpected visitors in the home were rarely welcomed. Sarah F. of a small town in Alabama noted, "I was most positively impacted by Christians who asked for permission to meet me or talk with me. The cold-call visitor to my home was a pain. I ended up accepting Christ through the witness of a church member who took me to lunch on three different occasions. I knew what her agenda was, but at least she invited me to lunch."

But not all cold calls are ineffective, the unchurched told us. We heard numerous stories about Christians who always seemed to be able to share their faith in casual conversations. They were not invited by the unchurched to talk to them, but these churchgoers often seemed to find a way to move a conversation to eternal issues.

"Eric is a trip," Peter W. of San Diego told us. Peter is a U3 (neutral) unchurched man who works with Eric. "We will be talking about the Chargers or the Padres, and before I know it, he's telling me something about his church or God. I really respect him, you know. He doesn't beat me over the head with his beliefs, but he sure isn't shy to talk to me about them. Most of the church people I know act like they are ashamed of what they believe."

The bottom line of cold-call evangelism seems to be to make the most of every opportunity God gives you. Pray for such opportunities. But showing up at someone's home without an invitation was one of the biggest turnoffs articulated by the unchurched. "I would be glad for church people to come talk to me in my home," said Millie B. of Odessa, Texas. "I just want to know when they're coming."

*Surprise #8: The unchurched would like to develop a real and sincere relationship with a Christian.* Our study of the unchurched continued over 2001 and 2002 with a noticeable intermediate point of September 11, 2001. The attack on our nation that day engendered many questions from American citizens, and many of the questions were about God. Though the door was open for Christians to develop relationships with nonbelievers before September 11, the opportunities increased after that infamous day.

The leader of the research team, Twyla Fagan, stated this issue clearly to me in a memo she wrote about the progress of our research project: "Most of the unchurched the team is interviewing would respond positively to a 'genuine' Christian who would spend time with them in a gentle, nonjudgmental relationship." Twyla continued, "Most of the unchurched can easily tell the difference between 'drive-by' evangelism and a person who really cares."

I learned how to share my faith by reading *Evangelism Explosion* by D. James Kennedy.[2] The manner in which Dr. Kennedy taught me how to start a conversation with a nonbeliever, and the way he taught me how to share a biblical plan of salvation are infinitely invaluable to me. Evangelism Explosion (EE) is one of the more popular training tools in personal witnessing. It belongs to a category of tools sometimes called "canned evangelism." The label "canned evangelism" is unfortunate, because it implies an uncaring, notched-belt approach to evangelism.

But EE originated from the heart of a man who is passionate about the lost and deeply concerned for the unchurched. When Christians use a canned evangelism tool to witness to the unchurched with no obvious concern for the person, the unchurched immediately detect this impersonal approach. "I had some people come to see me from the Baptist church just three blocks from here," Monte G. of Baltimore told us. "I felt like they were meeting a soul quota with me. They just wanted to spill their presentation and move on. But I would've been happy to talk with them for a long time if I thought they really cared."

The "soul quota" use of canned evangelism tools is neither the intent nor the desire of those who create these programs. But many of the unchurched quickly recognize the abuse of these good tools.

If we who call ourselves Christians *really* believe that a person is lost outside of salvation through Christ, we will make the lost and the unchurched one of our highest priorities. And if we *really* have broken hearts for these unchurched persons, we will take whatever time is necessary to get to know them and to share the love of Christ in word and deed. Winning the lost and reaching the unchurched are really not big mysteries. Millions of these men and women are waiting for one of us Christians to spend time with them and to show them we really care. Jesus desired that none would perish. In the midst of his packed schedule, he took time to show his love to sinners. Are we willing to do likewise?

> If we *really* have broken hearts for these unchurched persons, we will take whatever time is necessary to get to know them and to share the love of Christ in word and deed.

*Surprise #9: The attitudes of the unchurched are not correlated to where they live, their ethnic or racial background, or their gender.* The unchurched are not a monolithic group. That reality came through with the wide variety of responses we received. One cannot therefore expect a certain attitude from an unchurched person from Georgia just because he or she lives in a Bible Belt state. And we could not describe to you the common characteristics of an Asian

American unchurched person. The variety of responses within each ethnic group was significant.

The only pattern where we saw any correlation was related to income. The higher an individual's income, the more resistant to the gospel he or she is likely to be. Jesus himself warned us of the power of money to be like a god to us: "Again I say to you, it is easier for a camel to go through the eye of a needle, than for a rich man to enter the kingdom of God" (Matt. 19:24 NASB).

*Surprise #10: Many of the unchurched are far more concerned about the spiritual well-being of their children than of themselves.* A few years ago my research team and I studied the Bridger generation, those born between 1977 and 1994.[3] We discovered a large unchurched population among these young people, but we also discovered a generation highly receptive to the gospel. In my consultation ministry with the Rainer Group, I have found that churches that are highly intentional about reaching youth and children tend to be among the most evangelistic churches in America.

> The higher an individual's income, the more resistant to the gospel he or she is likely to be.

And now, in this research project, we found that the unchurched with children at home are deeply concerned about the spiritual welfare of their children, even if they articulate little concern for themselves. Perhaps in our encounters with these unchurched persons we need to mention their children. Perhaps churches in America need to be more intentional in reaching children and youth. And perhaps we need to heed more closely the words of the Savior, who exhorted us to let the children come to him.

### For Those Like Jack, Before It's Too Late

In the next several chapters, we will take a journey and listen to the unchurched at different faith stages. We will start with the most resistant and move to the most receptive. You will discover, with the small exception of the U5s, that the unchurched are usually nice and receptive people. They are family members, coworkers, and friends — the unchurched next door.

Before we proceed further, I want to point out that a person may move from one position on the Rainer scale to another in a short time. Nelson Searcy, who works for the North American Mission Board in the New York City area, told me that "almost everyone in New York City moved up one level after September 11." A U5 thus became a U4, a U4 became a U3, and so forth. But someone can move to a less receptive point quickly as well.

Take Jack from Toronto for example. Jack is a U4 who moved to a U3 but may soon move back to the more resistant U4 position. He is eighty-one years old and retired. He is really uninformed about religion in general and churches in particular. He has only faint memories of attending a Presbyterian church a few times when he was a child. Jack believes in heaven although he is not sure what it will be like. He does not believe that hell exists.

Jack's theology might be called "practical universalism." When we asked him how people get to heaven, he responded, "God will treat us all the same. It doesn't make any difference if you are honest or dishonest. He created us, so he'll take care of us." And about Jesus Christ, Jack's confusion was obvious: "He might have been a wonderful man on earth at some time, but I don't believe all I've heard about him. It's hard to believe that someone would be raised to life again. Maybe in a mental way but not a physical way."

Jack's own description of himself a year prior to our interview would have fit perfectly in the U4 category. He was resistant to the gospel but not antagonistic. Now he admits he is really neutral and no longer resistant, a classic U3. Why did this change take place? "My wife died less than a year ago." Jack said, then paused to regain his composure. "We were married sixty years."

We asked Jack if anyone had ever shared with him how to become a Christian.

"No, not really," he responded softly. "My wife tried to get me to go to church before she died. It's too bad we didn't know more about religion."

If Jack's words do not tear at the heart of Christians, I really don't know what will. Here is an unchurched octogenarian who cannot recall anyone telling him about Jesus. And even in the events of his wife's death, he heard from no Christian about Jesus. In my book *Surprising Insights from the Unchurched,* I shared with readers how receptive the unchurched were during times of crisis.[4]

The crisis could be a positive event, like the birth of a child. Or it could be a life-shattering event, like the death of a wife of sixty years. During these times, Christians need to be especially sensitive for opportunities to show love, concern, and the hope of Christ.

My concern for people like Jack is that he will soon revert to his old pattern of resistance to the gospel. He will once again be a U4 instead of a U2 or U1. Or perhaps the Holy Spirit is working in such a way that Jack would accept Christ as his Lord and Savior. But where are the Christians? For eighty-one years Jack has heard from no one. Do we *really* care?

## A Plea More Than a Project

For years I have been asked how churches can grow. I have consulted with hundreds of church leaders across America, leaders who sincerely desire that their churches reach people. "Why aren't we reaching people?" I am often asked. "Why is our society so resistant to the gospel?" many inquire.

After nearly a decade of research and almost fifteen years of consulting with churches, I am becoming more and more convinced that the answers to most of these questions can be found in the mirror. Nearly 130 million people in the United States alone would come to church if they were invited. And if they came, many would hear about the Savior who offers the only way of salvation.

I do not mean to be harsh or cynical. I am grateful for all the cutting-edge approaches to reaching the unchurched. I thank God for the innovative attitudes of many of our churches. Yet the more we research, the more we interview, and the more we listen, the more I become convinced that the answer to all the troubling questions about the church in America is very simple. We Christians have become disobedient and lazy. Investing our lives in the lives of lost and unchurched people is inconvenient and messy. And, as some missionaries have learned, it can be life threatening.

> We Christians have become disobedient and lazy. Investing our lives in the lives of lost and unchurched people is inconvenient and messy.

The end result of all the work our team has done is not really a project but a plea. We have listened to more than three hundred lost and unchurched persons across America. We have logged hundreds and hundreds of hours listening to the hearts of those who do not have the hope that you and I have. We have listened to your friends, your family members, and your coworkers; we have truly heard from the unchurched next door.

We have categorized the responses of these unchurched people into five different levels, which, as I said above, is what we are calling the Rainer scale. We have provided you with these categories so you can better understand why some unchurched persons respond the way they do. We will give you insights in this book on how you might reach these people according to their faith stages.

But now that the research and writing are done, I want to remind you that our work was not so much a project as a plea. I plead with you to ask yourself if lost people really matter to you. I urge you to look at your life's priorities and be brutally honest. Do your priorities *really* reflect a concern for lost people? If this book becomes but another nice research project, I will have failed. If it remains on your bookshelf and you have little change in your heart, I will have failed.

You see, lost people matter to God. And that which matters to God should matter to me. Many churches and many Christians have become caught up in the spirit of the "What have you done for me lately?" age. But the call of the gospel is to renounce self and follow Christ. And if we really follow Christ, he will take us to some messy places.

So please read this book for enjoyment. Read it for enlightenment and information. But, above all, read it with a prayer that God will touch you to become even more obedient in reaching the world for Christ. Thanks for joining me on the journey. Now let's enter the faith stages of the unchurched so we can truly reach the unchurched next door.

## Chapter 1

# The Unchurched Next Door

---

There was a person by the name of Jesus Christ.
He probably lived a very good and moral life.
I think he was an ethical person.
Whether or not he was more is not important.

*—Betty M.,*
*U4 from Baltimore*

---

Perhaps you would not expect John E., a college freshman in Wisconsin, to be interested in attending church. After all, John was raised with little Christian church background. Most of his days in any kind of religious setting were spent in a Universalist-Unitarian church. And of course the Universalist-Unitarians do not believe in a fully divine Christ since they do not believe in a Trinitarian God. But they do believe that all people will ultimately make it to heaven, a concept for which they have no clear understanding.[1] But now John is not attending any kind of religious institution. Yet he still gave this incredible response: "I probably would attend a church if someone invited me, and the closer the friend the more likely I would be to attend."

Researcher Travis Fleming is a Ph.D. student at the Southern Baptist Theological Seminary, where I serve as dean. Travis has a heart for evangelism. Yet Travis, like most of the researchers, admitted that this research exercise was an eye-opening experience.

In telling us about his encounter with John E., Travis noted: "I am grateful to Dr. Rainer for allowing me to work on this research team for unchurched persons. It has been an enlightening experience for me. It has made those of us on the team step away from the confines of the seminary classroom to enter into the minds and the lives of people who do not have an intimate relationship with Jesus Christ. Conducting these numerous interviews showed me there are people all over the United States who are just a conversation or a relationship away from being introduced to Jesus Christ."

The sad note about Travis's word is that John E. may never have heard the gospel unless this research project had intersected with his life. When asked about his concept of God, John gave a muddled yet sincere response: "He's a higher being. I picture him as ... I really don't know ... he's up there somewhere." Yet John, despite all his confusion, is ready to go to church if invited. But no one has invited him to church. And no one ever explained the gospel of Jesus Christ until Travis interviewed him.

Travis was grateful for the opportunity to interview John, who could best be described as a U4, resistant but not antagonistic toward the gospel. Yet Travis also quickly realized that other Christians would have to enter into John's life for him to become more receptive to the gospel. "I presume it is going to take one of John's friends to share Christ with him," Travis mused. "John *will* listen. That is why the local church and laypersons are so important. Each one must reach one! We must 'always be prepared to give an answer to everyone who asks you to give the reason for the hope that you have'" (1 Peter 3:15).

## Why This Book Is for You

I cannot know what caused you to begin reading this book. Perhaps your pastor suggested you read it. Perhaps you were intrigued by the title and you have a desire to reach out to your friends and neighbors who are not Christians and do not attend church. Or perhaps you know that you could be doing something more to be obedient to God's command to make disciples of all nations (Matt. 28:19).

Whatever your motivation, I am grateful to God for the opportunity to share with you the work of the research team. But it is my prayer and desire to see this book become more than an academic exercise. Indeed, as I was leading the team in one of our meetings, Travis commented that he wished this information would be written for all Christians, not just pastors, ministers, staff, and leaders in Christian organizations. I took Travis's suggestion to heart and wrote this book for all who are followers of Christ.

Readers who have read my earlier books will notice similarities in this book. You will see some statistics and some charts, but you will also sense the heart of a pastor. Before I came to Southern Seminary on February 1, 1994, I served as pastor of four churches in Indiana, Kentucky, Florida, and Alabama. One of my primary passions in pastoral ministry has always been to communicate God's vision for reaching the lost. Such is the heartbeat of this book.

## Before We Go Further: Eight Tough Questions

If you are willing to hear from the mouths and hearts of lost people, and if you really believe that lost people matter to God, let us pause a moment before we get into the interviews, data, and statistics. Let us be reminded that evangelism, including personal evangelism, begins with God. It is not some human endeavor that depends on magical words, the latest methodologies, or cutting-edge research.

Reaching the unchurched is spiritual warfare. Satan will oppose us at every effort we make to reach lost people. We cannot proceed in our own power. In my pastoral and academic ministries, I have seen Satan thwart the witness of believers in myriad ways. The following eight questions are meant to address some of those areas in which our opportunities to be a witness for the Savior can be stymied.

37

1. *How is your prayer life?* Most of us, if we are honest with God and ourselves, would admit that we are too busy for our own good. Life's demands sometimes cause us to replace the good for the best. Time in prayer is often the loser when we look at our checklist of to-do items.

Prayer is an awesome opportunity to come into the presence of the living God. Prayer is an incredible picture of the demonstration of God's desire to have fellowship with his creation. Immediately after the apostle Paul described the full armor of God for spiritual warfare in Ephesians 6:10–17, he said, "Pray in the Spirit on all occasions with all kinds of prayers and requests"(v. 18). Prayer is our source of power to fight the schemes of Satan as we try to reach the unchurched world around us.

We cannot expect to reach our unchurched friends, neighbors, and family members if we are not men and women of prayer. I encourage you to begin each day with a prayer similar to this: "According to your will, Lord, allow me this day to cross the path of someone with whom I can share the love of Christ." See how God will answer that prayer! How is your prayer life?

2. *Whom did you tell about Jesus today?* I recently finished a consultation visit with a church in the Midwest. In addition to my role as dean of a seminary, I am president of a church consultation firm called the Rainer Group. As part of the preparatory work, our consultation team interviewed dozens of church members.

One question I asked in a particular interview was a straightforward "Do you share your faith on a regular basis?"

In addition to the usual hesitation, excuse-making, and defensive behavior, the response of this person was not common in my interviews. "How *do* you," the middle-aged man asked, "share your faith on a regular basis?"

My response may have seemed curt at the time, but it also seemed the right thing to say. "Just do it," I replied.

Before I finished my work at this church, this same man approached me and began to speak with tears flowing from his eyes:

"I left our interview pretty offended. But your words would not leave my mind: 'Just do it.' I realized that my failure to share my faith was nothing more than disobedience, sin against God. I just wanted you to know that I told someone about Jesus for the first time in my life yesterday." The man really began to lose his composure as he barely got the last few words out of his mouth: "The person I told about Jesus accepted him last night. He was my sixteen-year-old son."

When we fail to share our faith, we sin against God. Jesus told us in his last words before he ascended into heaven, "You will be my witnesses" (Acts 1:8). No option or out was given. Whom did you tell about Jesus today?

3. *How is your family life?* The last three decades have provided clear evidence that one of Satan's most effective strategies against Christians has been to attack the family. When a Christian's family is in turmoil, his or her witness to the unchurched is damaged significantly.

I wish my best illustration of this reality were not so personal. You see, my speaking and consulting ministry involves considerable travel. All of my sons are now grown and living on their own or at college. But when they were at home, I found myself struggling to keep a right balance between my work and my family.

My wife, Nellie Jo, did a remarkable job of working with my secretary to make certain I missed very few of my boys' special events, particularly the athletic events in which they were so actively involved. Still, I began to accept more and more invitations. I can see now that my own ego and sinful self-centeredness explained my inability to say no.

One afternoon one of my sons brought one of his Christian mentors to our home. The young man asked me to sit down as my son shared something with me. Simply stated, my son said that he missed me. I may have been sitting in the stands of the athletic events cheering him on, but I had not been there for him just to talk, to spend time together.

I was crushed. I immediately started writing letters to cancel speaking engagements. Some people were angry at me. With others I lost credibility for breaking a promise to speak. I paid the price for my sin of self-centeredness, for my failure to put my family first in ministry.

The apostle Paul told church leaders that they could not lead the church if they did not manage their households well (1 Tim. 3:5). I have seen with painful clarity that my witness to the unchurched and lost is ineffective if my family life is in disarray. How is your family life?

4. *Do you need to reconcile with someone?* A remarkable act of God took place in a church in the southwest. The church had seen virtually no evangelistic growth for years. Then church members began to share their faith boldly and unchurched people began coming into the church by the dozens each week. The church grew rapidly.

What had happened in the once lifeless church? It seems, according to the reports of several members, that a long-standing dispute between the worship leader and the deacon chairman was resolved in a single night in a single event. The worship leader, at the conclusion of a Sunday evening service, asked those present to stay for a few more minutes.

With a trembling voice, the worship leader confessed his animosity toward the lay leader, took all the blame upon himself, and asked the congregation and the deacon for forgiveness. It was, as one person described the change, "as if we had been released from a deep darkness into bright sunshine." A new enthusiasm marked the lives of church members. They began to invite the unchurched and to share their faith. Revival took hold of the once lifeless church.

Imagine that you are praying to God with a significant request, and you hear the voice of God respond, "No way!" Though such a scenario may be unlikely, the theological truth is on target. Jesus said, "Therefore, if you are offering your gift at the altar and there remember that your brother has something against you, leave your gift there in front of the altar. First go and be reconciled to your brother; then come and offer your gift" (Matt. 5:23–24). At another point Jesus said, "But if you do not forgive men their sins, your Father will not forgive your sins" (Matt. 6:15).

Jesus obviously placed a high value on relationships between people. Is it possible that your enmity toward someone is rendering your witness ineffective? Do you need to reconcile with someone?

5. *Are you handling your finances and possessions biblically?* Such a question may seem unusual and out of place in a book on the unchurched. The primary purpose of this book is to motivate you and others to reach out in the name of Christ to the unchurched. And Jesus said very clearly that a preoccupation with the material world precludes our having a focus on the important matters of God.

Does your lifestyle honor Christ? If necessary, could you make some adjustments to downscale your lifestyle? Do you give abundantly and cheerfully, well beyond the tithe? Do you incur as little debt as possible? Do you put the priorities of God before the material amenities of the world? Are you handling your finances biblically?

6. *Are you committed to your church?* I have had the God-given opportunity to consult with more than five hundred churches. Additionally, the research team and I have studied thousands of churches and their members over the past decade. One trend is explicitly clear to me: A vast number of church members have developed a consumer mentality.

Comments like these are becoming commonplace: "I don't get my needs met at this church." "I don't like the times of the services." "This church does not have enough programs to meet my needs." "I am not fed at this church."

Certainly some of these concerns and complaints are legitimate. Many churches have become so inwardly focused that they fail to see the needs of others. But too many Christians have an attitude that asks what the church has done for them lately. The attitude of sacrificial service is all but gone for many church members.

Paul wrote nine letters to churches that became a part of the canon of Scripture. In all but one of the letters he expresses abundant joy and genuine thanksgiving for the ministry and people of the churches. None of the churches was perfect. Indeed, some of the churches had serious internal problems. Yet Paul found reasons for joy and thanksgiving.

The only letter in which Paul does not express an attitude of gratitude is his correspondence to the Galatian churches. In these churches the gospel itself was being deserted (Gal. 1:6), and only then does Paul communicate his great disappointment in the church.

I have pastored four churches. Since becoming dean of the seminary, I have served as an interim pastor of eight churches. I have seen firsthand how some people will abandon a church for the most trivial and self-serving of reasons. I have seen hard-working and God-honoring pastors and ministers criticized and ostracized for not meeting every perceived need in the church.

Do you truly desire to reach people with the gospel of Christ? Do you want to reach the unchurched next door? Do you care about being a witness for the Savior? You must love your church, despite its flaws and imperfections. Paul's letters indicate clearly that only serious doctrinal deviation can justify a critical spirit toward the church. Do you pray for the leaders of your church? Do you ask what you can do for God in the church rather than what the church can do for you? Are you an encourager to others in the church? Are you committed to your church?

7. *Do you love others unconditionally?* As you begin to hear the voices of unchurched people in the United States and Canada, you may hear at least one common theme. These men and women often wonder if anyone could truly care for them. Some are in lifestyles that they sense are wrong, but they don't why. As Nicole H. from California told the research team, "Look at me! Look how screwed up my life is! Do you really expect me to believe that anybody could ever have anything to do with me?"

It is too easy to write off people who are not like us. It is too convenient to avoid those who irritate us. It is simply a lot easier to spend time with people like us, people who think like us and act like us.

But if we truly love people unconditionally, we will seek those who are different. We will, in God's power, learn to love the unlovable. We will begin to see more people through the eyes of Christ. Do you love others unconditionally?

8. *Do you have an attitude of gratitude?* When I was a teenager, my high school football coach took time to talk with me. Coach Joe Hendrickson had many matters on his agenda, but he took time to talk with me. He explained to me how everyone is a sinner who has fallen short of the glory of God. He told me how Christ went to the cross to die for me, to be my substitute on the cross. And he showed me in Scripture how I could receive Christ as my personal Savior, how my sins could be forgiven, and how I could have the promise of eternal life.

On that warm evening in May, I accepted Jesus Christ as my Lord and Savior. Much has transpired in the thirty-five years since that most important point of my life. I have seen many good times. I have experienced many struggles. I have been given the gifts of a beautiful wife and the three best sons in the world. And I have preached the funerals of both of my parents and many others I love deeply.

In all of life's peaks and valleys, I have discovered again and again the consistency and constancy of God's love and mercy. And I know that one day I will see him face to face.

Is it any wonder then that I always have reason to rejoice? We who have been transformed by the presence of Christ in our lives always have reason to rejoice. Paul wrote to the Philippian church: "Rejoice in the Lord always. I will say it again: Rejoice!" (Phil. 4:4). Our rejoicing does not depend on the changing circumstances of life, but on the unchanging Christ who gives us life.

Do you show a joyous attitude at home, at work, and in your neighborhood? Such joy can be contagious and give you opportunities to tell others the source of your joy. Do you have an attitude of gratitude?

## A Profile of the Unchurched Next Door

In the introduction I shared some of the surprises uncovered by the research team in this project. Now I would like to introduce you more fully to the men and women who gave us hundreds of hours of their time. I could give you a detailed statistical profile here of the more than three hundred persons at the risk of boring you to death. Instead, I offer the statistical profile as an appendix for you Type A personalities (see appendix D). For the rest of you readers, I offer ten broad conclusions about the unchurched. As we delve into the different unchurched groups, I will provide more specifics. For now, let us look at ten key issues to consider.

1. *The unchurched are not antichurch.* As our interview team gathered for report meetings, I would ask different team members about their perceptions thus far. John Tolbert provided this common response: "These people don't have the negative attitudes about the church that I expected."

Indeed, one of our specific questions asked the unchurched to describe their own attitudes toward the church. The responses indicate the general positive perception the unchurched have about the church even if they have never attended.

### Table 1.1

| What Is Your Attitude toward the Church? | |
| --- | --- |
| Antagonistic | 5% |
| Resistant | 11% |
| Neutral | 36% |
| Friendly | 27% |
| Very friendly | 11% |

Four out of ten of the unchurched actually have a friendly or very friendly attitude about the church. And only 16 percent have negative attitudes. These results confirm our earlier point: Most of the unchurched would welcome an invitation to church.

Researcher Warner Smith interviewed one of many of the unchurched who demonstrated this positive attitude toward the church. Pamela F. is a friendly, talkative woman who has just moved from North Dakota to Arizona. Her husband is an airline pilot, and they live in a beautiful resort community. Pamela was raised in

Minnesota and baptized as an infant in the Catholic church. Her family rarely attended church; she has a memory of attending in the sixth grade.

> These results confirm our earlier point: Most of the unchurched would welcome an invitation to church.

Pamela is thirty-two years old, twice married, and the mother of two. Her major source of spiritual guidance has been the writings of Ayn Rand. When asked who God is, Pamela responds, "I have no idea." Her views of Jesus are similarly enigmatic: "When it comes to Jesus, I'm a walking contradiction. It's hard for me to believe that he is what people make him out to be. I believe they were needing it to happen."

With such a view of God, one might expect Pamela to be totally resistant to the gospel or even to an invitation to church. To the contrary, Warner classifies her attitude toward the gospel as a U3 on the Rainer scale. Remember, U3s are neutral toward the gospel, expressing no hostility or antagonism. Indeed, Warner believes that Pamela might quickly move to being more receptive to the gospel if someone would befriend her and simply invite her to church. The problem is that very few Christians share their faith or invite someone to church.

Very few Christians share their faith or invite someone to church.

Listen to Warner's summary of his interview with Pamela: "Pamela is open to someone talking with her about Christ. She is open to being befriended by a Christian. One loving, authentic Christian friend can win this woman and her family to Christ."

How many opportunities do you have to befriend an unchurched person, a neighbor, a coworker, or even a casual acquaintance? Yet most Christians today commit the sin of silence. They use excuses that say they do not want to impose their beliefs on others, that they do not want to offend others, or that the unchurched are not really interested in the church.

Our research, however, shows quite the opposite. Many of the unchurched *are* looking for Christian friends. They *are* open to an invitation to church. They *do* want to know what Christians believe. And you could be that person who will make the eternal difference in the life of an unchurched person.

The good news is that Pamela is seriously considering attending church even though she has yet to be invited. Warner notes, "As God had ordained it, a new nondenominational church has opened within walking distance of her home. Pamela and her husband are thinking of going." I pray that they will find unashamed Christian friends who can share with them the only way of salvation.

*2. Over 17 million people will accept Christ if presented with the gospel. Another 43 million are close.* I realize that statistics cannot speak for the mind of God nor presume upon the sovereignty of God.

Over 17 million unchurched persons are waiting for someone to share Christ with them. Where are the Christians to share the Good News?

I also realize that our research is fallible, so I am making these declarations very carefully.

Our research estimates that there are 160 million unchurched people in America. This assumption is based on our surveys of more than two thousand people, asking them how often they attend church. If they said five times or less in a year, we classified them as unchurched. Now, among the unchurched, 11 percent are U1s. Remember, a U1 on the Rainer scale is someone who is highly receptive to the gospel; many U1s are waiting on God's messenger in order to accept Christ. If the 11 percent holds for all the unchurched in North America, that means that more than 17 million people are waiting to hear the gospel. Where are the Christians to share Christ?

Consider one more issue. Another 43 million Americans are U2s. On the Rainer scale that means that they are open and receptive to the gospel. Again, the vast majority of the receptive unchurched people in America told us that no one had ever invited them to church or shared the gospel with them.

Do you see what a difference you could make? You may think that you could never tell someone about Christ. While I would probably disagree with your self-assessment, I know you could invite someone to church. That simple act could make an eternal difference. How will you respond?

> Again, the vast majority of the receptive unchurched people in America told us that no one had ever invited them to church or shared the gospel with them.

3. *Most unchurched persons believe in the existence of both heaven and hell.* As you seek to be obedient to get involved in the lives of unchurched persons, you need not feel apologetic or defensive about your beliefs. Most of the unchurched have some fairly orthodox views about eternity. Consider, for example, beliefs among the unchurched on the existence of heaven.

### Table 1.2

| Belief among the Unchurched in the Existence of Heaven | |
| --- | --- |
| Believe heaven exists | 79% |
| Do not believe heaven exists | 13% |
| Don't know/other | 8% |

Almost eight out of ten unchurched persons believe in the existence of an afterlife called heaven. Admittedly, their view of heaven does not always closely correspond with the biblical picture of heaven. But the numbers do picture an overwhelming sense that there is more to our existence than these few years we call life. Our interviews with unchurched people across North

America confirmed not only a belief in heaven, but also an eagerness to talk about it.

Think about the increasing interest in books, movies, television shows, and other media that deal with end-time events and glimpses of the "other side" of eternity. Talking about heaven may be an excellent point at which to start a conversation with an unchurched person. Yet most of the unchurched we interviewed indicated that no Christian had ever initiated such a conversation.

Even more fascinating from our perspective was the widespread belief in the existence of hell among the unchurched. But the belief in hell was directly related to the unchurched person's receptivity to the gospel. In other words, a U1 on the Rainer scale, someone almost ready to accept Christ, was far more likely to believe in hell than a U5, someone antagonistic toward the gospel. The chart below clearly indicates this trend.

## Table 1.3

| Do You Believe in the Existence of Hell? | | | |
|---|---|---|---|
| | Yes | No | Don't Know/Other |
| **U1** | 96% | 4% | 0% |
| **U2** | 82% | 6% | 12% |
| **U3** | 70% | 21% | 9% |
| **U4** | 51% | 41% | 8% |
| **U5** | 20% | 67% | 13% |
| All Unchurched | 70% | 21% | 9% |

One of our reasons for providing you characteristics of unchurched persons by faith stages is to help you better understand the issues and objections you may experience with different unchurched people. You may encounter a U1 or U2 who is receptive to discussing matters of faith. These people likely will have views on hell very similar to yours. On the other hand, a U5, one antagonistic toward Christianity, is likely not only to reject a concept of hell, but to become very angry at the idea of anyone believing in hell. Dirk J., a U5 from Minnesota, expressed these sentiments clearly: "You Christians are scum! I would tell all of you to go to hell, but I don't want to make you feel good about your stupid view that there is a real hell!"

4. *September 11 taught us an important lesson about the unchurched.* The research team did almost half of our interviews before September 11, 2001, and half after that fateful day. For the most part, attitudes toward Christianity among the unchurched changed little after the twin towers fell. There is, however, one noticeable exception to this general conclusion. For those interviews dated September 15 to September 30, there is a keen interest in matters of faith. Even the U5s interviewed before September 11 had a much mellower attitude for the few follow-up interviews we had in the two weeks immediately after the tragedy.

But by late October 2001 the attitudes were pretty much business as usual. In other words, we saw a small window of opportunity to share the gospel immediately after September 11. It would appear that the moments during or immediately after a national or personal crisis are key opportunities to share our faith. But how many Christians are intentional about sharing the gospel during times of crisis? How many churches are strategic about sharing Christ during such trials? Do *you* intentionally share the love of Christ when someone you know is going through difficult times?

5. *Unchurched persons are nervous but willing to talk about matters of faith.* Researcher Guy Fredrick expressed amazement about how much information an unchurched person was willing to share: "As I began interviewing people for this project, I was struck by the unchurcheds' candor with a total stranger." In fact, Guy discovered one of his interviewees from an Internet search of local phone directories in Minnesota. Even that "cold call" approach yielded a willing and talkative subject.

Many Christians get nervous when they start sharing their faith. Guess what? So does the person to whom you are speaking. But most of those persons hope you and they get over their nervousness, because they really want to talk about matters of faith. Do not let your butterflies and apprehension stop you from talking. The next several words you say could make an eternal difference in the life of the person who is listening.

6. *Most of the unchurched have a fairly high view of the Bible.* About one-third of the unchurched believe that the Bible is totally true and that it is God's Word. Another 46 percent believe that the Bible is generally true, and applicable in some areas. In other words, three-fourths of the unchurched see the Bible as an inspired book, one that is unique among all literature.

Contrary to some conventional wisdom, most of the unchurched are not turned off by Christians who cite biblical passages or discuss biblical truths. While followers of Christ never should be ashamed of God's Word, it may provide some level of comfort to realize that a majority of the unchurched will gladly hear scriptural truths. Indeed, in many of our interviews, it was the unchurched who initiated questions and discussions about the Bible. Marilyn U. from Connecticut notes, "I've never been to church in my life except for some weddings and funerals. But I would really like to find some people who could teach me about the Bible. I would like to learn as much as possible."

> Indeed, in many of our interviews, it was the unchurched who initiated questions and discussions about the Bible.

Once again, however, we saw a significant disparity in the response of the unchurched at different faith stages. Over half of the U1s actually affirmed the Bible to be God's Word, even though they are not Christians. But none of the U5s saw the Bible to be the Word of God.

## Table 1.4

### What Is Your View of the Bible?

| | God's Word/ Totally Truthful | Some Truth | Myth | Don't Know |
|---|---|---|---|---|
| **U1** | 55% | 33% | 0% | 12% |
| **U2** | 43% | 41% | 2% | 14% |
| **U3** | 24% | 55% | 1% | 20% |
| **U4** | 10% | 51% | 14% | 25% |
| **U5** | 0% | 40% | 33% | 27% |
| All Unchurched | 30% | 46% | 5% | 19% |

*7. Most of the unchurched would rather talk to a layperson than a minister about religious matters.* Harland G. is a native Floridian who attends church on Easter "about every three years." Two pastors have contacted Harland after two of his Easter visits, but a layperson has never talked to him about Christ.

"You know," commented Harland, "the two ministers who talked to me were nice enough but I, I mean, like that's their job. But I'd like to get into a conversation with a church person that's a normal person like me. Why is it that regular church members never talk about religious stuff?"

Harland's views were expressed in myriad ways by many of the unchurched we interviewed. The sad reality we discovered in our study was that very few of the unchurched population have heard about Christ from a layperson. Yet the unchurched as a rule would like to talk to someone other than clergy about religious matters. The silence of Christians may be one of the greatest tragedies in the church today.

*8. Easter is still a key time to invite the unchurched.* In retrospect, I wish one of our standard questions in this project would have been: "How many times have you attended an Easter service at a church?" Unfortunately, I did not include that question in the surveys conducted by the research team. Because of two key issues discovered in our interviews, however, I can say with a high level of confidence that Easter is a significant time to invite the unchurched.

> The sad reality we discovered in our study was that very few of the unchurched population have heard about Christ from a layperson. Yet the unchurched as a rule would like to talk to someone other than clergy about religious matters. The silence of Christians may be one of the greatest tragedies in the church today.

First, the anecdotal information from the interviews is overwhelming. Even when we did not specifically ask, the unchurched would tell us about attending on an Easter Sunday. "The only time I really ever go to church," said Kathy A. of Ohio, "is on Easter." "Why Easter?" we asked. "Well, it's the time everybody really thinks about church and religion. It's just the thing to do." Kathy's comments were repeated in similar fashion in the majority of our interviews.

Second, in asking the unchurched how often they attend church, we found that half of those interviewed had attended at least one time in the past year. I think we can surmise with some level of confidence that the most common day attended was Easter Sunday.

At this point you may think our emphasis on Easter Sunday is interesting but not very helpful in your reaching out to lost friends, neighbors, and family members. And after all, since so many people come on Easter, why do we need to emphasize this day as a key strategy for reaching the unchurched?

The reality is that most of the unchurched who do visit on Easter will have few meaningful connections with church members. They will simply attend because "it's the thing to do," then return to their world of the lost and unchurched.

A few church leaders realize how important Easter is in evangelizing the unchurched. Like other leaders, they will expect big crowds on Easter, but they will go further. They will encourage, strategize with, and, perhaps equip laypersons to be ready to reach the large numbers of unchurched who enter the church doors on Easter. They will not be content with large numbers alone; they will have a plan in place to connect with the unchurched who do attend.

Have you ever been intentional about inviting unchurched persons to an Easter service? Have you offered to take them to church and to lunch afterwards? Have you seen this day as more than just a time when your family will worship together? Are you asking God to give you opportunities to invite the unchurched this next Easter?

> Have you ever been intentional about inviting unchurched persons to an Easter service?

9. *Many of the unchurched wonder why their Christian neighbors and coworkers do not invite them to church.* Elmer Y. from Mississippi was a delightful interviewee. A native of Meridian, he moved to

Jackson seven years ago. "I see several of my neighbors leave for church on Sunday morning," Elmer tells us. "I'm usually on the porch reading the paper, or sometimes I mow my lawn. Every time I see them leave, I feel a little catch in my throat. I mean, I know I should be doing something religious, but I just haven't attended church most of my life. My parents hardly went either."

Elmer is thirty-two years old and works as a bank loan officer. "I know these neighbors who go to church," Elmer continues. "We talk about a bunch of stuff. But I have never heard them say anything about their church, God, or anything religious. Why is that? If church matters so much to them, why don't they ever say anything about it?"

> "We talk about a bunch of stuff. But I have never heard them say anything about their church, God, or anything religious. Why is that? If church matters so much to them, why don't they ever say anything about it?"

But such sentiment is not limited to the Bible Belt of Mississippi. Sharon W. of San Diego echoed Elmer's feelings. She does not see her neighbors leave for church on the weekend, but she does have two Christian coworkers at her brokerage firm. In fact, she and her two friends were among the top brokers in Southern California last year.

"Mike and Jenny [her coworkers] and I make more money than any of us ever dreamed. But we've all talked about how the money hasn't really made us happier. I know that they go to church regularly, so I sometimes hint to see if they'll say anything about it," she told us.

"One time we got into this real serious discussion about the important things in life," Sharon continued. "I decided just to ask them outright if church was that important to them. You should've seen how red their faces turned. They said a few things like, 'Of course it is,' but you could tell they weren't comfortable at all talking about religious issues. I just can't understand it. I think I'm really searching for something, but no one seems to want to talk to me."

We categorized Sharon's attitude as a U2, receptive to the gospel and to the church. If you include the U1 and U2 categories, there are about 60 million people living in the United States alone who would be willing or even desirous to talk to someone about Christ. But if our interviews are indicative, the vast majority of these receptive unchurched persons have never had such a discussion. And many wonder why.

10. *Most of the unchurched have a spiritual view of life.* We found very few atheists in our study. To the contrary, most believe in God, and many were willing to talk about religious matters.

Researcher Jon Beck interviewed Sarah R. from Colorado. Sarah is a thirty-eight-year-old stay-at-home mom busy raising a family. She was raised as a nominal Roman Catholic but rarely attended church. Her husband was raised as a Baptist, but he likewise attended church infrequently as a child.

They have a Bible in their home, but Sarah does not believe any of the family members have ever read it. "That's my husband's Baptist influence," she quips. When asked about any spiritual influences in her life, Sarah responds quickly. "I do daily meditation — get in touch with my higher power. And both me and my husband have been studying some information on Eastern religions."

Jon then asked Sarah about her view of heaven. "Oh, for sure there is a heaven," she quickly responds. "You can get there by how loving and kind you are to others in this life. We must live in harmony with all things: earth, spirit, animals, and people."

Sarah can recall only one Christian talking to her about Jesus in her entire thirty-eight years. "She was a business client. She impressed me because she was always talking to me about her relationship with Jesus. She didn't try to force anything on me, but in her own kind way, she shared her beliefs with me."

Only one person in Sarah's entire life had told her about Christ. But we have no doubt that Sarah is interested, even seeking

> My point is to remind you repeatedly that the world of the unchurched is not a world of fire-breathing pagans.

strongly, truth in spiritual matters. My point is to remind you repeatedly that the world of the unchurched is not a world of fire-breathing pagans. Most believe in the existence of God. Most pray on a regular, even daily, basis. Most believe the Bible to be something more than just another book on spiritual guidance. And many are waiting to hear from you about the Savior in whom you have placed your trust.

## A Plea from a Formerly Unchurched Person

At the risk of redundancy, I want to remind you that the heart and much of the wording of the research project was shaped by our previous research, the results of which are published in my book *Surprising Insights from the Unchurched*. Again, that project focused on interviews of new Christians who were newly churched. Those men and women spent all of their lives to the point of our interviews as unchurched and lost persons. Then someone invited them to church. Then someone showed they cared about them. Then someone introduced them to Christ.

These formerly unchurched influenced our study of the unchurched significantly. They gave us insights, helped us to form questions, and helped me to interpret many of the responses of the unchurched. Before we conclude this chapter, I would like you to hear from one of those formerly unchurched people. Marian is a one-year Christian from Indianapolis. We asked her to share with us what church members and Christians should hear from someone who was lost without Christ for the first forty-one years of her life.

"Tell them," Marian begins, "that the world and Satan will give them many reasons not to be bold in telling others about Jesus. They will even have many reasons not to invite someone to church." She pauses with obvious intensity in her face. "But tell them never to accept those excuses. The unchurched do want to be invited to church. The lost do want to be told how to be saved."

Marian is now holding back tears. She continues slowly. "But what if Paula had not cared enough to invite me to church? What if no one had been there for me during my divorce? What if no Christian had the guts and the conviction to tell me about Jesus? Tell them, Thom, to stop listening to the lies of Satan and the world and to be obedient. There are millions of people who were like me, waiting on someone like them to be unashamed of what they believe."

No author or researcher could state it better. Enter with us now into the world of the unchurched. We will listen to people at several different levels of receptivity to the gospel. But they are all lost and unchurched. And they all need someone, to use the words of Marian, with "the guts and conviction to tell me about Jesus." So we may enter this world of the unchurched not merely as an academic exercise, but with a prayer that God will speak to us and convict us.

Thanks for joining me this far. The challenges may seem many. But we serve a God of hope and power. We go now into the world of the unchurched, not in our power, not in our strength, but in the power of the Spirit of the Lord Almighty (Zech. 4:6).

## Chapter 2

# Faith Stages of the Unchurched

---

Why don't you just keep your stupid beliefs and Bible
out of my face?

*—Frances M.,*
*U5 from Massachusetts*

You will never know how much I appreciate your
sharing your beliefs in Jesus with me.

*Naomi T., a U1 from California*

"Some seed fell along the path, and it was trampled
on, and the birds of the air ate it up. . . . Still other
seed fell on good soil. It came up and yielded a crop,
a hundred times more than was sown."
*Jesus, Luke 8:5, 8*

---

Why not?" I asked myself. The retreat for the leaders of the seminary where I serve as dean had lasted many hours on consecutive
days. We finally had a break, and the options were many. Sleep. Read.
Paperwork from the seminary. Catch up on telephone calls. Watch television. Walk. Go to the bookstore. My choice surprised me. I *would*
take a walk, but I would have a specific purpose in mind.

The executive cabinet of Southern Seminary had convened in Cambridge, Massachusetts, for our annual retreat. The four days we spend together are always profitable and mostly exhausting. Some meetings last until almost midnight. The president of the seminary does not realize that some of us older men (he is a few years my junior) need more than four hours of sleep.

So when the option came for a few hours of free time, the temptation was to take a nap to be prepared for the long evening session. But sleep would not come, so I decided to walk to meet with someone I did not know.

The walk on that warm August day was beautiful. Harvard University was next to our hotel, so the sightseeing was limitless. But I was walking to keep an appointment.

You see, I had decided to interview one more unchurched person. This interview would not be a part of the database, since I did not have an interview form in hand. That was not really important to me. I just wanted to see how a person off the street would respond to my question.

My approach was simple and above board. I would stop someone, tell that person I was a Christian researcher, and ask for a few minutes of his or her time to ask questions. The first person, a thirty-something man, ignored me. The second person, Frances M., was willing to speak to me. Actually, she seemed eager to speak to me. In fact, I thought she might kill me.

This fifty-something woman restrained herself for all of about fifteen seconds, then she let me have it. "You Christians are so hypocritical. You look down on everyone else. You have a fairy-tale belief system. And most of you look like you are from the twilight zone!" (I do not think I was wearing polyester that day.)

It would be a misnomer to call our session an interview. It was, to the contrary, a ranting monologue. Many of Frances's words cannot be repeated in a Christian book. I did not feel alone in the attack, because Frances ranted about many Christians: Jerry Falwell (Neanderthal), Billy Graham (narrow-minded), James Dobson (misogynist), Mother

Teresa and the pope (lunatics on abortion), Franklin Graham (neo-Neanderthal).

Nevertheless, Frances seemed very intelligent despite her belligerent attitude. She knew a lot more about Christian issues than many Christians do. She seemed to be a hurting woman; she was definitely an angry woman.

Frances literally screamed her final words at me: "Why don't you just keep your stupid beliefs and Bible out of my face?" Okay, so much for a pleasant afternoon walk.

I fear that many Christians think my encounter with Frances is a typical encounter with unchurched persons. They therefore avoid the hostile encounter and console themselves that someone more gifted will share his or her faith.

Yes, Frances is an antagonistic unchurched person. We would place her in the category of U5, the most gospel-resistant category. But her attitude is not typical among unchurched persons. To the contrary, she is a rare exception. Only about one out of twenty unchurched people would have an attitude close to the belligerent nature of Frances's perspective.

On the return flight home, I sat next to a pleasant and talkative African American man whom I would place in his late thirties. I confess that I had neither prayed nor planned to share my faith on the ninety-minute flight. I was tired, and any kind of conversation was not on my agenda.

God and Will J. had other plans. "How you doing?" Will greeted me. "Great," I mumbled. Ten seconds of blessed silence. "What do you do?" Will asked.

*Oh boy,* I thought, *this response will get him quiet.* "I am a Baptist minister," I responded with clarity.

It seemed as though my prediction was true. Will became quiet and seemingly thoughtful. No conversation took place while the plane taxied down

> Only about one out of twenty unchurched people would have an attitude close to the belligerent nature of Frances's perspective.

the runway. Will remained silent as we ascended to 33,000 feet. Then the question came.

"Do you mind if I ask you a couple of questions?" Will inquired softly. "I'm having some difficult times in my life, and I just need to know where to turn."

*Okay, Thom,* I thought. *You have been disobediently silent. Now is the time to get back on God's agenda.*

Will was hurting deeply. This tall and muscular man was like a child on the inside. He had experienced many blows in his life. And he had tried to find ways to fill the void he constantly felt. None had satisfied. None had filled. Until now.

I listened for a full hour. Recognizing that the plane would land shortly and Will and I would be separated, perhaps for a lifetime, I finally spoke. "Will, I cannot solve all of the problems in your life. But I want to talk to you about Someone who will be all you need."

Will listened with urgency as I explained that Christ died for sinners like him and me. Tears began to well in his eyes when I told him that Jesus loved him so much that he died on a cross for him. And expectancy filled his expression when I shared with him how he could receive Christ as his Lord and Savior.

As the seat-belt sign went on to announce our initial approach into Cincinnati, Will prayed to receive Christ. He became a child of the King. As my friends know well, I am not a hugging type of person. But as Will and I departed from one another in the Cincinnati/Northern Kentucky International Airport, we did embrace. And I knew that if I did not see him again in this life, I would see him in heaven.

## Understanding Faith Stages

On the one hand, Frances and Will had something in common. They were lost without Christ. They were both unchurched. On the other hand, their personalities were very different. And their attitudes toward Christians, Jesus, and churches could not have been more in contrast.

Frances is a U5, a person who is antagonistic toward Christians and Christianity. Will was a U1, someone so receptive to the gospel of Christ that he was waiting on someone to tell him the old story. Review the various points on the Rainer scale again.

## Figure 2.1. The Rainer Scale

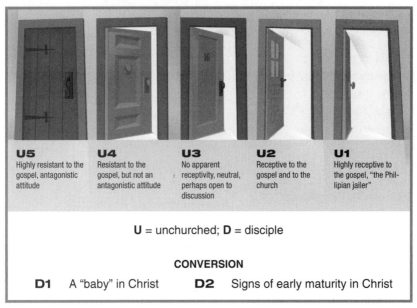

| U5 | U4 | U3 | U2 | U1 |
|---|---|---|---|---|
| Highly resistant to the gospel, antagonistic attitude | Resistant to the gospel, but not an antagonistic attitude | No apparent receptivity, neutral, perhaps open to discussion | Receptive to the gospel and to the church | Highly receptive to the gospel, "the Phillipian jailer" |

**U** = unchurched; **D** = disciple

**CONVERSION**

**D1**   A "baby" in Christ          **D2**   Signs of early maturity in Christ

The first purpose in my writing this book is to plead with urgency for Christians to share their faith. The second purpose is to show Christians that the unchurched are a diverse group of people in many ways. My third purpose is to share with Christians characteristics of different types of unchurched people with whom you might have confidence speaking in everyday encounters.

In this chapter you will get a more complete introduction to the concept of faith stages and the way we present it on the Rainer scale. But we view our research as more than sociological analysis. We see this concept discussed two millennia ago. The Bible provides the best description of faith stages.

## The Parable of the Seed and the Soils

Sometimes Luke 8:4–15 is called the parable of the sower. But the parable told by Jesus himself is also about the seed and the variety of soils. In verses 4 to 8, Jesus tells the story of the seed and the soil on which it fell.

While a large crowd was gathering and people were coming to Jesus from town after town, he told this parable: "A farmer went out to sow his seed. As he was scattering the seed, some fell along the path; it was trampled on, and the birds of the air ate it up. Some fell on the rock, and when it came up, the plants withered because they had no moisture. Other seed fell among thorns, which grew up with it and choked the plants. Still other seed fell on good soil. It came up and yielded a crop, a hundred times more than was sown."

When he said this, he called out, "He who has ears to hear, let him hear."

> The first purpose in my writing this book is to plead with urgency for Christians to share their faith. The second purpose is to show Christians that the unchurched are a diverse group of people in many ways. My third purpose is to share with Christians characteristics of different types of unchurched people with whom you might have confidence speaking in everyday encounters.

In this parable the seed is the gospel message. The ground or soil represents those who hear the gospel and their different levels of receptivity. Listen as Jesus explains further in verses 11 to 15:

"This is the meaning of the parable: The seed is the word of God. Those along the path are the ones who hear, and then the devil comes and takes away the word from their hearts, so that they may not believe and be saved. Those on the rock are the ones who receive the word with joy when they hear it, but they have no root. They believe for a while, but in the time of testing they fall away. The seed that fell among thorns stands for those who hear, but as they go on their way they are choked by life's worries, riches and pleasures, and they do not mature. But the seed on good soil stands for those with a noble and good heart, who hear the word, retain it, and by persevering produce a crop."

While we cannot demonstrate a one-to-one comparison between the soil in Jesus' parable and each level of receptivity on the Rainer scale, there are similarities. The greatest similarity is that lost and unchurched people hear and receive the good news of Jesus Christ with different responses and different levels of receptivity. We believers will benefit from understanding something about the attitudes of the different unchurched people we encounter. Thus, one of the purposes of this book is to introduce you to the concept of faith stages.

## Faith Stages 101

One chapter of this book is devoted to each faith stage, so we will not spend too much time going into detail about each level of receptivity. This section is, therefore, a primer to introduce you to the concept of faith stages.

Keep in mind the title of this book, *The Unchurched Next Door,* as you read. My sincere desire is to communicate to you that there are unchurched people only a walk, a desk, or a classroom away who are eager to hear from you about your faith in Christ. These unchurched people next door often wonder why you are so reticent to say anything about the most important aspect of your life.

Several million unchurched will eagerly listen to you. Many will be ready to receive Christ when you talk to them. The largest portion will probably appear noncommittal, but they will not reject what you have to say. And only a small number will be resistant; an even smaller number will be hostile. And even that hostile group, the U5s, will not likely cause any more harm to you than a good tongue lashing. What do you have to lose? Please read carefully as I provide some introductory comments to each of the groups on the Rainer scale. We will begin with the most antagonistic, the U5s.

### The U5s: The Antagonistic

Jerry J. is a fifty-five-year-old man from Tennessee. Though Tennessee is often considered part of the Bible Belt, we found that such

More than one-third of the U5s live in small towns or rural areas.

geographical labeling is losing its validity. The mobility of people in our nation makes regional religious descriptions less clear.

Jerry is forthrightly antagonistic about any religion. "Religious people are intolerant," he insists. "And the million-dollar palaces called churches are a big turnoff. How can you square spending that money that could be used to help other people?"

Jerry lives in a small town of under 2,500 in population. Interestingly, we found that the U5s and the U1s were more likely to live in a rural or small town area than the other unchurched groups. Perhaps these places have some interesting town meetings!

As I have said, U5s represent only a very small portion of the unchurched population. Indeed, our data indicate that the number is only about one in twenty.

Nevertheless, sometimes it is one single encounter with a U5 that causes a Christian to retreat into a shell of silence. Any discussion of religion in general and Christianity in particular can lead to an unpleasant conversation. So at least be informed about the characteristics of the U5 next door. Do not be surprised when he or she responds in a hostile fashion.

As an introduction let us look at the encounter between Jerry J. and researcher Warner Smith. We will explore U5s in greater detail in the next chapter, but Jerry provides a descriptive microcosm of this group.

It is not unusual to find that a U5 has some church or religious background.

It is not unusual to find that a U5 has some church or religious background. For Jerry the background was Southern Baptist. He is uncertain how many times he attended the Baptist church in Tennessee, but he knows he stopped attending when he was a child. Jerry does not want to elaborate on the reasons he stopped attending. We are not sure he even knows why.

Jerry's self-description of his attitude toward the church is "neutral," but it is obvious to Warner that this guy is anything but neutral. For example, he refused to see any possibility of Jesus as a historical figure. "He is not a real person," Jerry insists. "He is just an idea that was made up to make people do the right things."

And Jerry leaves little doubt that he has no room whatsoever for a Christian to share his or her beliefs with him. "My biggest turnoff by Christians is their trying to impose their beliefs on me," he informs us. Indeed, Jerry sees his attitude as the growing attitude toward religion in America. "Religion in America will continue to decline," he insists. "There are a lot of people like me who have no regard for it."

Our interviews were, of course, not full-fledged endeavors in psychoanalysis. There were times, however, when we would have loved to delve deeper into some issues.

Jerry, you recall, indicated some modest church affiliation with a Southern Baptist church as a child. As we asked him our series of questions, the next in sequence was about the greatest influence in his life. Without hesitation Jerry responded, "My dad." But it was the response to the next question that shocked us. Have any Christians been influential in your life? With little expression, Jerry responded, "My dad. He was a deacon at the Baptist church."

Any attempt to follow up on this issue met a wall of resistance and resentment. What happened in that Baptist church? Why was Jerry's dad's influence not sufficient to lead Jerry to faith in Christ? Did something traumatic happen in the Baptist church in Tennessee? What ever happened to his father?

Many of the U5s did have certain trigger points in their lives that seemed to

> Many of the U5s did have certain trigger points in their lives that seemed to have made a negative impact on their views of the Christian faith.

have made a negative impact on their views of the Christian faith. But some of the U1s and U2s, the more receptive unchurched, had negative experiences as well and moved beyond them. What is the relationship between the antagonism of the present and a negative event of the past? That question for us remains unanswered.

We cannot know fully what took place in the lives of the U5s to turn them against the Christian faith. We can, however, admonish Christians who avoid resistant and antagonistic unchurched persons. They too need to hear the gospel. As we will see later, the way one approaches and deals with a U5 is typically different than the approach to other unchurched persons. But different does not mean that we should neglect them.

There is one other matter we should mention before we leave our introductory session on the U5s. The researchers found that it was not uncommon to be the recipient of some hostile invectives from this group. They learned not to take the negative responses personally.

Such is our word of encouragement to you the reader. Many Christians have told us that one of their primary fears of witnessing is rejection. One important lesson we learned from the U5s is that the unchurched do not reject the Christian. Rather, they seem to have a plethora of other issues that have little to do with the one who gives a Christian testimony. Thus, fear of rejection is simply no excuse for silence.

*The U4s: The Resistant*

There is a subtle but distinguishable difference between a U4 and a U5. The U5s are hostile in their conversations and antagonistic toward anything that looks Christian. The U4 is equally resistant to the claims of Christ, but he or she does not express that resistance in a hostile manner. In other words, you can carry on a pleasant conversation with a U4, but do not expect receptivity to anything you have to say about your faith.

We found two broad categories of U4s. One group resembled the U5s in many ways. They were resistant to anything of a religious nature. The other U4s were religious in some sense, perhaps even a part of another religion, but they were highly resistant to Christianity. In the chapter on U4s, we primarily deal with the former group. So for this brief introduction, let us look at a religious U4 who happens to be a Mormon.

Joyce B. is a senior adult living in Oklahoma. Her religious background is the Church of Jesus Christ of Latter-Day Saints, more commonly known as the Mormons. Her conversation with researcher Patrick Hanley went well, and Joyce's attitude was friendly.

While some U4s resist anything religious, Joyce prays at least once a day. She is committed to a relationship with God because "He is our heavenly Father. He is our creator."

On views of heaven and hell, Joyce's Mormon influence was obvious. "There are three levels of heaven," she explained. "Everyone goes to one of the three levels, but the bad people go to the lowest level of heaven." On hell she simply responded, "I'm not sure if hell is what they say it is."

Patrick explains: "Mormon theology has played a major role in Joyce's theology. She believes in levels of heaven and that there is no hell. The work you do here on earth dictates where you go in heaven."

Joyce has been presented the gospel on a few occasions. Interestingly, the greatest Christian influence in her life is her son, who is now a Baptist minister. Yet she remains to this day late in her life unwilling to accept the truth claims of Christ.

Patrick says of the influence of Joyce's children: "Her sons and daughter have all been influential in her life. She has been exposed to the Christian faith through Easter presentations and felt moved by them." But Patrick is not optimistic: "I don't think she will accept the gospel, because she has lived too long in her Mormon faith."

An encounter with a U4 can leave a Christian feeling empty. The U4 may not respond with fierce opposition, but he or she just seems unmoved by anything the Christian may do or say. The story of Joyce provides a good example of how some churches and Christians have been effective in at least presenting the gospel. The U4s are willing to go to special presentations such as those at Easter or Christmas. They may not respond immediately, but they gradually become more receptive. The U5, to the contrary, is unlikely to attend any special Christian event.

Although we cannot explain why with statistical certainty, since our total interview size was just over three hundred, the U4 category was dominated by males. While our full study group was almost equally divided by gender, more than 60 percent of the U4s were male. It seems that for many females, if they were resistant to the gospel, they were antagonistic as well and thus fell into the U5 category. If our sampling is accurate, perhaps we can one day discern why females were less likely to be U4s than any other unchurched group.

Researcher Deborah White seemed to have a propensity for finding some of the more interesting unchurched persons. She met Rene M. of Arkansas at a truck stop. Rene is a more typical U4 than Joyce. The fact that he is male, uninterested in any religion, but willing to carry on a decent conversation makes him more stereotypical U4.

Rene is a Hispanic, and for reasons we do not know, the Hispanics had the highest proportion of U4s than any ethnic group. Rene has the typical lackadaisical attitude toward religion that is common in the U4s: "I'm Catholic, but I don't practice anything."

Deborah asked, "Do you pray to God, Rene?"

"Nope," he replied, "I think he's make-believe. Nothing has ever proved different to me."

"And what do you believe about the Bible?"

"It's a myth. How could it be real? It was written by men."

"Do you believe in the existence of heaven?"

"Nope."

"Hell?"

"Nope."

And then Deborah attempted to get Rene to be a bit more verbose by asking him an open-ended opinion question: "What is your view of the typical minister?"

"They are a joke," Rene exclaimed. "They teach something that isn't real. It's all hype. They don't care about people!"

Well, we did want him to open up.

Deborah summarizes her encounter with this more typical U4: "Wow, what a guy! He most definitely was resistant toward God. He originally claimed to be an atheist but then said that maybe 'atheist' was too harsh a word. He says he went to church as a child, but I can't tell he learned anything at all."

Deborah did see, however, at least some glimmer of hope for Rene, so she did not classify him as a U5. "He says he has some Christian friends," she writes, "but they haven't had much impact on him yet. If they would keep after him, maybe they could convince him to at least attend with them, but I just don't know. He was a pretty hard case."

Thus far the case for presenting Christ to the unchurched may seem a disheartening endeavor. But we presented the U5s and U4s first, and they account for only 26 percent of all unchurched persons. Stay with me. The task is more palatable with the U3s, U2s, and U1s.

### The U3s: The Leaners and the Apathetics

The U3s are the largest segment of the unchurched population. Of the 160 million unchurched people in America, they account for more than 57 million, 36 percent of the total.

This group was the most difficult to describe. Sometimes we called them "neutral," but they were not always noncommittal. Sometimes we described them with the phrase "no apparent receptivity or resistance," but few really met that criteria cleanly. Yet they fit none of the other categories either. Perhaps the first descriptive statement we can make about U3s is that they are somewhere between a U4 and a U2. But as we interviewed more and more U3s, three distinct subgroups emerged.

> The U3s are the largest segment of the unchurched population. Of the 160 million unchurched people in America, they account for more than 57 million, 36 percent of the total.

The largest group, perhaps one-half of the U3s, were called "the apathetics." For these unchurched, religion seems to be a nonissue. They act neither interested nor offended when someone talks to them about matters of faith. One of our researchers noted with accuracy: "These people put religion in the category of just one of many choices in the world today. For them, religious issues have the same importance as deciding the week's menu."

Another subgroup was "leaners." Although they did not demonstrate the clear characteristics of U4s or U2s, they tended to lean toward one of those two groups. As Michel G., a new Christian from Vermont told us, "Your category of U3 is on target. But it is a category that someone will pass through quickly. He will either become more receptive [U2] or less receptive [U4] pretty quickly."

Paul P. is a typical U3. Interviewed by researcher Todd Randolph, Paul gave responses that could almost be anticipated.

> "I sometimes went to a Methodist church growing up."
> "I would describe myself as neutral in most religious matters."
> "I pray to God every other month."
> "The Bible is truthful and applicable in some areas."
> "Both heaven and hell exist in perceptions of one's mind."
> "I don't know about Jesus, but I do believe in God."
> "I enjoy Easter and Christmas events at churches."
> "I like most pastors, but one was very disrespectful to my father when I was a kid."
> "I would attend a special event, but I'm not likely to attend a regular worship service."

Researcher Brad Morrow interviewed Patsy S. of Louisiana. His conclusions were similar to many of the U3 summaries: "This interview was a real hodgepodge. She knows some of the answers but does not seem to have a genuine personal relationship with Jesus Christ. She really is not antagonistic toward the church, just apathetic. She is an intelligent woman who has been shaped by different tolerance and diversity movements. She sees no reason to be in church. She seems to be depending on a works theology for salvation."

Patsy seems to be a "leaner" toward the U2 category. On the one hand, she has a strange view of eternal life: "Heaven and hell aren't places you go. It's what happens with your spirit. It will be happy or sad forever." On the other, her view of Jesus is close to orthodox: "He is the one who sacrificed for us. He is willing to forgive us no matter what we do. He was a real person born in Bethlehem, and he became a spirit. He is the one we answer to." Yet Patsy seems confused about salvation in Christ. "To get to heaven," she said, "you have to ask God to be in your heart and life, and be a good, moral, giving person."

Our researchers had two perspectives about U3s like Patsy. Some felt that her beliefs in some of the cardinal doctrines of the Christian faith would make her a good candidate to be more receptive to the true gospel of Christ. But others felt that her mixed-up Christian/works salvation/New Age beliefs would make her less receptive to the simple gospel message.

Such is our introductory description of the U3s. Sometimes we describe them more by what they are not than what they are. They are not as resistant as the U4s. But they are not as receptive as the U2s. Perhaps a discussion of the next group, the U2s, will clarify some of those differences.

> Sometimes we describe them more by what they are not than what they are. They are not as resistant as the U4s. But they are not as receptive as the U2s.

### The U2s: The Seekers

Much has been written and said about the seeker movement, about seekers, and about seeker services. I have yet to see a consistent definition for seeker. I do know, however, that this group of U2 unchurched persons is truly seeking something in their lives. And many of them are fully aware that they are seeking God himself.

The U2s are the second largest group of unchurched persons in America. We estimate that there are 57 million U3s, the largest group, and 43 million U2s. More than one out of four unchurched fit the description of the U2. Chances are that someone you know in your neighborhood, at work, at school, or in the marketplace is a U2.

The U2s were the youngest of the unchurched groups. Nearly six out of ten were under the age of thirty-six. They are the unchurched with the most females — 62 percent of the total. The U2s' view of biblical authority is not significantly different from that of evangelical churchgoers. And 95 percent of them believe heaven exists, while eight out of ten believe hell exists.

While these demographic descriptions tell us something about U2s, it was their responses to questions about spiritual matters that set them apart from previous unchurched groups as depicted on the Rainer scale. These men and women knew something was missing in their lives.

Twyla Fagan, our lead researcher, interviewed Marianne S., recently from California but just moved to Dallas. She is a forty-something homemaker who attended a Catholic church some as a girl. She describes her attitude toward the church as "friendly" and even has begun visiting an evangelical church in the Metroplex of Dallas. She prays every night and believes in a God of miracles. She also has a rather strong belief in the presence of guardian angels.

Marianne is truly a seeker. She is once again visiting a church, she is praying to God on a regular basis, and she believes in the supernatural. But she has not yet found Christ. Her views of Christ are biblical to a point. "I believe Jesus died for us and that he was the Son of God," she says. Then she demonstrates her struggles with who Christ really is. "Are Jesus Christ and God one and the same?" she asks.

"How do you believe you get to heaven, Marianne?" Twyla inquired.

"Oh, you must believe in God, believe in your own religion whatever it may be. And then if you're a good person . . . You know — you have to give a little to get a little."

This seeker has one strange theology!

Marianne has warm memories of going to church as a child. And when asked if she would attend a church if invited, she responded quickly and enthusiastically, "Of course!"

I pray that in the midst of our statistics and interviews, you hear from God, for nearly 60 million people like Marianne are searching for answers. They are the unchurched next door. They wonder why churchgoers with whom they work and live are silent about their faith. They are waiting on you to open your mouth and your heart.

> Nearly 60 million people are searching for answers. They are the unchurched next door. They wonder why churchgoers with whom they work and live are silent about their faith. They are waiting on you to open your mouth and your heart.

As you travel with me through the pages of this book, I pray also that you will see the numerous opportunities to share your faith. You may on occasion meet a belligerent U5 or a resistant U4. And you will most likely come in contact with one of those ubiquitous U3s. But you will also have numerous opportunities to talk to a receptive U2. They are very close to becoming Christians, and they have many questions. Most of them would be excited to be invited to your church.

And there is still one more group of unchurched to whom I want to introduce you. They are the U1s, the most receptive of the entire unchurched population. The next few paragraphs should motivate you to do something now, for the U1s are ready to receive Christ as their Lord and Savior.

## The U1s: Waiting on You

We estimate that there are 17 million U1s in America, representing about 11 percent of the total unchurched population. They tend to be younger to middle-age adults; 83 percent of them are below the age of fifty-one. They are the group that overwhelmingly said "busyness" was the number one reason they did not attend church.

Most all of the U1s pray regularly. Most believe in both heaven and hell. Almost half have a grace/faith understanding of salvation, though most of them admit some confusion.

Now listen to this statistic very carefully: More than 97 percent of the U1s said they would be "somewhat likely" or "very likely" to attend church if invited. These unchurched are waiting on you. Do you hear their cries for help?

> More than 97 percent of the U1s said they would be "somewhat likely" or "very likely" to attend church if invited. These unchurched are waiting on you. Do you hear their cries for help?

We will share many stories of the U1s in chapter 7. For now let us tell you one story, the story of William D.

As I said earlier, I have served as an interim pastor of eight churches since becoming dean at Southern Seminary. In reality I do very little pastoring because of my other responsibilities. Primarily my role is preaching.

At a recent interim pastorate in Kentucky, I noticed a large man standing in the back of the church one Sunday after services. He kept looking at me, and I decided that if he wanted something, he could ask me. Because of the large size of the church and the fact that I did little outside of preaching, I sometimes would not know if a person was a guest or a member. The man in the back was visiting for the first time, I would learn later. But I was just too busy for him that Sunday.

The next Sunday he showed up again. And again he looked at me, this time from a closer vantage point. Maybe God was finally getting through my thick skull and busy lifestyle. This time I went to him.

William D. seemed both fearful and relieved that he had finally gotten my attention. I introduced myself, and he informed me that this visit was only his second ever in a church. He also told me that he was a police officer and that he was struggling with the many tragedies he sees.

"I held a fourteen-year-old boy in my arms as he died last month. He was in an awful accident," the burly man said softly. "It's just too much to handle at times. Sometimes I wonder if there is any purpose to life whatsoever."

I knew my time was limited. William had already told me that he went on duty at two that afternoon. He would have to leave shortly.

Prayerfully, I made a quick decision. Instead of responding to all the questions William was throwing at me, I would ask him a question.

"William," I asked, "have you ever accepted Jesus as your Lord and Savior?"

He seemed taken aback by the change of the conversation. "No," he responded with hesitation. "But I have started reading the Bible."

I told William that reading the Bible was great but that it would not get him to heaven. I then presented the gospel as clearly as I could in God's power.

People were still mingling in the church sanctuary. It would not be the most comfortable setting, but I could not let this moment pass. I asked William if he would like to ask Christ into his life.

"I, uh, I need time to think about it — you know, to get my life together," he stammered.

I am not usually this persistent in my witnessing, but I really sensed that God was doing something in William's life. Once again I could not let the moment pass. I told him that he would never get his life together without Christ and that he had no excuse for delaying his decision.

William's response caught me off guard. "You're right," he said, "I'm ready."

And on that day on a warm autumn afternoon in Louisville, Kentucky, William D. became a child of the King.

What if I had ignored the impulse to share my faith with William? What if I had been my usual too-busy self? What if I had taken William's first and minor resistance as a clear sign to back off? I cannot answer the kind of questions that remain in the hands of a sovereign God. But I do wonder how many times I have been disobedient in my silence.

By our estimates 17 million U1s are waiting to hear the gospel, waiting for someone to give them hope. They are waiting for you. One out of ten unchurched persons is a U1. In the course of a day, you may come in contact with fifty unchurched people; five of those are waiting for you to tell them about Christ. They are ready. Are you?

## The Unchurched Next Door: Different People, Different Approaches

The purpose of this chapter is far greater than describing characteristics of the unchurched people in America. The purpose has not merely been to describe a typology called the Rainer scale. Rather, the primary purpose has been to move you to a greater point of commitment and desire to share the good news of Christ.

Deanna K. is from Hawaii. A little less than a year ago she accepted Christ through the witness of a soldier stationed there for several months. Deanna is very excited about her newfound faith. She immediately became involved in a local church where she is growing in Christ every day.

A month prior to my conversation with Deanna, she signed up for a Bible study advertised in her neighborhood. When she arrived, she was very surprised to see so many of her neighbors that she knew fairly well.

"I looked around the room right before we began," she told us. "I said, 'Jennifer are you a Christian?' and Jennifer said, 'Yes.' I then asked Debbie Jo if she was a Christian, and she said she was too. In fact, I asked five of my neighbors that same question, and they all told me they were Christians.

"I guess I was kind of obnoxious that day. I told each of them that I had been a Christian less than a year. I told them that I had lived in the neighborhood for eight years and none of them had even told me they were Christians. I got too emotional and told them that they might as well have told me to go to hell, because that's what their silence said."

My prayer for you and for me is that we will cease committing the sin of silence. I pray also that when you come across a U1, you will be equipped and ready to share your faith on the spot. And when you come across a U5, you will not take the resistance and antagonism personally but will be prepared to do something to help move that person to a greater level of receptivity to the gospel.

That is where we will go next — to a more detailed description of the resistant U5s. From a human perspective, you may see these recalcitrant people as hopeless. But you do not go to them in your own power. Through God's power all things are possible. With anticipation, then, join me in the world of the U5s.

**U5**
Highly resistant to the gospel, antagonistic attitude

**U4**
Resistant to the gospel, but not an antagonistic attitude

**U3**
No apparent receptivity, neutral, perhaps open to discussion

**U2**
Receptive to the gospel and to the church

**U1**
Highly receptive to the gospel, "the Phillipian jailer"

## Chapter 3

# "Religion Is Okay
for the Weak-Minded"

*The World of the U5*

---

Aren't Christians supposed to be nice?
My impression is that Christians are snotty.
Also, my first impression of preachers is that
they are scary. Christians just think they are
better than everyone else.

*—Becky B.,
U5 from Ontario, Canada*

---

Cynthia M. is a U5 from Indiana. Remember that U5s are the most resistant, even antagonistic, to the church and to the gospel. But also remember that, among the unchurched, U5s account for only 5 percent of the total. We must not stereotype all unchurched persons as U5s, for they represent only a small minority. So when we tell the stories of people like Cynthia, keep in mind that they are not your typical unchurched persons.

Deborah White, who interviewed Cynthia, made a noble effort to share the gospel with her. Deborah commented, "I took a shot and tried to share my faith. Well, she totally shot me down so fast she made my head swim. I could see in her face the disgust with many of the questions about God and heaven and hell."

Like many U5s, Cynthia seems to be struggling with deep personal problems. She is an alcoholic who married at age sixteen and strove to raise three children. Her marriage has been shaky. On at least one occasion she and her husband con-

> Among the unchurched, U5s account for only 5 percent of the total. We must not stereotype all unchurched persons as U5s, for they represent only a small minority.

templated divorce, though they remain married today. Cynthia's middle daughter had a child out of wedlock. Her oldest son has a drug problem and is presently serving prison time.

Like many of the unchurched in the U5 group, Cynthia never goes to church and would not go if invited. For her, church "is not reality. It's not issues of today. The sermons are the same, and I don't agree with any of them." Of course, we are not clear how she has become so informed about sermons when she never attends church. We do not see Cynthia as a viewer of television preaching either.

The two words Cynthia used to describe Christians are "hypocritical" and "preachy." She seems to have no level of comfort with Christians or with any aspect of the church. And she resents God for all that has happened in her life. How can we reach people like Cynthia? Though the U5 group is indeed a small number of all unchurched, they still represent about 8 million people in the United States alone. And since many U5s do not even believe in the existence of God, they are indeed the most difficult to reach. Nevertheless, we must not ignore them.

I debated whether my chapter on U5s should go near the beginning of the book or toward the end. My desire is to communicate clearly, on the one hand, that U5s do not represent most unchurched persons. On the other hand, however, I want readers to hear that this group cannot be ignored. My choice to begin the discussion of the Rainer scale with the U5 reflects my desire to deal with stereotypical issues of the unchurched early, recognizing that a U5 has many of those stereotypical characteristics.

As you listen to some of these men and women, you will hear hurt, anger, and confusion. And you will hear fierce resistance to the gospel and to the church. But God's grace is sufficient for even the most estranged person. We listen now to the U5s with a prayer that God will use us to bring them one step closer to him.

## U5s Are the Wealthiest Unchurched People

Jesus said bluntly, "It is easier for a camel to go through the eye of a needle, than for a rich man to enter the kingdom of God" (Matt. 19:24 NASB). Our Savior made his point clearly: Wealth and the accumulation of possessions can be a hindrance to receiving Christ. Wealth becomes the object of devotion and precludes faith in Christ.

We found a very clear relationship between wealth and the attitudes of the unchurched. Indeed, the U5s in our study include some of the highest-income individuals. The following comparison is telling.

### Table 3.1

|  | Percent of U5s | Percent of All Unchurched |
|---|---|---|
| Income $50,000 to $99,999 | 33% | 24% |
| Income over $100,000 | 13% | 7% |
| Total | 46% | 31% |

A U5 is almost twice as likely to have an income above $100,000 as the general population of the unchurched. And almost half of the U5s earn over $50,000, compared to 31 percent of the total unchurched population.

While our research cannot prove a direct relationship between wealth and resistance to the gospel, the evidence seems compelling that such is the case. Sandra S. is a U5 from Alabama. Her income is well above $100,000. Her beliefs, or lack of beliefs, seem consistent with many of the wealthy unchurched we interviewed. She "can't believe that Jesus is God." She does not even have a religious system that believes in any kind of higher being. Sandra states simply and forthrightly, "There is no god."

A U5 is almost twice as likely to have an income above $100,000 as the general population of the unchurched.

The rest of Sandra's responses to our interview became predictable. "The Bible is a myth." "There is no heaven or hell. We create our own heaven or hell here on earth." And her objection to the local church, curiously, centers on money. "The budgets of most churches are just too big," Sandra told us. "The sizes of the staff are too large, too much money spent on personnel costs."

Not all wealthy persons are agnostics, atheists, or U5s. A person of lofty financial means can be a Christian. Jesus did say of the wealthy entering the kingdom, after the disciples asked him if the rich can be saved, "With people this is impossible, but with God all things are possible" (Matt. 19:26 NASB).

The U5s were the most educated persons among the unchurched.

If our primary contacts are among the wealthier of society, or if our churches are located in more affluent areas, the likelihood exists that we will find greater resistance to the gospel.

Perhaps the growing wealth of our own nation at least partially explains the decline in conversions over the past fifty years. Evangelism among the wealthy in our society is difficult, but they need Christ as much as any of us.

## U5s Are the Most Educated among the Unchurched

While wealth seems to be one major obstacle to receiving Christ, advanced education may be another. More than 39 percent of the

U5s had a master's or doctoral degree, compared to 14 percent of the total unchurched population. And over one-fourth of the U5s had a doctoral degree, compared to only 4 percent of all the unchurched.

Mark J. from Maryland is a typical highly educated U5. He claims to be an agnostic, one who is uncertain about the existence of God, but he sounds more like an atheist, one who firmly denies the existence of God. Mark received his Ph.D. in economics some twenty years ago. Like many of the highly educated U5s, he sees religion as a crutch for the less educated. In fact, Mark attributes his denial of the reality of God as a natural consequence of his advanced learning. "The more education you receive, the more you realize that religious beliefs just don't make sense."

> Like many of the highly educated U5s, he sees religion as a crutch for the less educated. In fact, Mark attributes his denial of the reality of God as a natural consequence of his advanced learning.

Interestingly, Mark's biggest turnoff by Christians is their prayer lives. Mark believes the exercise of prayer is futile. "The Christians I know pray for everything," he lamented. "I can't stand it when they pray for trivial things that just aren't important. In my mother's church, some of the people were praying for their new pastor to find a good place to live. Isn't that ridiculous?"

As you can see in appendix C, one of our regularly asked questions to interviewees was to name the person who influenced them the most. A common response among U5s was a teacher or professor. One of Mark's economics professors urged the students to see everything rationally, a process the professor claimed would exclude religious beliefs. "He really opened my eyes," Mark said. "He is probably the main reason I don't believe in the existence of God."

Please do not hear that our study implies that education is evil. Like wealth, however, the attainment of knowledge and education can be one's own god. And the most resistant to the gospel, the U5s, were more likely to have such an attitude toward education.

## U5s Are Likely to Be over Fifty Years Old

At first glance the discovery that U5s are more likely to be over fifty years old surprised us on the research team. The most resistant to the gospel were the oldest unchurched persons. But then we realized that the real story was that the younger unchurched are more likely to have an interest or belief in spiritual matters. Our research and the research of others has confirmed the growth of spiritual interest among young adults and youth in America.

Still the findings are interesting. Look at the stark contrast we uncovered.

### Table 3.2

| Unchurched over 50 Years Old | |
| --- | --- |
| All unchurched | 20% |
| U5s | 40% |

The number of unchurched over fifty years old was twice as prevalent among the U5s as compared to all unchurched. And while we cannot claim from our limited data that there is a direct correlation between older age and resistance to the gospel, we did attempt to discover reasons behind this unusual scenario.

Doug L. is approaching retirement. He works for the U.S. Army as a civil servant. He currently resides in Virginia, but he looks forward to retirement years in Montana. Doug was a real case study for us because he is in his sixties, earns more than $100,000 per year, and has a Ph.D. degree.

Doug is a typical U5. He never goes to church, and he sees the church as irrelevant. He is probably an atheist, and he certainly does not believe in heaven or hell. Jesus, Doug tells us, was likely a historical figure, but "what you hear about him today is nothing but myth. There was a good man named Jesus who did good works and was probably martyred, but he wasn't resurrected." No Christian has ever been an influence in Doug's life. No Christian has ever shared the gospel with him. If someone invited him to church, it is "not likely at all" that he would attend.

Doug does represent an interesting pattern in our study. Most of the U5s over fifty years old went to church at least some as a child. Doug's experience was in the Congregational Church in Montana.

Researcher Warner Smith, upon interviewing Doug, found that Doug was resistant, even antagonistic, to the claims of Christianity but that he did not vent any frustration toward him as the interviewer. Notes Warner, "Doug was honest when he asserted three times during the interview that his lack of time and interest are his major obstacles to attending church. His short answers were not because he was rude or because he was uncomfortable. He seemed to believe sincerely that these things just do not apply to him."

Patsy D. of Tennessee, fifty-five years old, gave us similar answers. She too went to church as a child, first as a Nazarene then as a Baptist. The Nazarene church was her parents' church, and the Baptist church was her choice because of the youth group. She even attended a Church of Christ early in her first marriage but "quit when the minister condemned the Equal Rights Amendment."

Patsy's view of God is different. "The universe is God," she told us. "God is in me and God is in you. Anything that we can produce is God. Air is filled with God. God is immanent but not transcendent. Transcendence seems possible, but I have not known one to do so."

Patsy does not believe in a literal heaven or hell but does believe "they both exist in one's mind." She also believes one can get to heaven "by good works." Of course, we were unclear what it meant to get to heaven in one's own mind. Patsy too was "not likely at all" to attend church. She cited her negative experience decades earlier with a Church of Christ minister as the primary reason for her antipathy toward the church.

We could repeat stories like those of Doug and Patsy several times. Common themes seem to run through many of their stories: Most attended church some as a child, most would not attend church

> These men and women have resisted the gospel for at least five decades. Now their hearts are hard and resistant.

today, and many had negative church experiences in their childhood or early adulthood.

Still this pattern of information does not provide us with a definitive explanation for the disproportionate representation of those over age fifty in the U5 category of the Rainer scale. Perhaps the answer cannot be found in the research. Perhaps the most obvious explanation is the best. These men and women have resisted the gospel for at least five decades. Now their hearts are hard and resistant. Their stories are heartbreaking, and though it may appear that our efforts to reach them are futile, we cannot surrender these souls to Satan.

## U5s Are Not Likely Ever to Attend Church

The fact that U5s are not likely ever to attend church may seem self-evident. After all, does not the description of a U5 at least imply that U5s do not attend church? If they are resistant or antagonistic to the gospel, why should we expect them to attend church?

I would have had the same reaction prior to this research project. But one of the amazing surprises of our research was discovering that most of the unchurched do attend church at least once or twice a year. The U5s, however, rarely if ever attend church.

This resistant group tends to have a very skeptical view of anything supernatural. They attempt to provide rational explanations for events we Christians would describe as miraculous. For the U5, then, Jesus may have existed as a good man who did good deeds, but he certainly was not the Son of God. And there most definitely, the U5s contend, was no resurrection. Heaven and hell do not exist as literal places. And the view called annihilationism, that we simply are no more when we die, was common among the U5s. Immortality is unthinkable to most U5s.

This antisupernatural bias tends to affect the U5s' attitude toward the local church. Why should they attend a place that advocates beliefs that are antithetical to their own? The U5s seem to desire to be consistent with their beliefs, or lack of beliefs, in their actions.

Jean S. of Maryland is stereotypical of this mentality. Researcher Rusty Russell discovered Jean through a mutual friend. Jean, an older U5, did attend a Catholic church some as a child. Today she detests organized religion. "There is nothing for me there. It has no answers and I have no questions," Jean told us.

Rusty asked Jean if she would be interested in attending a Bible study at a church.

"I have no need for the Bible," she said. "The Bible was written for very simple people. It was written to give moral and ethical guidance to uneducated people."

Like many of the U5s, Jean's view of Christ is rationalistic. "Yeah, I do believe a person by the name of Jesus Christ lived on earth," she said. "He probably lived a good and moral life. I think he was an ethical person. Whether he was more is not important."

Rusty was stunned by the directness of Jean's responses. "Jean is the most inflexible person I have interviewed," Rusty commented. "I was stunned when she told me (she told me often) that she never thinks about spiritual things. She's convinced that religion is only good for children because it gives them traditions and roots."

It is the antisupernatural rigidity of Jean's views that best explains her unwillingness to see any value in attending church. Unlike the other unchurched persons we interviewed, the U5 typically has no room for God or anything that cannot be explained rationally. The church, therefore, is a waste of time, best left to those of simple minds and little education.

> Unlike the other unchurched persons we interviewed, the U5 typically has no room for God or anything that cannot be explained rationally.

## U5s Typically Do Not Pray

By now the fact that U5s typically do not pray should not surprise you. With their antisupernatural bent, U5s are unlikely to see any value in prayer. This trait sets them apart from many other unchurched persons. Look at how prayer diminishes in importance with each successive unchurched group.

### Table 3.3

| Do You Pray to God on a Regular Basis? | |
| --- | --- |
| | Percentage Who Answered Yes |
| **U1** | 90% |
| **U2** | 75% |
| **U3** | 63% |
| **U4** | 46% |
| **U5** | 13% |

Nine out of ten of the most receptive unchurched persons prayed to God on a regular basis; just over one out of ten of the least receptive U5s did so.

Jamie R. of Utah is a typical U5 in this respect. Her response to the prayer question was adamant: "I never pray to God. He is nothing to me. Why should I pray to something that does not exist? Prayer is something for weak people."

## U5s Have a Condescending View of the Bible

We would expect that the Bible is not viewed as an authoritative book by U5s. After all, the Bible becomes authoritative when it is seen as the supernatural work of God's hands. The following responses confirm our supposition.

### Table 3.4

| The U5s' View of the Bible | |
| --- | --- |
| Totally truthful/God's Word | 0% |
| Truthful and applicable in some areas | 40% |
| Myth | 34% |
| Don't know | 26% |

The low view of Scripture among U5s, however, is just part of the story. They also have a suspicious and condescending perspective of the Bible. They do not merely view Scripture as irrelevant for their lives; they see anyone who holds value in or depends on the Bible as weak and uninformed.

Jerry G. of Delaware was one of many U5s who could not understand why the Bible was still an attraction to people in "this enlightened and sophisticated age." Jerry is in his late fifties and grew up as a Baptist. The most influential person in his life, he told us, was his father. Interestingly, his dad was a deacon in the Baptist church.

Jerry is a self-described agnostic: "I don't know that there is a God or not." His wife is a Buddhist. He had a daughter late in life, and so he allows the ten-year-old girl to go to church on Easter and to go to vacation Bible school.

To our question "Do you believe the Bible is truthful/applicable in all areas of life?" Jerry's "Don't know" response does not tell the full story. On the one hand, Jerry admits that he does not know a lot about the Bible. "It's been so long since I looked at a Bible that I couldn't begin to tell you what's in it," he told us. In that respect Jerry was more forthright than many of U5s who castigated Scripture but seemed to have little knowledge of it. Jerry was one of the few U5s who professed a level of ignorance about Scripture.

> U5s also have a suspicious and condescending perspective of the Bible. They do not merely view Scripture as irrelevant for their lives; they see anyone who holds value in or depends on the Bible as weak and uninformed.

On the other hand, Jerry was no less condescending than most of his U5 peers. "But what I can't understand," he vented, "is how anybody can claim that a book has some kind of special power. You either have to be a nut or have a low IQ to believe that. I'm amazed at how many nuts really do believe there is something mystical and magical about mere words."

One would not be surprised then that U5s do not use the Bible as a source for spiritual guidance. Indeed, *none* of the U5s we interviewed claimed to use the Bible at all for help. See how they compare to the other unchurched groups.

## Table 3.5

| Number Who Said the Bible Is a Source of Spiritual Guidance | |
|---|---|
| U1 | 60% |
| U2 | 36% |
| U3 | 28% |
| U4 | 10% |
| U5 | 0% |

## U5s Tend to Have a Negative View of the Church

One of the overall surprises of our study was that unchurched persons as a whole do not have a negative view of the church. The U5s proved to be the exception to this finding. But even the U5s were not in full agreement in their assessment of the church. We therefore said that U5s *tend* to have a negative view of the church.

We can look at the U5s' perspectives of the church from several different angles. First, we can discover how many of these resistant unchurched persons have had negative experiences with a church. The numbers are overwhelming. Nearly seven out of ten, 69 percent, of the U5s had a specific recollection of a negative church experience.

> Nearly seven out of ten, 69 percent, of the U5s had a specific recollection of a negative church experience.

The U5s were not alone among the unchurched in their recollection of negative church experiences. In fact, the majority of the unchurched in all categories had a negative recollection. The defining issue for the U5s, however, was the intensity of their hurt and the bitterness they still carry to this day.

Donna M. from Kentucky, when asked if she had ever had a negative experience in a church, responded quickly, "Very much so." But when we asked her to elaborate, she was unable to do so emotionally. All that she would tell us is that the experience was related to something that happened to her daughter.

Chapter 3: "Religion Is Okay for the Weak-Minded"

Perhaps some other insights Donna provided us shed light on that negative experience. For example, she said that the only way you could have a positive church experience was "to follow their rules and regulations." And then, at a later moment, Donna commented how church members "take their beliefs and try to push them down everyone's throats."

> The defining issue for the U5s, however, was the intensity of their hurt and the bitterness they still carry to this day.

Researcher Travis Fleming commented in his summary: "I think Donna is turned off by church legalism she experienced as a child. She is antagonistic toward any orthodox teaching or preaching on hell, wrath, or God's punishment."

Another indicator of the U5s' negative view of the church came when we asked why they thought many people did not attend church. Nearly one-third of the U5s said church was irrelevant. As a point of comparison, only 3 percent of the U1s, the most receptive unchurched group, viewed the church as irrelevant.

The reasons for the U5s' claim that the church was irrelevant varied. One group took their negative church experiences of the past and declared that those incidences were sufficient to pronounce the church irrelevant. Another segment never attended church but could find no value in doing so. Yet still another group viewed the church as a gathering of superstitious persons and could not understand why Christians were so unenlightened and still believed in the supernatural and the miraculous.

> Nearly one-third of the U5s said church was irrelevant. As a point of comparison, only 3 percent of the U1s, the most receptive unchurched group, viewed the church as irrelevant.

Another explanation for some of the negative views of the church can be tied to the U5s' view of the clergy. Remember, however, that most of the unchurched have a positive view of ministers. The negative views, as expected, increase with the more resistant unchurched persons.

91

## Table 3.6

| Negative View of Clergy | |
| --- | --- |
| U1 | 13% |
| U2 | 21% |
| U3 | 19% |
| U4 | 31% |
| U5 | 40% |

Shauntez H. of Michigan saw little positive in the lives of clergy. Of the typical minister, he said, "Most of them are criminals. They are always recovering from something, but people let them get away with anything. These men are no better than anyone else, but they always get exalted." Indeed, his attitude toward clergy was obvious as he responded to researcher John Tolbert, who is a seminary student. John asked Shauntez if he believed in the existence of hell, and Shauntez snapped back, "You tell me, Rev.!" That statement brings us to one last distinguishing characteristic of the U5s: their beliefs on heaven and hell.

## U5s Are Less Likely to Believe in the Existence of Heaven or Hell

The antisupernatural mind-set of the U5s was most evident in their views of heaven and hell. The contrast between the U5s, the least receptive, and the U1s, the most receptive, was stark. Look at the diminishing beliefs as you move from U1 to U5.

## Table 3.7

| | Heaven Exists | Hell Exists |
| --- | --- | --- |
| U1 | 100% | 94% |
| U2 | 95% | 82% |
| U3 | 83% | 70% |
| U4 | 54% | 51% |
| U5 | 13% | 20% |

A majority of all but one unchurched group believes in the existence of heaven and hell; the lone exception is our resistant U5s. We were somewhat surprised to find a few more U5s believing in the existence of hell than those who believed in heaven. But, overall, very few U5s believe in either hell or heaven.

Lila C. is a Canadian woman in her fifties. She was interviewed by Guy Fredrick of our team. Her religious background is Roman Catholic, although it has been more than thirty years since she attended any church. She describes Jesus Christ as "a great soul," and she never reads the Bible. Lila's biggest turnoff by Christians is their claim that they have truth. "They claim to have truth," Lila sighs, "when two billion Chinese and many others do not."

Like many of our U5s, Lila does not believe in the existence of hell "except in one's own mind." We heard similar statements like Lila's among the U5s, but we never received a clear explanation of what they meant. "Heaven," says Lila "does not exist in any recognizable form, so we cannot go there."

The U5s as a group almost seem to have a nonchalant attitude about eternal destiny. Many seem amused and condescending in their attitudes about others who believe such myths. How do we reach this recalcitrant group? What do we say to them? Is there any hope for their redemption? Should the church write them off and put their resources into more receptive unchurched groups? To those questions we now turn.

## Reaching the U5s

Several years ago I preached the funeral of one of the most loved members in our church. I was a pastor in one of the Southern states in a church that had begun to reach unchurched people. "Mabel" was seventy-seven years old when she died. A devout Christian, she had been used of God to lead many people to Christ.

Mabel, however, would weep over the one she desired to become a Christian more than anyone else — her husband, Gene. "Oh, pastor," Mabel would say, "God has used me to reach so many people for him, but Gene is as stubborn as ever." Her deathbed prayer was for Gene's salvation.

I saw Mabel's death as a rare opportunity to reach Gene. Surely he would now be receptive to spiritual matters. Certainly the death of his beloved wife of fifty-four years would soften his heart. I requested and received permission to visit Gene at his home a week later.

The new widower was clearly hurting. Despite his and his wife's spiritual differences, there was never any doubt of their love for one another. He had trouble holding back tears as we spoke about Mabel.

I then spoke softly to him: "Gene, wouldn't you like to be with Mabel in heaven one day? Wouldn't you like to become a Christian and have the promise of eternal life?" Gene's response was polite but blunt: "Pastor, I wish there was a heaven. I wish I could believe that Mabel is living somewhere else now. But it's all too silly. We all just have to come to terms that when we die we die and that's it."

I left Gene's home with a heavy heart. Even at a moment of crisis, this U5 seemed unmovable. Is there any hope of reaching this most resistant group? The research team discovered five key issues about reaching U5s.

### Understand That a U5 Is Not a Typical Unchurched Person

Although U5s comprise only 5 percent of all the unchurched in America, many churches devise strategies and allocate resources as if a U5 were the typical unchurched person in their communities. And then they wonder why they reach so few unchurched people.

While we would never presume upon the moves of a sovereign God, we have observed that very few U5s become Christians directly from the U5 category, as Saul did on the Damascus road. Often the best approach is to seek to move a U5 to a point of greater receptivity. And while we would never recommend abandoning attempts to reach the U5s because of their fierce resistance to the gospel, we do suggest that churches and Christians not allocate their heaviest resources to this group. One could probably reach fifty U1s in the same amount of time it takes to reach one U5.

But the U5s should not be neglected. They are lost persons who matter to God. Let us view a few approaches the research team discovered in their hours of interaction with the U5s.

### *Apologetics Can Be Effective with the U5s*

"Apologetics" is the word used to describe the defense of the Christian faith. A good apologetic approach will explain why Christ's resurrection is historically true. It will give empirical evidence for the validity of the Christian faith for two thousand years. It will show that the messianic claims of Christ must be taken seriously.

> One could probably reach fifty U1s in the same amount of time it takes to reach one U5.

The use of apologetics appeals to the U5 on an intellectual level. The educational level of these unchurched persons is far higher than other unchurched groups, and many of them like to be challenged with a deeper cognitive approach.

Remember, with the U5s you are dealing with people who typically deny the reality of heaven and hell, do not believe the Bible is a book of any significant value, have negative views of the church, and view Christians as people who need something spiritual as their emotional crutches. U5s need to be intellectually challenged to the proposition that the Christian faith makes sense and that many extremely bright and gifted people are Christians.

But you may feel intimidated by the prospect of getting into a deep discussion with a U5. Fortunately, there are abundant resources for you to use in your encounters with U5s. Some of the more widely used popular apologetic works over the past thirty years were written by Josh McDowell. His book *Evidence That Demands a Verdict* and its sequels have been of immense value to many Christians. The classic *Mere Christianity* by C. S. Lewis is a great book to put in the hands of agnostics and atheists, assuming of course their willingness to read it. Lewis's own progression from a philosophical agnostic to an evangelical Christian will appeal to some of the more intellectual U5s.

One of my favorite contemporary apologetic authors is Lee Strobel, author of *The Case for Christ* and *The Case for Faith*.[1] What is particularly appealing about Strobel's works is that he writes from the perspective of a former U5. Indeed, his former agnostic, highly educated background gives him insights that contribute greatly to the field of apologetics.

Many U5s must be intellectually convinced of the validity of the Christian claims. Apologetics is at least one starting point to reach them.

## Many U5s Are Ignorant about Christianity

Some of our more heartening interviews with U5s took place when they admitted their lack of knowledge of Christianity, the church, and the Bible. At least these resistant unchurched persons gave us a small window of opportunity to explain some of the issues when they admitted their ignorance.

Faye W. is a U5 from upstate New York. She has never been to church, and she cannot recall her parents ever mentioning their attending church. At age forty-two Faye is a classic second-generation unchurched person. We categorized Faye as a U5 because she sees absolutely no value in any religion and because she sees religion as a crutch for most people.

When we asked Faye why she viewed religion that way, she immediately began talking about the Bible. "One of the reasons I see religion as nothing more than a psychological prop for the weak is their view of the Bible," she told us.

"What view is that?" we asked.

"You know, the view that God literally dictated every word of the Bible, kind of like it dropped from the sky to us."

When we challenged her assumptions about Scripture, she readily admitted that her knowledge of this issue was anecdotal at best. Furthermore, Faye was kind enough to listen to our explanation about the inspired nature of Scripture. She seemed genuinely interested.

Now Faye did not become a Christian the day of our discussion. And to my knowledge she is not a Christian today. But I truly believe that a small crack in her armor of resistance was made that day.

The U5s represent the most "never churched" group of the unchurched. Paradoxically, this more highly educated group is often the most ignorant about Christianity. Such is not the case because they are unable to learn or even unwilling to learn. It is simply because they have had such little contact with the Christian world and with the church that faith has been almost a nonissue for them.

You may have the opportunity to correct the misperceptions about the Christian faith among the U5s. Do so with a gentle and loving attitude. You may see the wall of resistance begin to crumble ever so slightly. And someone may follow one day to lead the person to faith in Christ.

*Understand That You Are Often Dealing with Hurt and Anger among the U5s*

Though the U5s only accounted for 5 percent of our total unchurched survey, they accounted for a much higher proportion of the stories of hurt and anger among the unchurched. Often their resistance to the gospel seemed to be directly related to an event or series of events that had turned them away from God and the church.

When researcher Deborah White started interviewing Reid K. from Missouri, she discerned rather quickly that she was dealing with a man with some very negative perspectives on the church and the Christian faith. Reid described his religious background as "some Baptist, some Catholic, and a little bit of Lutheran." He has not attended church for many years. "I don't believe in all this God stuff," Reid expressed with indignation. "It's a waste of time." His self-described feelings toward the church are "antagonistic." And his view of Christians is a simple "hypocritical." Regarding ministers, Reid says, "Most of them I would rate between greed and selfishness." This guy is not a happy camper!

Perhaps by this point we should not have asked Reid if he had any negative views of churches that he would like to express. Well, he let us have it. "All churches are run by the greed and selfishness of their leaders," he exclaimed. "Those ritual services irritate me too. You know, where they repeat things over and over again and it gets to the point that it doesn't mean anything to anybody. The evangelistic church reminds me of Hollywood — nothing but a lot of hype."

While our role in this study is not psychoanalysis, it was interesting listening to Reid talk on a subject about which we did not inquire — his parents. He reminded us that it was his parents who got him to church a few times as a child, and he said many times that his parents had been the biggest negative influence on his life. Somewhere deep into our interview, Reid shared with us that his parents divorced when he was an older child. The event was obviously devastating to him.

In many ways it was difficult for us to discern when Reid was angry at the church or when he was angry at his parents. And somehow he seemed to relate the two. We are not certain of the details of Reid's life, but we have no doubt that he is a man with deep wounds and much bitterness.

Deborah summarized the interview as follows: "Wow! This guy is out there. He hates the church and God as well. I can't imagine what happened to him to make him so bitter. He spent some time in the church, but he sure is rejecting it now. One of his big problems seems to be his relationship with his mother and father; he has no appreciation for them. It would take someone whom he respected to show him the way to God."

We discovered on several occasions in our interviews that the anger we heard and felt from some of the U5s was the result of life's events for which they blamed God and/or the church. When you run into these angry and bitter persons, do not take their rejection of Christ and the church personally. They are obviously in deep personal pain. Pray for them. Encourage them. Serve them. And through your Christlike attitude toward them, they may leave the ranks of the U5s and become more receptive to the gospel.

*Long-term Relationships and the U5s*

We learned something very important about U5s from new Christians. In my book *Surprising Insights from the Unchurched*, we looked at 353 "formerly unchurched," men and women who had been unchurched most or all of their lives but were now new Christians. Some of these formerly unchurched could recall lengthy periods in their lives during which they were resistant and antagonistic to the gospel. They shared with us the events that moved them to a point of greater receptivity to the gospel and to the church.

A common theme we heard was the persistent and long-term concern of a Christian toward them. Barry Q., a formerly unchurched man from Sacramento, explained it this way: "Ten years ago I hated God, I hated the church, and I hated Christians. My dad was killed in an automobile accident when I was fifteen, and I blamed God for his death.

"Phillip was my best friend in high school, and he never forgot about me. Even when he moved to Philadelphia and we were thousands of miles apart, he stayed in touch with me. I knew he was a Christian, but he never judged me. Even when I would scream at him in my anger with God, he never retaliated.

"I can't explain any one event that caused my bitterness and pain to subside. It almost seemed like a gradual event. When I finally decided to go to church, I already knew that God was working in my life. And when I finally accepted Jesus, it was not a moment from hatred to love, from darkness to light. It almost seemed like the natural thing to do.

"The way we Christians use the phrase, I can't say Phillip 'led me to Christ.' He did not present the gospel, with me praying to receive Christ. Someone else did that. But if you ask me what one person is most responsible for my becoming a Christian, the answer is easy.

Phillip. He never stopped caring, never stopped praying, and never stopped being my friend."

The U5s are difficult to reach. Many have barriers of intellectual pride. Some have barriers of material wealth. Others have a life experience that has turned them against God and the church.

And I must persistently remind you that the U5s are a distinct minority of 5 percent of the 160 million unchurched. But that still means that, in the United States alone, there are approximately 8 million U5s. While the church and Christians should not spend all their time attempting to reach them, we must do something.

I hope that this chapter has been a reminder that the relatively few unchurched persons called U5s are difficult but not impossible to reach. All of your efforts and your church's efforts to reach this recalcitrant group may seem in vain. But you play a part in God's plan to move them to a greater level of receptivity. And then, as perhaps a U2 or U1, they will hear the gospel gladly and receive Christ.

Impossible, you say? Difficult but not impossible. Remember, with God all things are possible. Let us be about the business of loving and serving the U5s into a point of greater receptivity to the gospel. Maybe they will soon transition to the level of receptivity we call U4. And that group is the subject of the next chapter.

**U5**
Highly resistant to the gospel, antagonistic attitude

**U4**
Resistant to the gospel, but not an antagonistic attitude

**U3**
No apparent receptivity, neutral, perhaps open to discussion

**U2**
Receptive to the gospel and to the church

**U1**
Highly receptive to the gospel, "the Phillipian jailer"

## Chapter 4

# "Just What Is Truth?"

### *The World of the U4*

Joseph G. has lived in Indiana most of his life. The thirty-something man has vague memories of attending a Catholic church as a child. He does not attend church at all today, though he did say, "I go occasionally for special services." He describes his own attitude toward the church as "neutral." Researcher Deborah White did not feel that Joseph accurately described himself. "While he said he was neutral, I believe he was more resistant, a U4," Deborah said. "Though he was very pleasant to speak with and made it clear that he would do the interview and answer the questions, he wasn't at all interested in hearing any views of Christianity."

Joseph provided some interesting insights about his views on religion in America. "Religion plays a lesser role in society today," he told us. "My parents were brought up with no choice but to go to church." He seems thankful that his parents did not treat him the same way. "For me there was no pressure to go to church as a child. They never made it a demand on my life. I'm more open-minded today because of their attitude."

Like many U4s, Joseph could not be described as either an atheist or agnostic. Indeed, he told us that he prayed to God "a few times a week." But when we asked him to describe the God to whom he prayed, Joseph gave us the typical nebulous U4 response. "To me, God is not man or woman," he opined. "I try to keep his description vague, no specific details. He is just a supreme being."

If Joseph was uncertain about God's identity, he really squirmed when we asked what he believed about Jesus Christ. "Whew, that's a tough one!" he exclaimed. "He was helpful, the Son of God — I could go on for hours, but that's a tough one. He was wise and helped a lot of people, and he was a prophet who could see clearly."

> A common issue among many of the U4s was some negative event related to Christians and/or the church.

A common issue among many of the U4s was some negative event related to Christians and/or the church. "My father remarried at a Baptist church, and there were a lot of rules there that mentioned how you should act when you come in contact with other Christians. Look, I've been around a lot of religions. No person should tell another one what religion they should belong to. I don't like being told my way or someone else's way is wrong. But other people have done that to me, and it bugs me."

Also common to many U4s was a deep misunderstanding of the way of salvation. Listen to Joseph's words when we asked him what it takes to become a Christian. "Have faith," he started well. "Have a willingness to read the Bible, I guess; study the Scriptures; and live life accordingly." A common response to this question among the U4s was to resort to a works salvation.

The U4s are unlikely to attend a church function on the first invitation.

Joseph indicated that he probably would not go to church if invited. "I guess the only way I would go would be if Mom asked me to go with her somewhere." Unlike the antagonistic U5s, the U4s seem to be careful not to offend the Christian interviewer. Even though Joseph was largely resistant to any attempts to share Christ with him, he assured us that he might change his mind at some point. "My views have changed over the years and continue to change when necessary," he told us. Of course, his malleability did not offer us much encouragement.

## U4s, Not Like U5s

In some ways a good starting point for understanding U4s is to note how significantly different they are from U5s. Whereas the other categories on the Rainer scale change in degree, U5s are virtually a category that stands alone. So when we start looking at the U4s, we will see a dramatic change from the previous category.

> In some ways a good starting point for understanding U4s is to understand how significantly different they are from U5s.

## The Heaven and Hell Issue

The difference between the U4s and U5s is no more dramatic than the two groups' views on heaven and hell. Only 13 percent of U5s believe in the existence of heaven, but the number jumps dramatically to 54 percent among the U4s. That the majority of the U4s believe in heaven, however, should not be misleading. More often than not, the heavenly view is far from orthodox.

Peter D. is a U4 from Oregon. Like the peers in his group, Peter is not antagonistic toward the church, but he certainly was not receptive to any of our overtures to explain the way of Christ. When we asked him to talk about heaven, however, he was effusive. "Something happens, you know, when we die," he pondered. "There just seems to be too much evidence that this life is not all that there is to it. I got a friend in Eugene that swears he talks to his dead mother every week. Who am I to question his beliefs?"

Another common characteristic of U4s is their willingness, if not desire, to affirm the beliefs of virtually everyone. Speaking further of his friend from Eugene, Peter comments, "It's not like he's some kind of wacko. I mean there are television shows about people who talk to the dead. There's just got to be more than this life."

Our interview questions did not specifically ask respondents to describe their picture of heaven. Yet it was not uncommon for the unchurched persons to elaborate on their perspectives of heaven. Peter was among the more loquacious. "Man, it's not easy to describe what heaven is like because no one has ever come back from there to tell us. It's got to be a place that's pretty cool. I mean, whenever you hear about spirits or ghosts trapped here on earth, most of them just want to leave and get to heaven. They obviously want to be in a good place or they wouldn't want to go there."

Peter also sees the plurality of religions as further evidence of some type of heaven. "Every religion seems to have some kind of belief in another life. I don't think they are all wrong. There has to be something to it." But he remained vague about describing this next life. "You just can't know," he insists. "I just believe that it is something as good as this life, probably better. I really don't believe in that reincarnation stuff. To me, that is the really stupid belief. I can't imagine being a cat in another life. Really stupid."

> While the majority (54 percent) did affirm the reality of an afterlife called heaven, approximately one-third (34 percent) did not believe in heaven.

The U4s had a significant minority group, however, that did not believe in the existence of heaven. While the majority (54 percent) did affirm the reality of an afterlife called heaven, approximately one-third (34 percent) did not believe in heaven. Kirk Y. of Kansas is representative of the minority group.

"It's just not rational," Kirk murmured. "I mean we are just physical beings. We are born, we start breathing, we stop breathing, and we die. That's basically all there is to it. How can we expect to live after our bodies die? It just doesn't make sense. I think it is the wishful thinking of some people who are afraid to face reality."

Though I did not personally interview all of the unchurched for this study, I read every report submitted to me by the research team. We also had several meetings at which we compared notes and experiences. A consensus among our team was that the U4s do think of heaven; they do wonder what happens when we die.

"They're so different from the U5s," researcher Jon Beck commented. "When you talk to a U5, you feel like you've run into a brick wall. It's like their hearts are hardened. But the U4s, whether they say they believe in heaven or not, really want to talk about heaven."

Christ has called you to be his witness (Acts 1:8). He expects you to be about his business of telling the Good News to others. When you meet a person who is resistant but not antagonistic, a classic U4, our research indicates that conversations about an afterlife may prove fruitful. That conversation is typically about heaven, but some U4s we interviewed seemed just as eager to talk about hell.

We were surprised initially to discover that a slight majority (51 percent) of the U4s believe in the existence of hell, while 41 percent do not. Like the concept of heaven, however, the perspectives on hell were far from orthodox. Indeed, many times the views would simply be off the wall.

"Yeah, I believe there is a hell," said Mandy R. of Florida. We waited expectantly to hear from an unchurched person to give us her unique perspective. "You see, I think it is a mind thing," she told us with all seriousness. "When we die our mind does not die. It goes on forever. So hell becomes our most negative thoughts that last forever. We are doomed to rethink our worst thoughts over and over again. It's a cycle that does not end."

We asked Mandy how she came up with this idea of hell, and she looked at us like we were crazy or ignorant or both. "It's the only thing that makes sense!" she exclaimed. "Our thoughts are separate from our bodies. Our bodies don't last forever, but our minds do. If we are evil and think evil thoughts in this life, we are punished with hell thoughts forever." She continued to look at us as if we just didn't get it. Well, we didn't get it, so we moved on to the next issue.

> Hell is just not as believable to the U4s as heaven is. The ever-present question of a loving God having a place of eternal torment and separation was pervasive in this unchurched group.

Hell is just not as believable to the U4s as heaven is. The ever-present question of a loving God having a place of eternal torment and separation was pervasive in this unchurched group. "If there is anything that ticks me off about you Christians, it is your crazy ideas about hell," George G. of Pennsylvania told us. "I think you would do a lot more good and convince a lot more people if you could get over that issue."

Though the numbers indicate that a slight majority of U4s believe in the existence of hell, the numbers who hold to the biblical and orthodox perspective are really rather small. Some of the U4s want to believe that there is a place for the "bad" people and for the "good" people, but few see hell as a literal place of eternal agony.

There was, however, a momentary "blip" that went contrary to this perspective. In the several weeks after September 11, 2001, the orthodox view of hell gained in popularity. Such sentiment was an obvious but temporary emotional response to the tragedies of that day.

"I believe Osama Bin Laden and his kind will burn in the hottest fires of hell," said Pedro F. of New Mexico. "There is no torture that is cruel enough for him and those that hate America." We interviewed Pedro on September 25, 2001, exactly two weeks after the towers fell and the Pentagon was hit.

We asked Pedro for a bit of indulgence in diverting from our planned questions. Though he was not at all receptive to any of our overtures to the gospel, he was polite as we took a different path in the interview. "Pedro," we queried, "did you have this view of hell before September 11?"

"In all honesty, probably not," he admitted. "First, I don't guess I thought too much about hell. Second, if you asked me earlier, I probably would have thought that hell was some kind of warped fantasy of Christians."

"I believe Osama Bin Laden and his kind will burn in the hottest fires of hell," said Pedro F. of New Mexico. "There is no torture that is cruel enough for him and those that hate America." We interviewed Pedro on September 25, 2001, exactly two weeks after the towers fell and the Pentagon was hit.

What was it about September 11, we asked, that changed his mind? "I guess it's the first time I gave much thought to real evil," he responded. "And I believe in a God of justice, and a God of justice will not let this go unpunished."

We did not interview Pedro again after this time together. But if he was typical of the U4s, he would be more reticent today to affirm the reality of a hell for condemned persons. Such was the September 11 effect. Many opinions changed dramatically for a season, only to revert back to their more passive positions in just a matter of weeks.

Still, Christians can be challenged by the U4s' views on eternal life. The majority believe something exists beyond this life, though they cannot identify it with specificity. The door is open, however, to speak of eternal matters with this group and to speak of God. But when you enter into a conversation about God with a U4, be aware that you may be speaking of two very different ideas. Such is the topic of our next section.

## Who Is God?

Our interviewers were in the early stages of this research when they realized that any discussion of God by a U4 needed clear definitions. While very few of the U4s were atheists who did not believe in God or agnostics who doubted the existence of God, the views of those who held to some type of theistic view were strange to say the least.

Barrie B. of Kentucky was interviewed by researcher Bland Mason. For Barrie, God is "something greater than yourself. All religions worship and believe in the same God. Whether you are Mormon, Muslim, or Christian, you believe in the same God." Barrie's perspective was common among U4s. Most of them have a view that is commonly known as pluralism, which advocates the equality of beliefs of many religions.

Erik G. of Washington State is but another example of this pluralistic perspective. Deborah White interviewed this twenty-one-year-old man who is already rising rapidly in the communications industry. Erik's mother is Catholic and his father is Protestant, although he has no idea of his father's specific church identity. He is also dating a Catholic young lady who "insists that I come to church, but she doesn't pressure me."

Unfortunately, Erik has some negative experiences with church and former girlfriends. "Some of my worst experiences have been with ex-girlfriends who were religious," he told us. "One once gave me an ultimatum: Go to church or get lost. I couldn't believe that. She condemned me for not attending church services."

Erik may have written off churches for now, but he still has a belief in the existence of God. He has attended a church service only twice in his life. One of those services was on September 12, 2001, at St. Patrick's in New York City, where he "really sensed the presence of God."

But just who is God to Erik? The St. Patrick's service put it in perspective for him. "The service really moved me because it wasn't a denominational thing," he commented. "They all pulled together and just believed in good things, not a particular God." But again God had no clear identity. He certainly was not the God who revealed himself in Jesus Christ. For the U4s who believe in the existence of God, ambiguity is the best description for God among this group.

The large minority of U4s who do not believe in the existence of God are hardly the hard-core resisters found among the U5s. In fact, the atheistic and agnostic U4s almost sound like the theistic U4s. They leave room for the possibility that they are wrong; they just do not want to limit God to some clear definition, particularly the Christian understanding of God.

> The large minority of U4s who do not believe in the existence of God are hardly the hard-core resisters found among the U5s. In fact, the atheistic and agnostic U4s almost sound like the theistic U4s.

Karl D. of North Dakota is a good example of the "open atheist." In his interview with researcher Warner Smith, he denied the existence of heaven and hell and mostly denied the existence of God. While it may seem surprising that one would equivocate on such an important matter, such responses were not uncommon among the U4s.

Karl is a senior at the University of North Dakota majoring in chemistry. He plans to do master's-level work in chemistry as well. In his education and training in science, he has accepted an "intellectual and scientific argument against the existence of God." Nevertheless, this college student's upbringing in the Lutheran church still tugs him back to considering a belief in God. Indeed, in what may seem like a contradiction, Karl denied the existence of God and heaven and hell, but he was open to the possibility of life after death. "I don't know what might go on after death," he told us. "I choose to believe there is more to us than biology, but I have no idea what that is. I hope there is an afterlife."

On the one hand, Brandon G. from Vermont might seem to be a hard-core atheist. On the other hand, his willingness to admit that there may be answers beyond him gave our interviewer Twyla Fagan a small amount of hope that Brandon might one day be open to the gospel.

Brandon never attends church. He is an avowed atheist. He believes all churches have direct ties to the Republican Party. He denies the reality of both heaven and hell. He obviously does not pray. And he has no memory of ever being invited to church. This brief description makes Brandon sound like a near hopeless case. Yet Brandon made some statements that led us to believe that his case may not be hopeless after all. His view of typical Christians is that "they are loving." He sees the typical church pastor or minister as "committed." His parents have just started attending church after many years of religious inactivity. And he admits that he is "somewhat likely" to attend church if invited, but "I cannot see the benefit to a committed atheist."

And though Brandon several times reminded us of his atheistic beliefs, he still seemed open to the possibility that he might be wrong. Researcher Twyla put it this way: "Right now Brandon is at a very black and white stage of his life, but he realizes that there are greater questions out there. He has been able to reason many answers out, but he is also beginning to realize that there might be something even greater than reason." Perhaps Brandon will discover that "something" is God.

Our study found that about 21 percent of the unchurched would best be described as U4 on the Rainer scale. It is conceivable, if not likely, that the number of U4s will grow in our increasingly secular culture. How should the Christian respond? We are called to be witnesses to U4s. What will we do? What will we say?

First, you as a Christian must not be intimidated by the multiple arguments offered by the U4s. And you must not depend on your own power or strength, but on the presence of the Spirit of God (Zech. 4:6). Second, understand that most U4s are confused and searching. They may offer arguments of passion and persistence, but often they are hurting and questioning beneath the veneer of self confidence.

Finally, realize that some things have not changed. The first-century world to which the early church witnessed was secular, pluralistic, and often argumentative. But an explosion of evangelistic growth took place in God's power with the church's obedience. It happened then. It can happen again today.

## Who Is Christ? Who Do Men and Women Say That He Is?

If there is confusion over the identity of God among the U4s, the identity of Christ really presents a challenge to this unchurched group. On the one hand, there is a reticence to see Jesus as the unique Son of God. On the other hand, the U4s do not want to assign Christ anything less than an important role in history. Some of the attempts to do so proved to be awkward and sometimes humorous.

For example, Brandon G. from Vermont, from whom we just heard, tried to see Jesus as a very important historical figure while still holding to his atheistic belief. "He definitely was a historical person, but he was not resurrected," Brandon mused. "He was an incredible role model, a symbol of how human beings are to treat each other. Jesus showed us the great capacity of the human being to do good."

> On the one hand, there is a reticence to see Jesus as the unique Son of God. On the other hand, the U4s do not want to assign Christ anything less than an important role in history.

The U4s typically refused to see or did not realize the inconsistency of their statements. They desire for Jesus to be a great teacher and role model, but they refuse to see him as the Son of God. But Jesus himself claimed deity and insisted that he is the only way of salvation (John 14:6). The U4s either must deny the historical accuracy of some of Jesus' claims or conclude that he was a liar. They seem willing to do neither.

Stuart B. of Indiana was interviewed by Rusty Russell of the research team. His religious background includes Church of Christ,

Buddhism, and agnosticism. Throughout all of his religious and non-religious phases, he has held tremendous respect for Jesus. "If I could go back in time in a time machine, I know exactly where I would go," he said excitedly. "I would love to talk to Jesus more than anyone else in history."

Stuart continued with an effusive description of Jesus: "I believe he was a remarkable healer, both physical and spiritual. I believe he had great clarity of thought and the ability to communicate truth. I have great respect for Jesus." His was a fairly lofty perspective for someone who is resistant to the gospel.

Julie P. of Colorado provides another example of a person who is resistant to the gospel but positive about the person of Jesus Christ. Julie grew up with a nominal United Methodist background. She sometimes attends a church service for a special occasion such as Christmas or Easter. But her overall perspective of the church is that it has too many rules. "We are basically spiritual by nature; all the church rules prevent us from finding true spirituality," Julie reflected.

Julie's thoughts about spiritual matters seem to be some strange mix of New Age and Eastern religions. Her prayer is constant, she says, because "I am in touch with a higher power through meditation." To get to heaven we must "live in tune with self and our spiritual oneness." When researcher Jon Beck asked Julie about her spiritual journey, she responded that her goal is "to live a life that is kind to all beings and the world; to live a life in harmony with all beings, earth spirit, animals, and people."

Despite her off-the-wall responses, Julie affirmed the significance of Jesus. "He was a great person that lived in biblical times. He was a good man, a spiritual leader. He played a great spiritual role in history."

U4s seem to have a good deal of caution when they speak about Jesus. These unchurched persons are very careful, even to the point of political correctness, in choosing their words about Jesus. And it is not easy to discern their motives for their fear of offending. That same group had no hesitation in telling us what was wrong with Christians like us, with the narrow-minded beliefs we hold, and with the churches we attend.

Though further study is needed, it appears that one of the few open doors for discussion with U4s is a conversation about Jesus. The mere mention of his name elicits a pause and can often move a conversation from resistant to pleasant. Although the U4s as a rule have little patience for Christians and the established church, in an ironic twist, they have tremendous respect for Jesus. The possibility for open dialogue is high unless the Christian decides to talk about one key issue regarding Christ: the truth that he is the only way of salvation. No single issue makes the blood of a U4 boil more than that of exclusivity, the doctrine that says that belief in Jesus Christ is the only way to heaven. The words of Jesus himself in John 14:6 are cited to affirm that the Savior is the only way, truth, and life, and that "no one comes to the Father" except through Jesus.

Our researchers rarely mentioned this foundational truth of the Christian faith, because the U4 was likely to raise the issue himself or herself. For example, in our earlier conversation with Julie P. of Colorado, she was quick to point out that her biggest turnoff by Christians is "when they try to tell me Jesus is the only way."

Exclusivity was seen as intolerant, narrow-minded, and bigoted by many U4s. These unchurched men and women could not fathom a rational person holding to a belief in such a narrow way of salvation. Ken T. of North Carolina was interviewed by researcher Todd Randolph. Ken viewed the belief that Jesus is the only way to be the classic example of "when religion overrides common sense."

> Exclusivity was seen as intolerant, narrow-minded, and bigoted by many U4s. These unchurched men and women could not fathom a rational person holding to a belief in such a narrow way of salvation.

The tolerance movement in America has made a huge impact, and nowhere is the impact more evident than on this issue. More often than not, we did not merely hear mild objections to exclusivity; we heard emotional tirades from the U4s. Words do not do justice to the outbursts we often heard. The reader cannot see the red faces and looks of indignation. "Christians would do a lot better in this world if you did not have the arrogance and stupidity to act like you've got all the answers. I don't know anyone else that makes arrogant claims like you people," screamed Jackie F. of Idaho.

Perhaps you can sense a bit of the emotion in Jackie's words. If you had been present during her outburst, however, you would have seen an anger and indignation that is difficult to describe with the written word. The U4s are simply furious that basic Christian doctrine holds to a single way of salvation.

How then do you the Christian respond? I fear that a few may take this description of the U4s and become totally reticent to share Christ as the only way of salvation. We cannot compromise the essence of the gospel. The world may reject the message we have to share, but we cannot fail to share it.

> The response of the U4s to the exclusivity of salvation through Christ is a caution for wisdom, not an admonition for silence.

The response of the U4s to the exclusivity of salvation through Christ is a caution for wisdom, not an admonition for silence. We did these interviews so that we could learn something about the mind-set of the unchurched world. You should not, therefore, be caught off guard by negative responses or even emotional outbursts by U4s. Be wise in your words and timing, but do not remain silent.

## The U4s and the Bible

Interestingly, the Bible can become a topic of common interest between a Christian and a U4. As you might expect, the U4s have a wide range of views on the Bible, but most have some level of respect for God's Word. As I have shown at different points in this chapter, it is fascinating to see the shifts in perspectives from the U5s to the U4s. This divergence is certainly true with views of the Bible.

### Table 4.1

| Views of the Bible | | |
|---|---|---|
| | U5 | U4 |
| Totally truthful/God's Word | 0% | 10% |
| Truthful and applicable in some areas | 40% | 51% |
| Myth | 33% | 14% |
| Don't know | 27% | 25% |

None of the U5s and only one out of ten of the U4s believe the Bible to be God's Word, totally truthful in all areas. But six out of ten of the U4s believe the Bible to be totally truthful or mostly truthful. And only 14 percent of the U4s view the Bible as a myth.

The Christian therefore has much more common ground than he or she might expect when relating to the resistant U4. These unchurched persons will not automatically regard any discussion of the Bible as irrelevant.

> The Christian therefore has much more common ground than he or she might expect when relating to the resistant U4. These unchurched persons will not automatically regard any discussion of the Bible as irrelevant.

A typical perspective of the Bible from a U4 was that of Dan C. of Iowa. Dan comes from a Jewish family but claims no particular allegiance to Judaism today. Interestingly, Dan told us that he is engaged to a Christian, but he refused to elaborate.

Something negative obviously took place in Dan's life, because he informed us that he "had a negative experience with every Catholic he has ever met."

We were therefore surprised that Dan held the Bible, both Testaments, in high esteem. His view of Scripture is that it is "true and applicable in some areas." On the one hand, he regards the Bible as "man's interpretation of God's work." On the other hand, when we asked Dan for advice to churches, he said that they need to "follow Scriptures more closely and stop misinterpreting the Bible."

Unlike the antagonistic U5s, we noticed a reticence among the U4s to be critical of the Bible. Once again, their responses were cautious, almost politically correct. Only one out of seven U4s was willing to call the Bible a myth. Most had something positive to say, or they said nothing at all.

As in most of my research projects, I see in retrospect several changes I would have made. On the issue of the Bible, I would have asked the unchurched persons an open-ended question to discover their views of the Bible and the impact it had on their lives. Unfortunately, we phrased the question in such a way that they could choose one of four responses and say no more.

Yet on occasion an unchurched person would elaborate beyond the objective choices. Frieda V. from Oklahoma was one such person. Frieda is a rare U4 who has never attended a church. "The Bible is the greatest book ever," she gushed. "I read it every day and sometimes twice a day. It's my fix; I can't live without it. It's just like God is talking directly to me."

Frieda reads parts of the Bible randomly. "I just open it and start reading," she says. "I mean, if God wants me to see something, he will lead me to it. It's always exciting to see where he'll lead me every day."

We would wish that most Christians would have Frieda's enthusiasm for the Bible. But we would also hope that someone like Frieda could get insights from a Christian for more coherent Bible study. Indeed, we see the possibility, if not likelihood, that a significant number of the U4s would be receptive to a home or neighborhood Bible study. They are unlikely to enter a church, but perhaps they will come to your home.

## Those Praying U4s

The number of unchurched who pray to God on a regular basis increases from 13 percent among the U5s to 46 percent among the U4s. The number would be significantly higher if we asked for those who pray at least occasionally. Simply stated, this resistant unchurched group sees value in prayer.

Tony G. from Texas was interviewed by Twyla Fagan. The twenty-something Hispanic has a Catholic background. He is quick to point out, however, that he went to the Catholic church "only because my mom made me. I don't consider myself a Catholic. I'm nothing now."

In one of our more fascinating conversations, Tony told us that he does not "even know a Christian, so I've got no views of what a Christian is like." Such statements were not uncommon at all levels on the Rainer scale. We on the research team were grieved to find how many unchurched people had no relationship at any level with a Christian.

Tony was yet another U4 who never attends church. No one has ever shared with him how to become a Christian. He is not likely at all to attend church if invited. He told us that "my brother invites me occasionally," which seemed curious since he had just told us that he does not know any Christians. How does he respond to his brother? "I appreciate it," he says, "but I'm not going. It just doesn't interest me. My daughter can go on her own if she wants, but I am not going to force her."

When we came to the issue of prayer, Tony said that he prays occasionally. What are the occasions? "I pray only when bad things are happening. Most of the time God helps those who help themselves. He really doesn't want to be bothered by us. I do pray to my grandmother who passed away two years ago. She was really religious, and I feel safer with her." Twyla would explain in her interview summary: "Obviously his grandmother influenced him quite a bit.

She was supposedly the most religious person he knew, but by the things he said, she was not a Christian."

A significant number of the U4s prayed to have something like a spiritual safety net. They do not know if anyone hears prayers, but they have little to lose by praying. Irene S. is an eighty-year-old Canadian from Toronto who expressed those sentiments. "Yes, I pray to God every night and even during the day," she told us. "Now I don't know if there is a God up there or not, so I just figure he's up there watching over us. But I don't think anyone knows."

> A significant number of the U4s prayed to have something like a spiritual safety net. They do not know if anyone hears prayers, but they have little to lose by praying.

The point I am trying to make throughout this chapter on U4s is that this group of unchurched persons as a whole is not unspiritual and anti-God. To the contrary, the U4s tend to be very spiritual and very confused about their spirituality. While we recognize that they may not enter our church doors any time soon, we do have significant points of contact and commonality with the U4s. Our failure to reach out to them is inexcusable.

## Will They Ever Attend Church?

I am not certain how you the reader will respond to this chapter. Will you see the U4s as a resistant and hopeless lot for whom our time and energy expended is just a waste? Will you see some of these beliefs of the U4s as so far out that any point of connection seems highly unlikely? Or will you view their spirituality and comments on the Bible and prayer as a potential starting point for sharing the gospel? Before you come to a definitive conclusion, listen to the comments of some U4s.

> While we recognize that they may not enter our church doors any time soon, we do have significant points of contact and commonality with the U4s. Our failure to reach out to them is inexcusable.

One of our standard survey questions was: "If a Christian friend or family member invited you to a church function now, how likely would you be to attend?" Remember, the U4s are resistant to any presentation of the gospel and to becoming a Christian. Look at their responses:

### Table 4.2

| Likelihood of Attending Church If Invited | |
| --- | --- |
| Very likely | 17% |
| Somewhat likely | 45% |
| Not likely at all | 38% |

From the research team's perspective, these responses are nothing less than amazing. Among the U4s, the second most resistant unchurched group, 62 percent indicated that they were either very likely or somewhat likely to attend church if they were invited. A repetitive theme that you will hear throughout this book is "If you invite them, they will come."

Our further questions found that most of these unchurched are uncomfortable entering a church building alone. They would rather you take them to church or meet them there. But the key issue is that the vast majority will come if invited.

> A repetitive theme that you will hear throughout this book is "If you invite them, they will come."

Now, the probing question for you and me is: "When is the last time you invited an unchurched person to church?" We in the churches are searching and agonizing over ways to reach the lost and unchurched world, yet the research indicates that a simple invitation may be the most cutting-edge approach we can employ.

When speaking of those who would enter the kingdom, Jesus said in the parable of the dinner, "Go out into the highways and along the hedges, and compel them to come in, so that my house may be filled" (Luke 14:23 NASB). Though the analogy between the kingdom and the local church is not perfect, the principle is close. We have been mandated by Christ to urge people, to invite people, even to compel people to come to church and to hear the gospel. What have you done to obey the Savior?

## What Are the U4s' Excuses for Not Coming?

We know that most Christians are woefully lacking in their obedience to invite the unchurched to church. What then are the reasons cited by the U4s for not attending? This group was candid in their responses. Although we asked them to explain why most people do not attend church, their responses really indicated their own stories. Let us compare them again to the U5s.

### Table 4.3

| Why Do You Think Many People Do Not Attend Church? | | |
| --- | --- | --- |
| | **U4** | **U5** |
| Laziness | 8% | 15% |
| Too busy | 29% | 8% |
| Church is not relevant | 19% | 31% |
| Christians are hypocrites | 10% | 8% |
| Other | 34% | 38% |

Notice the change in the response "Church is not relevant." More than three out of ten U5s cite this reason for not attending church, but only two out of ten of the U4s do so. Again, the point is simple: The U4s are much more receptive to spiritual matters and even to the church despite their resistance to the gospel. What are you doing to reach them?

## Listening to the Formerly Unchurched Again

As I indicated at the beginning of this book, the formerly unchurched guided this research project in many ways. Because their recent past was one of being unchurched, they gave us significant insights into the types of questions we should ask the unchurched. At different points in my research and writing, I would seek feedback from the formerly unchurched.

I shared with David M., a formerly unchurched businessman from New York, the information you have just read on U4s. David read the essence of this chapter and responded with a lengthy email. With his permission, I share with you a portion of his correspondence.

*Hey Thom, I just finished reading the material on the U4s. Boy, could I identify with those people. I was probably a U4 just about five years ago. I never was antagonistic toward the church and Christians, but I was resistant to anyone trying to convert me.*

*I look back on those years, and the best way I can describe it was that it was a time of fog. I didn't think or see much clearly in those days. Most of the time religious matters were not at the top of my agenda, but they were kind of hanging in my conscience. I guess the Holy Spirit was trying to get my attention.*

*The most amazing thing about that period is that I can't recall one person over several years who ever said anything to me about Jesus or even the church. I had Christian neighbors who never opened their mouths. I had Christian coworkers just two offices down from mine. Never a word from them.*

*Looking back now, I think I would have welcomed a word from a Christian. I didn't know it at the time, but I was hurting deep inside. And I probably would have put on some act of bravado to let people know I didn't need God as a crutch. But I still would have loved to have heard something from a Christian.*

*I guess I moved to a more neutral position, what you call a U3, after watching a Billy Graham crusade on television. I bet if someone invited me to church then I would have gone. You know the rest of my story. I finally visited a dynamic church in town and became even more receptive to the gospel. Finally someone from the church asked me to lunch. Mike, who is now my best friend, shared with me how to accept Christ. A few months later I did pray to receive Christ.*

*But do hear what I am saying. I had to go to a church before someone talked to me one-on-one! For the first 42 years of my life, no one witnessed to me or invited me to church. I pray that I will never make that mistake. You know, the mistake of keeping my mouth shut. No, it's more than a mistake, it's a sin.*

*Thom, I pray that your next book will be used of God to open some mouths that are sinfully shut. If I had to depend on most Christians in America for hearing the good news, I guess I would still be hell-bound. Please let your readers know that most of the unchurched people out there would welcome a word from a Christian. Please tell them before it's too late for some.*

Thanks, David. But I will not need to tell them. You already did.

**U5**
Highly resistant to the gospel, antagonistic attitude

**U4**
Resistant to the gospel, but not an antagonistic attitude

**U3**
No apparent receptivity, neutral, perhaps open to discussion

**U2**
Receptive to the gospel and to the church

**U1**
Highly receptive to the gospel, "the Phillipian jailer"

## Chapter 5

# "Church Is Just Not My Thing"

### *The World of the U3*

---

Sure, I believe in God and Jesus.
I have no problem with the church.
It's just that I don't need the church in my life.
It's just not my thing.

*—Leah M.,*
*U3 from Minnesota*

---

The candidate I was supporting had run an excellent race to this point. But I had to admit that the opposition candidate was doing very well also. Election day was only nine days away, and I devoured any piece of information I could get.

Finally, a new poll was scheduled to be released the next day. I woke up early in the morning to check the Internet for the definitive poll. At noon the poll results were released. Now with only eight days until the election, my candidate held a slight lead with 45 percent of those polled compared to 43 percent for the opposition. Twelve percent of those polled were undecided.

I could feel my face redden when it hit me that more than one out of ten of the voting population was undecided with elections only a week and a day away. And it wasn't as if the candidates had identical positions on the issues. To the contrary, voters had a clear choice. The positions of the candidates were clearly defined and, for the most part, diametrically opposed.

*Undecided!* I screamed silently. *How could anyone following this political race remain undecided, especially this close to election day?*

If an election of some importance has a large pool of "undecideds," how much more amazing is it that matters of eternity can likewise have such a significant number without a clear opinion? Such seems to be the case with the unchurched. The largest single group of the unchurched was classified by our researchers as being neutral in their attitudes toward the church and the gospel.

To say that these U3s are undecided is not to say that they are without opinions. To the contrary, this largest category of unchurched on the Rainer scale often had outspoken views. But when questions were asked on the matters of church and eternity, they refused to commit.

## The Big Part of the Bell Curve

Since it has been several chapters since we have reviewed the specifics of the size of each of the groups on the Rainer scale, let us see again the relative numbers of each group.

### Table 5.1

| | |
|---|---|
| U1 | 11% |
| U2 | 27% |
| U3 | 36% |
| U4 | 21% |
| U5 | 5% |

The Rainer scale forms an imperfect bell curve. A perfect bell curve would have the U1s and the U5s as both the smallest and equal in number. The U2s and the U4s would again be equal in size and represent the second largest groups. The U3s would stand alone and be the largest in number.

The U3s in our study were definitely the largest in number. To put their numbers into perspective, remember that we estimate that there are approximately 160 million unchurched persons in the United States. If our sample size of 36 percent is also reflective of the national norm, we estimate that there are more than 57 million U3s in the United States. More than one out of three unchurched persons are U3s.

> There are more than 57 million U3s in the United States. More than one out of three unchurched persons are U3s.

Over the next several pages, I hope to help you understand better this large group of unchurched men and women in America. The task is not easy because, more than any group we studied, this group often defies categorization. Let's listen to a prototypical interview to get a perspective of the challenges we faced.

## Patsy S. from Louisiana Speaks

Patsy S. is a fifty-something U3 from Louisiana. She is well educated, having earned a master's degree several years ago. Interestingly, she grew up as a preacher's kid. Patsy's father was a pastor in the Wesleyan church. Her self-description of her attitude toward the church is "friendly," although researcher Brad Morrow viewed her responses as neutral.

Patsy does attend church on occasion, "less than five times a year" she thinks. Her inactivity in a church is primarily due to a busy schedule, she tells us, although she "uses the television medium as a primary source for religious help." Although she rarely attends, she does believe that "churches do a lot to provide different services for different age groups."

Patsy's views of Christians are about as confusing as her attitude toward the church. She describes Christians as "committed, loving, and hypocritical." And though she believes the Bible to be "totally truthful, God's Word," she depends on self-help books more than the Bible for guidance.

Eternity is also an ambiguous issue for Patsy. On the one hand, she denies the reality of a literal heaven or hell. On the other hand, while "heaven and hell are not places to go," there is "a sense that it is true, because your spirit will be either rewarded or punished. Your spirit will be either happy or sad forever." We wonder how closely Patsy listened to her father's sermons.

Then there is the issue of salvation. We asked, "How do you believe someone gets to heaven, Patsy?"

Her response began positively. "You have to ask God to be in your heart," she told us. It seemed as though her response might be headed toward something related to grace and faith. But then she added, "And you must be a good, moral, and giving person." Like many of the U3s, Patsy would not see salvation as a free gift from God; she had to add the human-centered works to the response.

Perhaps we are reading too much into Patsy's responses, but the two greatest influences in her life are her mother ("She taught me the importance of family and giving") and her best friend ("She helped me appreciate the diversity in others"). We found it interesting that she never mentioned her father, the Wesleyan pastor, as an influence.

Today Patsy is only an occasional visitor to the church. She later admitted that she mainly attends special events, "those that are celebrations and positive experiences like first communion, baby dedications, and musicals." She says that she alternates between three churches, the Methodist, Baptist, and Catholic. Patsy is certainly an ecumenical unchurched person.

Researcher Brad described Patsy the way we see many U3s. "Her beliefs are a hodgepodge of beliefs. She has all kinds of answers, but she doesn't seem to have a personal relationship with Jesus Christ. She is not antagonistic but rather apathetic toward the church. She is an intelligent woman who has been shaped by issues of tolerance and diversity. She sees no reason to be in church. Patsy also seems to be depending on a works theology for salvation."

Such is the world of the U3s. Clear definitions are difficult. For many of our researchers, they were the "other"; they simply did not fit neatly into any category. In this chapter, however, we will attempt to look at U3s from three different perspectives. First, we will look at the large group that truly seems to be neutral in matters of faith. Then we will examine the two "leaning" groups, one leaning toward U4 and the other toward U2. Let us begin with the neutral U3s.

## The Strange "Neutral" U3s

Todd Randolph interviewed Paul B. of Tennessee. His conversation reminded me of conversations I once had with my three teenage boys. Fortunately, they are now grown and are able to carry on a decent conversation with their old man. But in the past the conversation went something like this:

> Such is the world of the U3s. Clear definitions are difficult. For many of our researchers, they were the "other"; they simply did not fit neatly into any category.

"Hey Jess, did you have a good day?"
*(Pause)* "Yeah."
"What did you do today?"
*(Look of absolute boredom)* "Nothing."
"Well, I haven't seen you in thirty-six hours. Have you even breathed during that time?"
*(Obviously tuned Dad out totally)* "Naw." *(Male teenage speak for "no")*

The neutral U3s often gave us monosyllabic responses, at least feigning total disinterest. Listen to Todd's conversation with Paul:

Todd: What is your religious background?
Paul: Methodist.
Todd: Would you like to elaborate?
Paul: No.
Todd: What should churches do to attract more people?

Paul:    Nothing.

Todd:    Do you pray to God on a regular basis?

Paul:    No.

Todd:    If you decided to go to church, what day would you prefer?

Paul:    Sunday.

Todd:    Do you believe heaven exists?

Paul:    Yes.

Todd:    How about hell?

Paul:    Yes.

Todd:    What do believe about Jesus Christ?

Paul:    God exists.

Todd:    Who has been the greatest influence in your life?

Paul:    Grandparents.

Todd:    Can you tell us more about them?

Paul:    No.

Todd:    Has anyone ever shared with you how to become a Christian?

Paul:    No.

Todd:    If someone invited you to attend church, would you go?

Paul:    No.

Not all the interviews with neutral U3s were as curt as Paul's. Yet the neutral U3s simply would not give us many indicators as to their spiritual state. We could not tell if they were intentionally avoiding our questions or if their hearts were truly hardened to spiritual matters. About one-third of the U3s were categorized as neutral. According to our estimates, that percentage would translate to 19 million Americans.

> About one-third of the U3s were categorized as neutral. According to our estimates, that percentage would translate to 19 million Americans.

## U3: Leaning U4

The category of U4 on the Rainer scale is indicative of the unchurched who are clearly resistant to the gospel and to the church. A significant number of the U3s, about one out of five, were slightly resistant. They were not, however, so resistant that we could call them U4s. So we placed them in the U3 category, realizing that "neutral" is probably not a precise description of them.

Erin P. from Florida, for example, would be one of the U3s leaning toward U4. Erin is in her twenties and was raised as a Presbyterian. She is quick to note, however, that "my family goes to a Baptist church now." We are not clear why she chose to give us this information, but we did hear her say clearly "my family" in a way that excluded her. She would tell us later that she only goes to church for special events.

We discerned that Erin's childhood in church was not that pleasant. She told us a number of times that "parents should not make their children go to church. That's wrong. They should go because they want to go." Her description of Christians reflects the ambiguity of many of the U3s: "loving, open-minded, and narrow-minded."

For Erin prayer is irregular. "No, I don't pray on a regular basis," she told us. "Maybe ten times a year when someone is sick or even about current events." She also is quick to inform us that regular prayer is not necessary because "God is everything: breathing, talking, sleeping, eating."

Like many of the U3s, Erin affirms the existence of heaven and hell, but she certainly does not hold the biblical view. "I believe you create your own heaven and hell," she said. "You know, like if you committed suicide, that's personal, and you'd spend forever doing that over and over. I believe it's like that movie, *What Dreams May Come*. Most people will be in heaven or a good place to them, or maybe I should say however nice they make it themselves." We really were not sure what Erin was saying. Such was the case with many of the U3s.

> Like many of the U3s, Erin affirms the existence of heaven and hell, but she certainly does not hold the biblical view.

Erin's views of Jesus almost sound orthodox. "I completely believe that he came back from the dead. He is with us now. He's completely good and did well to others on earth. Oh, and he died for our sins."

Now, that didn't sound too bad, so then we asked, "How do you become a Christian and get to heaven, Erin?"

"You must be truthful to yourself and others," she responded readily. "Live the best life you can. Don't sin. If you do, ask for forgiveness. God forgives everything."

Again, this U3 has some knowledge of the Christian faith, but she still is confused about the gospel. And she does show some signs of resistance. This Orlando woman said she found the ideal church at, of all places, Disney World. "At Disney World they have all kinds of churches come and have concerts. It's great! It brings all sorts of people together to believe in one thing." Erin is more likely to return to Disney World for a religious fix than to visit a church in her area. Her attitude sounds something like the U4s, but we could not categorize her responses as resistant.

Researcher Deborah White summarized the interview with Erin well: "Comparing heaven to a movie was very interesting. I'm not sure what she did during those years at church as a child, but she didn't learn a lot about God or his Word. She reads the Bible a couple of times a week, has a Christian family (supposedly), prays a few times a year (when she needs something), and she's planning on creating her own heaven (where she assured me she was going when she died)."

Deborah concluded, "She says she knows who God is but that she does not need the church. There is just too much complacency. I tried to tell her what I believed, but she said it was 'too stuffy' and 'too rigid.' She needs prayer and consistent Christian friends before it's too late."

## U3: Leaning U2

Slightly fewer than one-half of the U3s showed some signs of receptivity to the gospel but not enough to indicate that they were clearly in the receptive category of U2 on the Rainer scale. Researcher Patrick Hanley talked to Park H. of Indiana, a man in his early forties. Park's background includes some level of involvement in a Presbyterian church as a child.

Park admits that his failure to attend church is due to "busyness and lack of time." His view of Christians, despite his own un-churched status, is friendly. And this man has no negative views of ministers. He considers them "friendly, outgoing, willing to help in times of need, and good speakers." Wow! I don't think the four congregations where I served as senior pastor would give me those high marks.

The most significant influences in Park's life are his mother-in-law and father-in-law, both churchgoing Christians. And he responded that he is "somewhat likely" to attend church if invited.

So why is Park a U3? Why is he not a more receptive U2? Though Park has a favorable attitude toward Christians and the church, he still resists attempts to share the gospel with him. In fact, he indicated to us that the only negative issue he has with Christians is "when people try to convert me." Indeed, Patrick Hanley summarized his time with Park by saying, "He feels fine about the church, really no negative comments. The only time he seemed to be irritated was when he began talking about people trying to convert."

Such was the case with about one-half of the U3s. They are very affirming of Christians, they rarely make negative comments about the church, and they generally have a belief in Jesus as the Son of God, though their theology tends to be weird beyond that basic affirmation.

> About one-half of the U3s are very affirming of Christians, rarely make negative comments about the church, and generally have a belief in Jesus as the Son of God, though their theology tends to be weird beyond that basic affirmation.

We have thus seen the distinguishing characteristics of three subgroups of U3s. The group as a whole, however, has certain marks that are common to all U3s. To those common points we now turn.

## Waiting to Be Invited

I hope you have not become lost in the stories of these unchurched persons, as intriguing as many of them are. And I hope you have not become mired in the pool of statistics I have written on these pages thus far. You see, I have a primary motive behind the statistics and the stories. I have prayed that, as you learn more about the unchurched, you will be more motivated to share your faith on a regular basis.

The day before I began writing this chapter, I attended a chapel service at Southern Seminary in Louisville, where I serve as dean. The chapel speaker was well-known pastor and author John MacArthur. Dr. MacArthur related some of the natural consequences of maturing as a Christian. He spent most of the time talking about the mandate for Christians to share their faith.

Dr. MacArthur related the story of an airplane flight where he found his seat assignment to be "the dreaded middle seat." During the flight, he had his Bible open as he studied God's Word. One of the passengers sitting next to him was a Muslim, who inquired about Dr. MacArthur's beliefs, particularly asking questions about the plurality of beliefs in America.

> You will hear this theme throughout this book. The vast majority of the unchurched would gladly come to your church if you invited them and walked with them into the church building.

The Muslim, who had recently moved to the United States, gave Dr. MacArthur an open door to share the gospel. Dr. MacArthur told him about the God he could know personally. And he told him of the only way of salvation. Though the Muslim seat companion did not accept Christ on that plane, he was given much to ponder.

In a way that was self-effacing, Dr. MacArthur simply shared from Scripture how evangelism is a natural outcome of growth in Christ. He implied that Christians who are not sharing their faith on a regular basis are not growing in Christ due to their disobedience.

You will hear this theme throughout this book. The vast majority of the unchurched would gladly come to your church if you invited them and walked with them into the church building. Even if you are not sharing your faith on a regular basis, you surely can invite someone to church.

With each more receptive group on the Rainer scale, the number who say they will attend church if invited increases. In the case of the U3s, 63 percent indicated they are "somewhat likely" to attend if invited. Another 23 percent said they are "very likely" to attend if invited. Do the math. Nearly nine out of ten U3s are at least somewhat likely to attend church if you invite them.

> Nearly nine out of ten U3s are at least somewhat likely to attend church if you invite them.

Rusty Russell interviewed Chris M. of Virginia. Chris indicated he would be at least somewhat likely to attend church if invited. The way Rusty summarized the interview powerfully tells the story of Chris. "He just doesn't feel like religion is right for his life. But at other times he blows me away with comments that seem full of faith in God. I think he's standing on the edge, waiting for something to push him one way or the other."

That was the sentiment we sensed from many U3s. They were waiting for something to push them one way or the other. And from the information we have gathered, it would seem that the push they need may be something as simple as inviting them to church.

## Church Is Relevant

We are not quite sure how the unchurched evaluate the relevancy of church if they never or rarely attend. But most of the more than three hundred unchurched persons we interviewed were happy to give their opinions on this matter. When we asked the U3s why many people do not attend church, the responses were revealing.

### Table 5.2

| Why Many People Don't Attend Church | |
|---|---|
| Too lazy | 6% |
| Too busy | 39% |
| Not relevant | 14% |
| Hypocrites in church | 11% |
| Other | 30% |

The revelation to us on the research team was not the factors that received high responses; rather, it was the factor that received a relatively low response: Only 14 percent of all the U3s thought church was irrelevant. This response was close to the U4s' response, where only 19 percent saw the church as irrelevant.

Think about the implications of this one piece of data. Most unchurched people, even those in somewhat resistant postures, do not view the church as irrelevant. They may not be coming to church, but they are giving us other reasons for their unchurched status.

Have you ever hesitated to invite someone to church because he or she may think the church would have nothing to do with their lives? Look at the responses of the largest unchurched group in America, the U3s. Only a small number would call the church irrelevant.

Martha R. of Kentucky is a classic example of a U3 who does not attend church but believes people *should* attend church. If that statement sounded confusing, you are not alone. The researchers found themselves scratching their heads at many of the U3s' responses.

Martha comes from a Southern Baptist background. In fact, her grandfather was a Southern Baptist pastor. Her father is seventy-five years old, had been unchurched for many years, but is now attending church regularly.

> The revelation to us on the research team was not the factors that received high responses; rather, it was the factor that received a relatively low response: Only 14 percent of all the U3s thought church was irrelevant.

Our interviewer Warner Smith noted some of Martha's background and struggles. "Martha seemed very comfortable throughout the interview. She was very forthright and spoke faster than I could write. Her grandfather was a very strict Southern Baptist minister. Martha is currently living with a man, a relationship that is about five years old. She has no children and has never been married. She has survived breast cancer and continues to search for meaning after losing her mother to a heart attack a few years ago."

One might think that Martha would be resistant to the gospel and unfriendly toward the church. Her father was obviously burned out on church from his legalistic father. She has fought breast cancer. She has never married. And she still struggles with her mother's death.

Despite all this apparent baggage, Martha has a very positive attitude toward the church. If a friend or family member invited her to church, she would be "very likely" to attend. Her infrequent times in church are primarily for special events. The few she has attended were "very moving. They made me think more about the way you want to be."

Like so many U3s, Martha has a confused understanding of the gospel that includes Jesus plus good works. "If you want to be a Christian," she said confidently, "you must believe in Jesus; you must believe there is a God, and you have to read the Bible. You won't know what God is thinking if you don't read it. It will tell you what's good in your own heart."

She continued to add to her to-do list to get to heaven. "You also have to do the right things, follow the Lord's work, live right, and do what the Lord wants you to do. Also, be a kind and considerate person."

Martha sees Christians as "committed and open-minded." Pastors and ministers are "good and fair people who are willing to listen and have compassion." And on the issue of church, she said emphatically, "Church is good for anybody. Everybody should go, not because they are forced to go, but because they want to go. You need to be in church."

Now remember, Martha is unchurched. Yet her comments make her sound like she is the chairperson of the outreach committee for the local Baptist church. We found it difficult to reconcile many of the U3s' favorable opinions of the church with their own lack of attendance.

> We found it difficult to reconcile many of the U3s' favorable opinions of the church with their own lack of attendance.

Though our confusion remained long after the interviews with the U3s, we do know with little doubt that most of them have a positive view of the church. You, as the Lord's witness, cannot use the church's supposed lack of relevancy as an excuse for silence.

## Let Us Pray

One of these days I would like to lead my research team on a quest to discern the prayer lives of active churchgoing Christians. One factor of which we are certain is that most of the unchurched are praying people. And they see little disconnect between an active prayer life and an inactive church life.

> One factor of which we are certain is that most of the unchurched are praying people. And they see little disconnect between an active prayer life and an inactive church life.

For this project, we began with the simple question: Do you pray regularly? Though we did not provide a precise definition for "regularly," the U3s were quick to respond one way or the other. Nearly two-thirds, 63 percent, did indicate their practice of a regular prayer life.

Our next question asked the frequency of their prayer lives. In a simple open-ended question, we asked how often they prayed. The results were intriguing.

### Table 5.3

| How Often Do You Pray? | |
|---|---|
| Daily | 51% |
| Weekly | 13% |
| Monthly | 4% |
| Other | 32% |

The "other" response included numerous comments of U3s who pray more than once a day. We even had one U3 who claimed that she prayed in her sleep!

We see the significance of this data on prayer as twofold. First, these U3s are not unspiritual beings. They believe in some type of God who hears and answers prayers. Their understanding of God and prayer may be far from orthodox, but their beliefs are at least a point of connection for the one who shares his or her faith.

Second, the prayer lives of many of the U3s are indications of men and women who are searching for answers. They realize something is missing in their lives. Many of them are praying to an unknown God with the hope, as Gina H. of Nebraska said, that "someone up there has heard something and can do something about it."

Ryan G. of Wyoming prays to "a higher power. I pray to him, her, or it daily. It's probably not a typical prayer, but it is prayer. I just got to believe somebody is hearing me."

But for Melanie M. of Hawaii, prayer is a last resort for a desperate woman. "My boyfriend who was living with me was murdered last year. Six months later my dad died. I was laid off at work last month, and two weeks later I discovered I had breast cancer."

Melanie was emotional, so we waited for her to regain her composure.

"I seriously thought about suicide. I mean, what's left to live for? But I just couldn't do it. So I started praying. I bet I hadn't prayed ten times in my life before all the _____ hit the fan. Now I'm just hoping God will hear me and help me."

It was after Melanie's painful explanation of her prayer life that we had the opportunity to share the gospel. Frankly, with all the tragedies she had experienced, we thought she would be highly receptive to receiving Christ. We were wrong.

"I just have trouble believing that there is only one way to heaven," she told us politely. "I mean, I would like to know more about God. I really need him. But I have always been bothered by people who tell me that their way is the only way."

Because of Melanie's resistance to the gospel, we categorized her as a U3. But because she was so receptive to spiritual matters and even to the church, we could not call her a U4. And despite her unwillingness to receive Christ as Savior, Melanie did hear us politely. The open door was her discussion of her prayer life. Such could be the case for you as you talk to the unchurched next door.

## Heaven Is a Wonderful Place, but Hell Is Real Too

The higher one moves on the Rainer scale, the greater the likelihood that that unchurched person believes in the existence of heaven and hell. The following chart portrays the dramatic change in attitude.

### Table 5.4

**Belief in the Existence of Heaven and Hell**

|    | Heaven | Hell |
|----|--------|------|
| **U1** | 100% | 94% |
| **U2** | 95% | 82% |
| **U3** | 83% | 70% |
| **U4** | 54% | 51% |
| **U5** | 13% | 20% |

Once again Christians have a great opportunity to talk with unchurched persons because of their widespread acceptance of an afterlife called heaven and hell. But be forewarned. Almost all of the U3s had views of the afterlife that were anything but biblical. Listen to just a few.

Michelle R. of Vermont said that "heaven is not a place that you can physically go to. It is the mind-altered state that lives forever. It is like the most restful sleep ever with the most pleasant dreams. You know, the kind of sleep that you never want to wake up from."

We asked, "And what is your view of hell, Michelle?"

"I have come to the conclusion that hell is a real place. I kind of believed that before September 11, but that sealed it for me. I'm not sure how it will work, but I believe those terrorists will suffer forever."

Then there is Mike G. of West Virginia, interviewed by researcher Bland Mason. For Mike, heaven is real "but not the traditional model." We never did learn what the nontraditional model looks like.

Mike was about as precise as anyone on his understanding of hell. "Yes, I believe in hell. It is a place reserved for really bad people. Here's how it works. About 80 percent of people are normal and live a good life. Another 10 percent are extra good, and another 10 percent are extra bad. Those are the people who will go to hell." Maybe with Mike's statistical precision, he can one day get saved and become one of our researchers.

But Angela Y. of California had to be one of our favorites in the category of "most vivid descriptions." Sit back and listen.

"Heaven is the most wonderful place," she began. "It is mostly blue with the sun shining all the time. There are numerous meadows and lakes and a few beautiful beaches. You will have your choice of the music you want to listen to. Everyone will be rich and will have very nice homes. There will be no dirt or trash. You can sleep if you want to, but you won't need sleep. There will be all kinds of fun games to play."

With such a vivid description of heaven, we waited with anticipation for her description of hell. She had already affirmed with certainty the existence of hell. So we asked, "What is hell like, Angela?"

"Oh, it's like being married to my ex-husband, Mike."

And so the interview concluded.

## The Ministers Are Okay

U3s like the clergy. In fact, U3s have the most positive views of ministers.

Though we are uncertain why this unchurched group has such favorable opinions, the table below shows their positive perspectives on ministers.

## Table 5.5

| Positive Views of Clergy | |
| --- | --- |
| U1 | 68% |
| U2 | 65% |
| U3 | 73% |
| U4 | 54% |
| U5 | 53% |

For Kamal S. of Massachusetts, ministers are "nice people. They teach you good things. They offer you a lot of things." Rajes D. of Texas, originally from Malaysia, affirms, "They are good. They are trying their best to help people." And Judy T. of Oklahoma concurs. "They are the type who offer true leadership. Ministers are some of the few people you can count on for guidance. They are committed. They are someone to emulate."

Conventional wisdom says that ministers are viewed with skepticism and even disdain by the unchurched world. They are the televangelists who take income from widows. They are the adulterers and sexual predators. They do not see their mission as serving God and others, but as doing whatever is necessary for their own good.

Our research found that such conventional wisdom could not be further from the truth. The unchurched as a whole have very positive views of the clergy. The U3s in particular hold them in high esteem. Once again, we received information that takes away another excuse for Christians not to witness. The unchurched next door are waiting on you, and they already have a positive view of your pastor.

### The U3s and Small Groups

In another surprise by the U3s, we found that this unchurched group has attended Sunday school and small groups in churches in significant numbers. Seven out of ten U3s attended Sunday school as children, and another two of them attended small groups or Sunday school as adults. Only 9 percent of all U3s have never attended either.

Once again, the data seem to defy conventional wisdom. We are often told that it is almost impossible to get unchurched persons into a small group without first getting them to come to a worship service. Our research indicates that this common understanding may not be true.

> Our research found that such conventional wisdom could not be further from the truth. The unchurched as a whole have very positive views of the clergy. The U3s in particular hold them in high esteem.

The difference may be the manner in which people visited Sunday school in the past. There seemed to be a willingness on the part of visitors to go to a class on their own. Today the unchurched are highly reticent to go to a class unless someone they know accompanies them. Tina B. of Utah, a formerly unchurched person who was immensely helpful in aiding our understanding of the unchurched, told us, "I really wanted to go to Sunday school to study the Bible, but I was scared to death to go into a church building by myself. Thank God Evelyn invited me."

Evelyn is Tina's neighbor. And Evelyn had the courage and conviction to ask her unchurched neighbor to go to Sunday school with her. Tina eagerly accepted. "Evelyn was the first person ever to invite me to Sunday school. I am determined I won't make that mistake. I have already started inviting my unchurched friends to Sunday school. Of the ten I've invited, five have come with me so far. But the key is that I go into the church building with them and sit with them. That makes all the difference."

We in church leadership often come to the conclusion that the unchurched will not attend Sunday school or another small group because they no longer come on their own initiative. They *will* still come. We simply need to invite the unchurched next door.

Many of them are waiting on your call.

## Lessons Learned from the U3s

The U3s are the largest unchurched group in America. By our estimates there are some 57 million of them. We call them the neutral group, but that nomenclature may not be the most accurate. Some do seem to have no interest and no animosity, but others may be ready to move to a more or less receptive posture. What then have we learned from these men and women?

## Christians and U3s Have Many Points of Commonality

As I have the opportunity to speak to about two hundred Christian groups each year, I hear many common perceptions about the unchurched. One of the most common is the idea that unchurched people have no spiritual interests in common. If we have learned anything from the U3s, it is that they are as a whole very spiritual people.

Most of them believe in God. Most of them believe Jesus is the Son of God. The vast majority affirm the reality of heaven and hell. And even their views on the authority of Scripture are not significantly different from those of Christians.

> Most of them believe in God. Most of them believe Jesus is the Son of God. The vast majority affirm the reality of heaven and hell. And even their views on the authority of Scripture are not significantly different from those of Christians.

A U3 may see heaven as a place for "good people" but have no real understanding of the biblical view of heaven and how to get there. But most U3s are not dumb; they are simply uninformed. And most are eager to learn and willing to be corrected. The good news is that we are not, for the most part, dealing with atheists, agnostics, or the antagonistic. We have a point of common beginning. And most U3s are willing, if not eager, to hear more from us.

## The U3s Are Eager to Learn

As I write this book, my youngest son, Jess, is finishing his senior year of high school. He gets up early on Friday mornings to lead a Bible study for middle school kids before school starts. The kids, I am told, are really impressed that the captain of the football team gets up so early on game day to lead the study. My middle son, Art, is close to graduating from college. He has started a Bible study in his fraternity. Many were surprised to see several frat guys studying the Scriptures together in the evening. My oldest son, Sam, lives in Indianapolis where he works for a bank. He has started a weekly Bible study for men. All three of my boys tell their dad with enthusiasm that the Bible studies have several people in them. There simply is no shortage of people eager to study God's Word. And to the surprise of some, even the unchurched are eager to learn more about the Bible and the truths of the Christian faith.

Again, we turn to the insights of a new Christian, Kyle C. of Georgia, who tells his story about his eagerness to learn more from Scripture. "I am a CPA [certified public accountant] in a midsize firm. One day Gerald, another CPA, asked me if I would be interested in attending a Bible study in his home. His invitation was low pressure, and I accepted his offer a few days later."

Kyle continues his story: "I was really excited about studying the Bible. Over the next several weeks, I began asking questions. All the men in the group were very kind; they went out of the way to help me. When I accepted Christ three months into the study, it just seemed like the most natural thing in the world."

When we asked Kyle to evaluate his status on the Rainer scale prior to beginning the Bible study, he said "U3." Stories similar to Kyle's could be heard among many of the U3s. Invite the unchurched to Sunday school. Start a Bible study in your neighborhood, school, or workplace. Give people the opportunity to learn about the Bible. You might be surprised at their responses.

## Remember the "Leaners"

About one-half of the U3s seem to be at a point of transition. Some seem headed to greater resistance toward the gospel (U4). Others seem poised for a greater level of receptivity (U2). And apparently the primary instrument that God uses to bring these leaners closer to him is the witness of a Christian. But about 28 million of these U3s are leaners. With only one person becoming a Christian for every eighty-five church members in America, it does not appear that there are sufficient numbers of willing Christians to reach out to these men and women at such critical points in their lives.

## The U3s Are Waiting

The final lesson we learned from the U3s is redundant. They, like many other unchurched groups, are waiting to be invited to church. More than 86 percent of the U3s are either "very likely" or "somewhat likely" to attend church if invited. But, as we learned over and over again, many of these unchurched have never been invited to church.

The unchurched, in the final analysis, are not anti-God and antichurch. And the higher one goes on the Rainer scale, the more receptive the unchurched are to your invitation. You will see that even more profoundly in the next chapter on the U2s, where we will discover that 97 percent indicated they will come if you invite them. To that group we now turn.

**U5**
Highly resistant to the gospel, antagonistic attitude

**U4**
Resistant to the gospel, but not an antagonistic attitude

**U3**
No apparent receptivity, neutral, perhaps open to discussion

**U2**
Receptive to the gospel and to the church

**U1**
Highly receptive to the gospel, "the Phillipian jailer"

## Chapter 6

# "Jesus Is Just Alright with Me"

## *The World of the U2*

---

I believe in Jesus. I believe in God. I just believe it's
better to worship alone than to go to church.

*—Georgia C.,*
*U2 from Kentucky*

---

Georgia C. has lived in Kentucky all of her life. She lives in one of
the many towns that is within the metropolitan area of Louisville.
A high school graduate, she is in her late fifties and has a modest
income. Georgia also has many Christian orthodox beliefs, but she has
yet to accept Christ as her personal Lord and Savior.

Our interview with Georgia was one of the more pleasant we had.
She was polite and nonargumentative, and she agreed with most of the
tenets of the Christian faith that we mentioned. She seems somewhat
receptive to the gospel but chooses, at least for now, not to attend
church. Georgia watches a lot of church and religious shows on television. It was therefore no surprise that she would like to see churches
"offer more television ministries."

At no point during our interview did Georgia seem uncomfortable. In fact, she seemed happy to help a Christian cause. And Georgia probably prays more than many Christians. She prays "every day and wakes up in the middle of the night and starts praying."

Her attitude about Christians is that they are "loving and generous."

Georgia depends on the Bible as her source for spiritual guidance. She can even cite the translation she uses: "I have several Bibles, but I usually read the NIV." She believes in hell and heaven as literal places. And when we asked her what her biggest turnoff by churches was, she promptly replied, "None."

So why would we include Georgia in our study of the unchurched? Doesn't this woman seem more committed to Christ than many active churchgoers? The first answer is easy. Georgia is in our study because she is unchurched. But another reason we include Georgia is that we perceive she is not a Christian.

On the surface, the interviewer might conclude that Georgia is a Christian. Listen to her responses to key questions. What do you believe about Jesus? "I believe that he is the Son of God." How does someone get to heaven? "Believe in Jesus, that he is the Son of God."

So why would we perceive that Georgia is not a Christian? At no point could she tell us that she had a personal relationship with Christ. She could not articulate any point in her life where she repented of sin and placed her faith in Christ. For Georgia Christianity is a cognitive agreement with some of the cardinal truths of the Christian faith. But it is neither personal nor relational.

Researcher Deborah White summarized the interview well: "Georgia says she believes in God and who he is as well as Jesus Christ. But she showed no desire to have a personal relationship with Christ. She only wants to watch church on TV, though she claimed to me that she would start looking for a church. She tried to show me that she knew the right things to say, but I sensed no true relationship with Jesus."

Georgia is a typical U2. U2s are generally friendly, even receptive to the gospel. They may give seemingly orthodox responses to questions about the Christian faith, but they have yet to make a personal step of faith. Something seems to be holding them back from making that ultimate decision.

U2s account for about 27 percent of the unchurched population. By our estimates there may be as many as 43 million U2s in the United States alone. And they are typically receptive to overtures made by Christians.

U2s account for 27 percent, or more than one out of four, of the unchurched population. And these are the men and women who will welcome a conversation with you. They will probably enjoy the story of your faith in Christ. And they will likely join a Bible study if you invite them. They are your coworkers, your extended family, your neighbors, and your merchants. They are the unchurched next door. God will use you to reach them. I hope that the description of the U2s in this chapter will not only give you new insights, but will also give you confidence to share your faith with them.

In addition to their receptivity to the gospel, U2s have some other interesting characteristics. The first of these even surprised us.

## A U2 Is More Likely to Be a Female

Nearly two out of three, 62 percent, of U2s are females. In fact, the two most receptive unchurched groups, the U1s and the U2s, were predominantly female.

Our research team tried to understand this phenomenon. Indeed, another interesting gender-related statistic might provide connection. Females were the dominant gender not only in U1 and U2, but in U5 as well. For whatever reasons, the female unchurched were not comfortable with the middle range of the unchurched. They were either receptive or antagonistic and nothing between the two extremes. Our relatively small sample size of just over three hundred unchurched persons does not allow us the ability to make dogmatic conclusions. The research team did conclude anecdotally that a female unchurched person is more likely to be on the extremes of the unchurched scale.

Can we offer any reasons why females dominated these unchurched categories? Though we could offer some speculative responses, we must ultimately conclude that we really do not know. I do hope, however, that this bit of information may give the Christian who is witnessing a bit of insight into how some females might respond to the gospel.

## A U2 Is More Likely to Be an Anglo

The highest representation of Anglos on the Rainer scale was among the U1s and the U2s. Our study looked at five broad racial and ethnic groups: Anglo, African American, Hispanic, Asian American, and other. The point on the unchurched scale that was the highest representation for each of these groups was:

### Table 6.1

| | |
|---|---|
| Anglo | **U1** |
| African American | **U5** |
| Hispanic | **U4** |
| Asian American | **U5** |
| Other | **U3** |

Again we can come to no definitive conclusion about the racial and ethnic correlation any more than we could discover the reason behind the gender relationship. At this point with admittedly limited data, we simply say that a U2 is more likely to be female and Anglo.

Paula S. is an Anglo who lives in Florida. In many ways Paula fits the most common profile of a U2. She has a college degree and an annual income above $100,000. Like many U2s, Paula has attended church, but her last visit was several years ago. Indeed, Paula has not been in church since 1974. She gives three reasons why she dropped out of church — "legalism, a big controversy in the church, and a divorce." She attends religious services only for special events now.

But like many U2s, Paula does not have a negative attitude toward the church. She describes the typical Christian as "loving." Also like many U2s, she prays daily. Paula is somewhat different than most U2s in that she does not have a biblical view of God, whom she describes as "a loving, all-powerful deity that we probably really don't understand."

Paula does, however, believe in a literal hell and heaven. She reads the Bible "at least once a day." And she views pastors and preachers as people with "a challenging life. I admire them for their stand and conviction. I have great respect for them. My experience with them is nothing but positive."

## Yes/Heaven, Yes/Hell with a Difference

By now you have begun to see the trend. The more receptive a person is to the gospel, the more likely he or she will believe in the existence of heaven and hell. As the numbers demonstrate, the belief in heaven is consistently and slightly higher than the belief in hell. For review let us look at the numbers who believe in these two eternal destinations.

### Table 6.2

|  | Belief in Heaven | Belief in Hell |
|---|---|---|
| **U5** | 13% | 20% |
| **U4** | 54% | 51% |
| **U3** | 83% | 70% |
| **U2** | 95% | 82% |
| **U1** | 100% | 94% |

Note the slight but significant shift as one moves from U3 to U2 on the Rainer scale. Those who believe in heaven increased from 83 percent to 95 percent, a twelve-point increase. Those who believe in hell increased from 70 percent to 82 percent, another twelve-point increase. The increases are significant but not nearly as dramatic as the increases that take place from U5 to U4.

The real difference we saw in the U2s in their beliefs about hell and heaven is that their perspectives were more often biblical than not. A U3, U4, or U5 who said he or she believes in hell, for example, will likely have a view of hell that is anything but biblical. Ann S., a U4 from Pennsylvania, said she "most certainly believes in hell. It is the state of mind that lives over and over again until you get it right." Okay. I am not sure what she meant by that statement. It sounded like a theology from the movie *Groundhog Day*.

Darryl R., a U3 from Minnesota, affirmed the existence of heaven and described it as "that state of mind where our thoughts meld into the eternity and where we become as God." I really expected to hear background music from *The Twilight Zone* as I listened to these people.

But the U2s more often than not sounded like orthodox, Bible-believing Christians in their views on heaven and hell. "Heaven is the place where we live in the eternal presence of God," said Samuel B., a U2 from Indiana. "It is a place of continuous worship and joy. In heaven there are no more tears and no more pain." If Samuel gets saved, he will make a good theologian.

Chandra O. of Michigan sounds more orthodox than some theologians when she speaks of hell. "Hell is eternal separation from God," she said with intensity. "But it's not just being out of God's presence; it is agony and suffering forever." Not bad for an unbeliever. But Chandra's voice trembles when she utters some unexpected words: "I pray I will never go there."

Over 43 million unchurched persons are U2s. They represent more than one out of four unchurched persons. You are likely to encounter them at your work. They are in the schools and colleges. Some may be in your immediate and extended families. And they are in your neighborhood. They are the unchurched next door.

And so many of these unchurched persons next door have beliefs that are not significantly different than yours. They believe in hell and do not want to go there. They believe in heaven and would like to know how to go there. The opportunities each day are countless. Are you intentionally and prayerfully making efforts to reach out to these unchurched next door?

Some of the characteristics of the U2s are profound, such as their beliefs on heaven and hell. Others are more curious, such as the fact that U2s are more likely to be female and Anglo. And some just make common sense, like the income levels of the unchurched.

## U2s Have Less Family Income Than Any Other Unchurched Group

We already knew that U5s are the wealthiest of the unchurched and that their wealth is an obstacle to salvation according to biblical testimony (see Matt. 19:24), so we were not surprised to find that the more receptive groups, the U1s and the U2s, had the lowest family incomes.

Note how family income decreases with each more receptive unchurched group:

### Table 6.3

|    | Income under $50,000 | Income under $20,000 |
|----|----------------------|----------------------|
| U5 | 46%                  | 13%                  |
| U4 | 69%                  | 27%                  |
| U3 | 66%                  | 24%                  |
| U2 | 75%                  | 23%                  |
| U1 | 71%                  | 16%                  |

Among the U2s, three out of four persons have a family income under $50,000. And while this standard of living by no means suggests a lifestyle of poverty, it does indicate that the U2s might be less focused on the material gain of the world and more interested in spiritual matters.

The U2s had the lowest family income of all the unchurched groups.

Indeed, all the evidence in our interviews indicates that the U2s have few obstacles to hearing and receiving the gospel. Are you seeking to reach these men and women, these unchurched next door?

## Still Working Their Way to Heaven

The U2s seem very ready to hear the gospel; indeed, many are. The U2s are largely orthodox in their beliefs. Why then have they not taken the step to receive Christ as their Lord and Savior? Like all of the other unchurched groups, they are still clinging to a salvation by works. They simply seem blinded to the reality that salvation is a free gift from God.

> Like all of the other unchurched groups, they are still clinging to a salvation by works. They simply seem blinded to the reality that salvation is a free gift from God.

Researcher Bland Mason interviewed Richard M. of Virginia, "a friend of a friend." Richard lives in a rural area of Virginia and served many years in the military. He is in his mid fifties.

Like many of our unchurched persons, Richard has some church background. "I grew up Episcopal," he told us. "I stopped attending in my thirties; I guess I just lost interest." Richard blames his lost interest in the church and his busy schedule on keeping him out of church. "I work a lot on Saturdays and Sundays," he said. But our researcher noted, "I got the feeling that he is using work as an excuse not to go to church. He could find the time if he really wanted to go."

And like most of the U2s, Richard has fairly orthodox views of the Bible ("It is totally truthful, God's Word"). And God "is the Creator of all, the Almighty One." For Richard, both heaven and hell are real, and his attitude toward the church, ministers in particular and Christians in general, is positive.

But Richard seems to have that one stumbling block that is so common among the unchurched. He cannot grasp the concept of unmerited salvation. Bland asked Richard how he believes someone gets to heaven. With little hesitation and total confidence, Richard responded, "You must live by the Ten Commandments and be a good person."

Such was the case with the majority of the U2s. As you seek to witness to these friendly and receptive unchurched persons, be prepared to hear responses of works salvation. But you must be prepared to share the truth of the gospel. Many will probably respond. Unlike the U3s, U4s, and U5s, a significant number of these men and women have a good grasp on just who Jesus really is.

## "He Is Christ, the Son of God"

Compare the two conversations with Whitney F. of Rhode Island and Frances M. of Delaware. These two Northeastern U.S. women seem to be pretty close in their receptivity to the gospel. Whitney is a bit more reserved in her attitude than Frances, so we categorized Whitney as a U3 and Frances as a U2.

Whitney believes, like many of the U3s, that Jesus is a unique figure in history. "Oh, there's no doubt that Jesus is one of the most important people in history," Whitney said. "He will always be remembered as one of the great humanitarians and teachers of all time."

Most Christians would affirm Whitney's words. But of course we on the research team wanted to hear more. We asked, "Is Jesus the Son of God, Whitney? Is he God?"

"I really don't think anyone can know all those details," she responded with confusion. "It really doesn't matter though. The main thing is that we follow his teachings."

> While a majority (53 percent) of the U3s affirmed the biblical truths of Christ, eight out of ten of the U2s held the orthodox view.

We cringed when we heard unchurched people make comments like "it really doesn't matter" if one believes that Jesus is the Son of God or if he is indeed God. The contrast was noticeable among the U2s. While a majority (53 percent) of the U3s affirmed the biblical truths of Christ, eight out of ten of the U2s held the orthodox view. Look at the perceptible shifts in the views of Christ at each unchurched level on the Rainer scale, particularly from U3 to U2.

## Table 6.4

| Jesus Is the Son of God | |
|---|---|
| U5 | 7% |
| U4 | 34% |
| U3 | 54% |
| U2 | 80% |
| U1 | 84% |

If an unchurched person did not believe that Jesus is the Son of God, what did he or she believe about Jesus? The most often mentioned alternative response was that Jesus was simply a good person or good teacher.

## Table 6.5

| Jesus Is a Good Person/Teacher | |
|---|---|
| U5 | 53% |
| U4 | 44% |
| U3 | 25% |
| U2 | 16% |
| U1 | 3% |

We thus return to Frances M., a U2 from Delaware. We heard from Whitney, a U3 from New Hampshire who does not think the deity of Jesus is an important issue. Frances disagrees strongly. "I believe with all my heart that Jesus is the Son of God," she said. "I believe he died on the cross to forgive our sins. I believe he is the Savior of the world." Not too bad for someone who is not a Christian.

The point is simply that more receptive unchurched persons tend to be more orthodox in their beliefs. The U2s are among those who seem to have a biblical view of Christ. If you encounter a U2 in your evangelistic encounters, you will be talking to someone who believes many of the same truths of Scripture as you do. But remember, these people do not have a personal relationship with Jesus Christ. Do not let their orthodox beliefs lull you into a sense of complacency. Knowing Christ cognitively is not the same as knowing Christ personally.

> Do not let the U2s' orthodox beliefs lull you into a sense of complacency. Knowing Christ cognitively is not the same as knowing Christ personally.

## U2s and Parental Influence

One of the most moving interviews took place with Jessica B. of Florida. Jessica was one of the 51 percent of the U2s who declared that the greatest influence in her life has been her parents. She said: "Mom and Dad are the biggest influences in my life. They have always been there for me. I know I broke their hearts when I dropped out of church in high school. I can't believe it's been twenty years, and I'm still not in church." Jessica paused. She was having trouble maintaining her composure. "Dad died last year," she whispered. "The first time I have been back in the church was to go to his funeral."

Our interviewer allowed Jessica a few moments to let her emotions settle and then asked her what it was like to return to her home church.

"It was really weird at first," she said softly. "But after a while, I began to have a flood of memories. The old hymns, the stained glass windows, the preaching ..." She paused again. "I'm not sure what happened. What has happened these past twenty years? Why haven't I listened to my parents? Why did Dad have to die before I came back to church? Why did I have to come to his funeral to come back to church?"

This poignant moment was a microcosm of the many interviews we had with the U2s. Slightly over one-half of these unchurched men and women made a point to share with us the influence of their parents. And anecdotally, the topic typically turned to church and religion as the primary influence by their parents.

The reasons many of the U2s dropped out of church in their youth are numerous. But many of them mentioned the important role their parents played in their religious upbringing. It seems as if Christians have a good opportunity to talk about spiritual matters to many unchurched persons by asking about their parents. The conversations that follow are often prime opportunities to talk about Christ.

> It seems as if Christians have a good opportunity to talk about spiritual matters to many unchurched persons by asking about their parents. The conversations that follow are often prime opportunities to talk about Christ.

## The U2: Recipient of the Gospel Message

More than any unchurched group, the U2s have been on the receiving end of witnessing. More than eight out of ten (82 percent) of the U2s told us that someone had shared with them how they could become a Christian. Among the U1s, the most receptive group, 77 percent told us that someone had witnessed to them.

Bridget G. of Kansas is a typical example of a U2 who has heard the gospel. Bridget is well-educated, in her late twenties, and has a Roman Catholic background. She holds some of the typical views of God that we have heard from other unchurched persons. "God is creator of all things," she told us. "He is all knowing and beneficent."

She also sees Jesus as "both human and divine," but her biblical grasp of Christ stops there. "He came from God to make a connection with human beings. But he's not the only one who has come to talk to human beings. Buddha was also a messenger of God."

And even though Bridget has heard the gospel, her understanding of salvation is uncertain and leaning toward works. "Only God knows how someone gets to heaven," she mused. "I guess it means being humble and believing in the existence of a higher being and loving your neighbor." Bridget's response was somewhat different when we rephrased the question and asked her what is needed to become a Christian. "You must accept and believe the teachings of Jesus Christ and make an effort to follow his teachings," she said. "You also have to recognize Jesus' relationship to God, that he was God's Son and spoke for God." Bridget was one of many unchurched persons who seemed to recognize one set of beliefs to become a Christian and another set of beliefs to go to heaven.

But Bridget still remembers people telling her how to become a Christian. "Students at school where I grew up — they said something like I needed to accept Jesus as my Savior," she told us.

When the unchurched did indicate that they had heard from a Christian about Christ, all groups said that friends were the typical witness. The only exception was the U2s, where the most common witness to the gospel was a family member. Note the Christian influence of family members among U2 unchurched persons.

> Bridget was one of many unchurched persons who seemed to recognize one set of beliefs to become a Christian and another set of beliefs to go to heaven.

## Table 6.6

| Who Has Witnessed to the U2s? | |
| --- | --- |
| Parent | 9% |
| Grandparent | 3% |
| Other family | 27% |
| Total family | 39% |
| Friend | 21% |
| Other | 40% |

The formerly unchurched who were the subjects of my earlier book *Surprising Insights from the Unchurched,* helped shape our questions and our study. One issue that was common among them was the influence of family members in their becoming Christians. So these new Christians encouraged us to ask the unchurched who had shared Christ with them. Their presuppositions were confirmed. Family members did play a major role in sharing the gospel with lost parents, children, and siblings. And the U2s were the most likely group to be influenced by a Christian family member.

> Family members did play a major role in sharing the gospel with lost parents, children, and siblings. And the U2s were the most likely group to be influenced by a Christian family member.

As we speak to well-intending Christians in evangelistic churches, we often notice a reticence to share the gospel with family members. Somehow we must communicate that family members may actually be the most effective in reaching their loved ones with the gospel.

## The Negative Experience Factor

You might expect the U5s to cite some past negative experiences with churches. After all, they are the unchurched who are the most resistant and antagonistic to the gospel. But you might be surprised to learn that as many U2s recalled such negative experiences as U5s. The chart below is telling.

### Table 6.7

| Negative Church Experiences | |
|---|---|
| U5 | 69% |
| U4 | 61% |
| U3 | 64% |
| U2 | 68% |
| U1 | 61% |

Nearly eight out of ten U2s had a negative experience with a church in the past. Such an overwhelming number can be explained in two ways. First, many of the U2s have some type of church background. The likelihood, therefore, of their having a bad church experience is greater simply because they were in church more than some other unchurched groups.

That reason alone, however, does not explain their comment on negative church experiences. The U5s, those who have the least church background of all the unchurched groups, had the same level of negative experiences. It seems that many of the U2s we interviewed were regular churchgoers as a child until something traumatic (from their perspectives) caused them to stop attending church.

Leda K. of Florida provides a clear example of such an experience. Leda is a forty-four-year-old stay-at-home mom. She and Frank have been married twenty years, but neither they nor their children have attended church in that entire time. Her story is not uncommon among the U2s.

"I attended an independent Baptist church for the first fourteen years of my life," she began. "The youth program was great and I was really involved. I also remember a lot about the preaching. Brother Jack was a kind man, but he did not hold back anything when he preached. I remember holding him in awe because of his convictions and the stands he took."

Leda paused and then resumed her story. "You see, my mom was the one who took us four kids to church. Dad never went, but I didn't think much of it. There were a bunch of families in the church like ours.

"I idolized my dad. Yeah, I knew he didn't have much to do with church, but he was a good man. I mean, I bet he did more good things than most church people. I really believe he was one of God's favorites because he helped so many people."

At this point in Leda's story, we nodded knowingly. We were listening to another unchurched person who thinks that one earns salvation. Leda continued.

"One day after church, this man who was a deacon in the church, a real _____, comes up to me and starts telling me what an awful man my dad was for not coming to church. He then tells me I'd better talk with Dad because he's going to hell. I was so mad! I told deacon _____ that he was the one who was going to hell and that he better never talk about my dad like that.

"Well, old deacon _____ was caught off guard. That really shut him up. He just walked away, the coward. I haven't been back to church since."

Unfortunately, we heard many horror stories like Leda's. If just some of the stories are accurate, we will be able to write a book called *Christians Say the Dumbest Things*. I learned a great deal from these unchurched people. Seeker sensitivity does not have to be dumbed-down preaching or doctrinal compromise. It just needs to be common sense and common courtesy. Though I know these offensive Christians represent a small minority of all believers, our church members need to hear repeatedly that we are to share the witness of Christ in love and joy.

Diana K. of West Virginia had her own negative experience to tell. Diana is a twenty-something young married woman who attended a Baptist church infrequently as a child. She had all positive experiences in her childhood as she can recall. The negative experience took place shortly after she and her husband were married. Since her husband had a nominal Episcopal background, they decided they would try church as a married couple and that the first stop would be an Episcopal church a few blocks from their house.

"First of all," she said, "we didn't know that this Episcopal church was charismatic. We weren't comfortable with that. Then we heard that a homosexual man was attending the church, and someone went up to him and actually told him to leave. I could understand a church taking a moral stand against homosexuality, but these people humiliated this man. I felt so sorry for him. My husband and I just left at that point, and we haven't really been motivated to try church again."

We on the research team realize that some of the stories we heard could be excuses or lively imaginations of the unchurched. And we also realize that no church is perfect and that members will make mistakes. But so many of the stories we heard defy the imagination. A number of Christians just seem to be rude and insensitive. They may be small in number, but their voices are heard loudly. We wonder how many unchurched have been hindered from the kingdom because of the insensitivity and even stupidity of some Christians.

> A number of Christians just seem to be rude and insensitive. They may be small in number, but their voices are heard loudly. We wonder how many unchurched have been hindered from the kingdom because of the insensitivity and even stupidity of some Christians.

## The Invitation Issue ... Again

We have already said that if you will invite the unchurched and take them to church, they will come. The issue of inviting the unchurched is especially obvious among the U2s. Look again at the likelihood of the unchurched to come to church if they are invited.

### Table 6.8

| Very Likely or Somewhat Likely to Attend Church | |
| --- | --- |
| U5 | 20% |
| U4 | 62% |
| U3 | 86% |
| U2 | 97% |
| U1 | 97% |

Earlier we noted the dramatic increase in the likelihood of attending church from the U5s to the U4s. But look at the U2s and the U1s. Almost all of those interviewed indicated without hesitation that they would be happy to come to church if someone invited them. In fact, they seemed delighted to go to church. But they are intimidated by the church. Or they are out of the routine of attending church. Or they are uncertain what to do once they arrive at church.

Janet N. is a U2 from Maryland. Like many U2s, Janet has some church background, but it has been thirty-two years since the forty-seven-year-old boomer has walked into a church. "Kyle [her youngest child] will be leaving home in a few months. I guess I'm anticipating the empty-nest syndrome and wondering what I'm going to do with the rest of my life."

She then returns to our questions. "Maybe church needs to be a part of my future," Janet ponders. "I have to admit that I've thought about it several times. But I have no clue what it would be like to go to church after all these years. I mean, I wouldn't know where to go or how to act. It would be a big step for me to walk into a church these days."

We then ask Janet if she would be comfortable going to church if someone invited her and walked with her into the church building. "Sure!" she exclaimed. "That would be the ideal scenario for me. I really would like to give church a try, and that would probably be the best situation for me."

As we continued our conversation with Janet, we asked her if she had ever been invited to church.

"It depends on what you mean by 'invited,'" she explained. "I've received a call or two from someone in a church in the area, and one person has even come by the house. But I didn't know anything about those people. It really wasn't as much an invitation as a marketing effort. But no one I know personally has invited me to church."

"Do you know any Christians or active churchgoers?" we asked.

"I'm not sure." She responded. "I think Brett, a guy who works with me, might be active in a church. And Dianne, my neighbor — her car is gone a lot on Sundays, but she has never mentioned anything about her church. Now that you mention it, you just don't hear church people talking much about their churches. Isn't that odd?"

From our perspective *odd* is not the best word. *Tragic* is a more fitting description. Millions of unchurched people are waiting for us to take them to church. But, for most of us, we do very little. *Tragic* is indeed the best word.

## Reaching the U2s

What have we learned about the U2s that may help us to be more faithful witnesses for Christ? From our research, at least six issues are clear.

*The U2s are eager to study the Bible.* Our conversations with the U2s were clear: U2s desire to learn more about the Bible. Almost without exception, these unchurched men and women took the initiative to mention their eagerness to study the Bible. They told us they would come to a home Bible study. They also told us that they would attend Sunday school if someone would go with them. "I really would like to get with some people and learn more about the Bible," Jerome P. of Michigan told us. "I know there are a lot of Bible studies going on, but I would like to get in one with someone I know. I don't want to go to one with a bunch of nuts."

The unchurched next door want to learn more about the Bible. Have you invited someone to a Bible study?

*The U2s desire to talk about eternal issues.* A conversation with a U2 is in sharp contrast to the conversations we had with U5s. The U5s, for the most part, had little inclination to talk about matters of eternity. The U2s, however, eagerly embrace a conversation about Jesus, hell, or heaven.

Indeed, many of the U2s expressed curiosity at the apparent reticence of Christians to talk about matters of faith. We see with the U2s a great opportunity to share the gospel simply by engaging them in a conversation about eternal matters. It would seem, however, that a number of Christians hesitate to talk about such issues for fear of offending, appearing narrow-minded, or being rejected. In the meantime, the unchurched next door, particularly the U2s, wonder why we are ashamed of what we believe.

*The U2s are frustrated with their understanding of a works salvation.* You have heard the many expressions of works salvation articulated by the U2s. Our researchers noted that the U2s not only believed in a works salvation, but that they had a sense of frustration about their own beliefs.

"You could continuously hear the U2s say that they are going to heaven because they are basically good persons," one of our researchers noted. "But there always seemed to be that uncertainty. 'Am I really good enough to get into heaven?' 'How will I know if I am good enough?' I think that we have a great opportunity to reach these unchurched people with a clear and compelling message of grace."

I agree with the researcher. Now we must pray that more Christians will have the boldness to share that message of grace.

*The parental connection is a great way to open conversations about spiritual things.* Do not forget the significant influence of parents on the U2s. We see this issue as a point of connection between the Christian and the unchurched next door. Conversations that may seem to be headed nowhere are often opened with a simple inquiry about the unchurched person's family heritage.

*Talking about the unchurcheds' negative church issues of the past can open the door to further conversation.* We on the research team believe that the U2s had a number of negative experiences with churches in their past. In fact, the number of such experiences was noted more frequently by U2s than any other group. The U2s were either the group with the most negative experiences or the group most likely to mention them.

> In some ways, the eagerness of U2s to talk about their negative church experiences is an opportunity for the Christian to move the discussion to matters of faith and salvation.

How does the Christian respond to the unchurched next door who mentions a negative church experience? It would seem that the believer should acknowledge and express regret about the bad experience. But then the opportunity is open to talk about matters of faith. In some ways, the eagerness of U2s to talk about their negative church experiences is an opportunity for the Christian to move the discussion to matters of faith and salvation.

*The U2s want to be invited to church.* You probably do not need or want a reminder to invite the unchurched next door to church. But let it be said again that the U2s are waiting on your invitation. Prayerfully ask God to give you faces and names of people and opportunities to invite them to church. It is a simple but profound act.

We now turn to the most receptive group, the U1s. You will hear new information plus a renewed emphasis on information you have already heard. This group may be the most exciting, for they are not just waiting on an invitation, they are waiting on someone to tell them how to become a Christian. They are essentially asking the question of the Philippian jailer: "What must I do to be saved?"

**U5**
Highly resistant to the gospel, antagonistic attitude

**U4**
Resistant to the gospel, but not an antagonistic attitude

**U3**
No apparent receptivity, neutral, perhaps open to discussion

**U2**
Receptive to the gospel and to the church

**U1**
Highly receptive to the gospel, "the Phillipian jailer"

## Chapter 7

# "What Must I Do To Be Saved?"

### *The World of the U1*

---

Before this interview is over, will you tell me how I
can become a Christian?

*—Rick M.,*
*U1 from Maine*

---

On a warm day in May of 1967, I went to a meeting led by the football coach of our high school, Joe Hendrickson. Bullock County
High School in Union Springs, Alabama, was a small school. Grades
seven through twelve comprised the high school; we had no middle
school or junior high. I was a seventh grader, the youngest of all the
high school students. Our football team included all six grades, though
we younger boys got little playing time.

Coach Hendrickson had started a local chapter of the Fellowship
of Christian Athletes. He truly desired for the boys on the team to
become Christians and for the Christians to become more devoted
followers of Christ. That muggy day in south Alabama was the first
time I attended the FCA. In that meeting I heard the gospel explained

clearly for the first time in my life. I was an unchurched teenage boy. I had attended the local United Methodist church in town, but I had no recollection of hearing the gospel.

Many years have passed since that fateful day in 1967, I can remember so much of the meeting clearly. Coach Hendrickson shared with us that all were sinners. He told us that we couldn't get to heaven with sin in our lives. And he explained the cross and how Jesus died for our sins. Then he said quietly, "Men, I try to teach you the true joy and discipline of being an athlete. I try to let you know what's really important on the football field."

Then he paused for a moment. Coach Hendrickson was not a gifted speaker, but he was real and passionate. "But there is something so much more important than football or anything else," he said. "In fact, it is so important that where you spend eternity depends upon it." And then my football coach shared the gospel of Jesus Christ with us. I have to believe everyone there clearly understood his presentation.

I went home that night as a boy under conviction. Before I went to bed, I asked Jesus Christ to forgive my sins and to be my Lord and Savior. My life has never been the same since.

I was a U1 unchurched person. I was out of church but ready and eager to hear the gospel. I accepted Christ the same day I heard the gospel. And I would later wonder why no one had ever shared the gospel with me before my teenage years.

By the way, Coach Hendrickson was fired before the next school year began. His football record was not stellar. And actually he did not have a very talented team, but many leaders in our town were sports idolaters. They refused to see the eternal impact Coach Hendrickson was making on our young lives. Many of those boys accepted Christ, and a number were called into vocational ministry.

## The World of the U1s

Approximately 11 percent of the 160 million unchurched people in America are U1s. Nearly 17 million people are very close to accepting Christ as their Lord and Savior. And many of those 17 million are waiting for someone to tell them about the Savior. Indeed, a number of our interviewees accepted Christ after the interview.

A large number of these U1s were relatively young. Nearly half of them were age thirty-five or younger. And 83 percent were under the age of fifty. We saw no geographical correlation to where the U1s lived. They are in California and they are in Maine. They are in small towns and they are in large cities. Compared to the U5s their education level was lower, but they largely reflected the national averages. The U1s are the unchurched next door. And of all the unchurched groups, this is the group comprised of people who recognize that they are seekers. They are looking for answers. Will you be ready to respond to them?

One of the primary purposes of this book is to help you identify characteristics of each of the unchurched groups on the Rainer scale so you can know how to respond. But you should not have much trouble recognizing U1s. They are eager to hear biblical truths. They may even take the initiative to ask you questions. In this brief chapter, I hope to offer you a few more insights to this most receptive group.

## Church Background and the Baptists

More U1s have some church background than any other unchurched group. It was rare for us to talk to a U1 who had not spent some time in church in the past.

Researcher John Tolbert spoke with Jonathan R. from Michigan. Jonathan seems to have a basic understanding of key biblical and gospel issues. He notes that "God is a supreme being who is the Holy Trinity." And one gets to heaven, says Jonathan, "by asking for forgiveness and following Jesus." But Jonathan still

> More U1s have some church background than any other unchurched group. It was rare for us to talk to a U1 who had not spent some time in church in the past.

admits, "I don't understand all there is to becoming a Christian. Can you tell me the procedure?"

As with most U1s, Jonathan seems to have a biblical view of heaven and hell. Most of his responses indicate that his understanding of spiritual issues is not significantly different from that of churchgoing Christians. Researcher John commented, "This person is highly receptive to the gospel. It seems as if he is just resistant to the church because of some past experiences. He spoke highly of his childhood pastor. But since the pastor died, he has not returned to the church on a regular basis."

John's summary of the interview points to two interesting issues about the unchurched. First, these men and women are likely to have some type of church background. Their time in church may have been sporadic and short-lived, but the church is not a foreign and strange place to them.

> Another key issue is that the most common church background among the unchurched is Baptist. More than four out of ten of the U1s have attended or have been a member of a Baptist church at some point in their past.

Another key issue is that the most common church background among the unchurched is Baptist. More than four out of ten of the U1s have attended or have been a member of a Baptist church at some point in their past.

We on the research team were uncertain how to understand this issue. If we look at it positively, we might conclude that the Baptist churches did a good job of moving people to a greater level of receptivity to the gospel. Or, on the negative side, we could assume that the Baptists were unable to hold on to these persons who were so close to accepting Christ. And if we researched further, we would probably find truth in both suppositions among all the U1s.

U1s do not fit the stereotypical model of unchurched persons. They are not antichurch; to the contrary, most have some church background. The gospel and the Bible are not foreign truths to the U1s; in fact, some U1s articulated these truths better than Christians.

And U1s are far from resistant to the gospel. As many of our researchers observed, some of these unchurched would ask them how they could be saved.

## Pleasant Childhood Memories

The U1s we interviewed not only tend to have some church attendance in their background, but many of them have their best church memories from their childhood. Jonathan R., for example, not only has a church background; more specifically, he has a Baptist church background. His best memories of church took place in his childhood. He speaks warmly of attending Sunday school as a child in the Baptist church. Such memories tend to engender in U1s a desire to return to church. But many have gotten out of the habit of attending and are waiting with anticipation for your invitation.

Twyla Fagan interviewed Kerry D. from Texas. There is little doubt that Kerry has a strong church background. "I grew up going to a Baptist church. I went to church every time the doors were open. I guess I attended church every week of my childhood."

We could cite Kerry's beliefs, but you could anticipate them by now. He is a U1 who basically has orthodox Christian beliefs. Kerry was even baptized in the church, although he is still struggling to understand the truth of the gospel. Twyla indicated that Kerry uses various excuses to stay away from church, but "I sense he is really searching." She thinks it would not take much to get Kerry back into church and even to become a follower of Christ.

If these unchurched have some level of church background, the obvious question asks why they left. First, some of these U1s never really became regular church attendees. They came irregularly and often only for a short time.

Second, for those U1s who went to church for a few years on a regular basis, the reasons for their departure are too diverse to detect a pattern. One general observation we can make, however, is that very few U1s left the church because something negative happened to them while they attended church. To the contrary, most U1s report very positive past church experiences. Let us look at some of those experiences.

## The Positive Power of Church

Over 97 percent of the U1s recall positive church experiences in their past, the highest of any group on the Rainer scale. And while 61 percent of the U1s also could recall a negative church experience, they tended to be much more vocal about the positive experiences. Perhaps they were more favorable to the church because they were so receptive to the gospel. Perhaps the U1s' positive outlook toward the church is directly related to their own spiritual hunger. One factor seemed certain to us: Any conversation about the church or invitation to the church typically yields a favorable response from the U1s.

Researcher Brad Morrow interviewed Nancy H. of Mississippi. Brad describes Nancy as a clear U1: "Nancy is very friendly toward the church. She grew up in the church, but she has a confused theology. She believes that being a good person saves you. She would be willing to go to church and would probably be open to the gospel. It is obvious that the Holy Spirit is convicting her."

Nancy is forty years old. She lives in a rural area of Mississippi and has a healthy family income. Her church background is unique. She grew up in a church that was "Baptist, Presbyterian, and Methodist. Since we lived in such a small rural area, all three churches met together just so we could have enough people in worship." I bet some interesting discussions took place at this Baptimethopresby church.

In a rather interesting part of our conversation with Nancy, she shared with us about a time when she nearly died. Her description of the several days was "a near-death experience." She told us that "a minister helped me through that awful time. He was such a wonderful person. He didn't care if I was a member of the church; he just ministered to me."

Not only does Nancy have a positive perspective on the church and ministers, she remembers fondly her grandmother "who read the Bible to me and explained it every day." So much in Nancy's life seems to be in place to take the next and most important step, to receive Christ as her personal Lord and Savior.

We hope that as you have read through the pages of this book, you now see clearly that there is no such thing as a typical unchurched person. The U1s, about 17 million in the United States alone, are very receptive to the gospel. And, as you have seen in these pages, many of them have a church background, which has been a positive experience for them.

One more interesting comment from Nancy is noteworthy. She is like many of the U1s in that she says she will attend church if invited. But then she adds, "I really would like to go if my children invited me." This U1 is waiting on a lot of people. We pray that someone responds quickly.

## If They Are So Receptive, Why Aren't They in Church?

The U1s like the church, and they like the ministers of these churches. Many have positive memories of attending church in their past. And many others are seeking to understand the truth of the gospel. With all of these positive dispositions toward the church and Christians, why are these U1s not attending church?

When we asked the U1s the open-ended question, "Why do you think many people do not attend church?" these receptive unchurched persons tended to answer for themselves.

### Table 7.1

| Why Do You Think Many People Do Not Attend Church? | |
| --- | --- |
| Responses of U1s | |
| Laziness | 23% |
| Too busy | 42% |
| Hypocrites in church | 6% |
| Church is not relevant | 3% |
| Other | 26% |

Obviously, the U1s believe that busyness is the primary culprit keeping them from church. Laziness was a distant but significant excuse. For example, Nancy H. of Mississippi, whom I just introduced, said, "People are busy and working. They put that before church. We are worn down and worn out."

In his interview with Cindy I. of South Dakota, researcher Warner Smith found that busyness was one of her key reasons for not attending church. Cindy is a forty-year-old divorcee with a Catholic religious background.

"I am selfish with my time. I'd rather sleep late on Sunday morning personally," she told us. "I'm also of the opinion that many people try church and find that it's not fulfilling. I need to find a church that offers something for newly divorced people. I bet there aren't many churches out there like that."

Melissa N. of Indiana concurs: "It's just too early to get up." And Megan T. of Toronto expresses similar sentiment. "Some of us just don't make time for church in our busy schedules. We know that is an excuse, but we use it anyway. Our Sundays are a premium. And I have to admit, there is a bit of laziness on my part. I haven't made a conscious decision not to go to church. I just haven't made it a priority."

We noticed a difference in these interview responses among the U1s compared to other unchurched groups on the Rainer scale. The U1s tend to speak of their excuses not to attend church in the first person. They do not talk about other people as much as they speak of their own misplaced priorities.

> The U1s tend to speak of their excuses not to attend church in the first person. They do not talk about other people as much as they speak of their own misplaced priorities.

This self-awareness seems to be but one more indicator of the U1s' desire to learn more about spiritual matters. Church does matter to them even though they are not presently attending church. There are innumerable ways to touch the U1s, to start a conversation, and to share the gospel of Jesus Christ. Perhaps many U1s simply need that last bit of encouragement, that gentle shove to get them into church to hear the gospel. They know they are making excuses not to attend. It is almost as if many of them are waiting on Christians to ignore their excuses and to push them to attend church or hear the gospel. Remember, slightly more than one of ten unchurched persons are U1s. The fields are truly white unto harvest with the unchurched next door.

## Those U1 Prayer Warriors

If you have any doubt about the spiritual receptivity of the U1s, listen to them talk about prayer and all doubts will be removed. In fact, we on the research team thought the U1s had a more fervent prayer life than most Christians. Nine out of ten U1s indicated that they have a regular prayer life, and seven out of ten told us they pray daily.

Sometimes the U1s were effusive about their prayer lives. Patty M. of South Carolina once attended the United Pentecostal Church of God. "I used to be a holy roller!" she exclaimed. When we asked Patty if she prayed to God on a regular basis, she responded enthusiastically, "Yes! Every day! I must talk to him because he is everything to me. He is wonderful. He can make you feel so wonderful. I believe in his power so much!"

> Nine out of ten U1s indicated that they have a regular prayer life, and seven out of ten told us they pray daily.

Like many U1s, Patty has a supernatural view of life. She believes in a God who intervenes in the lives of people. But Patty is also like many of the unchurched who pray, in that she sees God mostly as the being who fulfills her wish list in prayer. She really does not pray for God's will to be done; rather, she prays to feel good and to get what she needs. Her view of prayer is largely limited to self-help.

Still, the evangelistic potential of reaching the praying unchurched is significant. Several years ago I served as pastor of a church in St. Petersburg, Florida. Early in my ministry at the church we began delivering surveys to hundreds of homes near our church. The survey was actually a door hanger. We would visit homes on Saturday from 10:00 A.M. to noon. When someone came to the door, we would introduce our church and ourselves and indicate that we were seeking our neighbors' help in becoming a better church in the community. We asked them, if they were willing, to complete the survey within an hour and hang it on the door when they were finished. We promised not to knock on the door a second time.

The response was incredibly high, over 50 percent. The survey asked many questions, but there was also a place on the back to write in any prayer requests. We were amazed at how many people requested prayer. They left their addresses and telephone numbers, and we responded to every one of them.

Pinellas County, Florida, in which my church was located, is almost 90 percent unchurched. So we knew that most of the respondents were unchurched. Yet we still connected with them through prayer. A number came to our church, and a good number of those became Christians.

One of the best ways for you to reach the unchurched evangelistically is to ask people regularly if they have any need for which you can pray. You may be surprised to see how readily your coworkers, friends, and neighbors respond to you. And you will see quickly how prayer is a point of connection to the unchurched.

## Heaven and Hell

The U1s believe in the existence of heaven and hell. Their understanding of both is, for the most part, a biblical view. As we have shown in the previous chapters, the greater the level of receptivity to the gospel, the higher the likelihood that the unchurched person will believe in the existence of heaven and hell.

### Table 7.2

| Believe in the Existence of | Hell | Heaven |
|---|---|---|
| U5 | 20% | 13% |
| U4 | 51% | 54% |
| U3 | 70% | 83% |
| U2 | 82% | 95% |
| U1 | 94% | 100% |

Almost every U1 you will encounter will have similar beliefs to you regarding heaven and hell. There will be no need for an extended debate on their existence. To the contrary, these unchurched men and women will be likely to engage you in a conversation if they happen to discover you are a Christian.

Michelle B. of Indiana is one of the few U1s in our study who had little or no church background. The forty-something U1 said, "I went to a church day camp with some kids in my neighborhood. I think it was called Bible school. But my family really did not attend church. The few times they did were at a Catholic church. I really don't remember anything about that."

> These unchurched men and women will be likely to engage you in a conversation if they happen to discover you are a Christian.

Like many of her U1 peers, Michelle says that "time is the biggest factor that I don't attend church. There are just too many things going on in my life. Our family is always on the run. By the time Sunday gets here, I just want to rest and to spend time at home with my family."

Michelle believes in both heaven and hell. In fact, her beliefs are probably not that much different than yours or mine. Indeed, it was the discussion of heaven and hell that seemed to engender some change in Michelle's demeanor. Ultimately, researcher Deborah White concluded that this unchurched person was close to becoming a believer.

"Michelle was extremely friendly. She appeared very friendly toward the idea of church and God. She is very illiterate about the Bible but seems interested in learning more. At the end of the interview I asked her if she had thought about visiting some churches in her area. She said that she and her husband had been discussing it.

"Although she was running short on time, she did allow me to tell her briefly the plan of salvation. I do know she was interested in talking more about heaven and hell. And I think she will soon go to church with a friend so she can get her child in church."

As you encounter these receptive unchurched people in the course of a week, understand that most of them are very interested in discussing matters of eternity. Such a discussion may be the first step in a change in their eternal destiny.

## A Confused Understanding of Salvation

Most of the unchurched in our study who claim to believe in the claims of Christ have a works understanding of salvation. The U1s have different views of salvation. They often told us that belief in Christ is what is necessary to be a Christian. Then, several minutes later in the interview, they would tell us that the way to heaven is to be a good person and to follow the teachings of Christ. As we listened to U1s, we noticed a consistency in their confusion. On the one hand, they want to use biblical language to describe what it means to be a Christian ("You must believe in Jesus"). On the other hand, they seem as if they cannot resist explaining the way to heaven as works oriented.

> On the one hand, they want to use biblical language to describe what it means to be a Christian ("You must believe in Jesus"). On the other hand, they seem as if they cannot resist explaining the way to heaven as works oriented.

Researcher Travis Fleming interviewed James S., who has lived in the same small Oklahoma town for most of his fifty-five years. He is a well-educated man who was "raised around Baptists." He explained further: "I've attended about every denomination you can think of."

Like many U1s, James thinks busy schedules are the primary reason people do not attend church. "A lot of people get wrapped up in their own lives. Some are taking care of elderly parents. But a church can happen at home if people are there who believe in the Lord."

James is a typical U1 in his attitude about spiritual matters. "I pray to God on a regular basis," he said. "Seldom does a day go by that I don't pray. I mean we are talking about our Creator, the Alpha and Omega, the Beginning and the End . . ." Further indication of James's receptivity is his view of the Bible. "The Bible is the Word of God; it is totally truthful. I go to the Bible almost every day for help. Psalm 23 is my favorite part of the Bible." And James wanted to be clear that we knew he believes in the existence of heaven and hell, "just as it is described in the Bible."

But then we began to ask questions about heaven and salvation, and James's confusion became obvious. His understanding of Christ is fairly clear: "He existed on earth. He is the Son of God. He is just what the Bible says about him."

Then when we asked James what it takes to be a Christian, his response became a bit muddled. "You've actually got to believe in him; you've got to set your life on that kind of person. You can't follow everything else on earth. If you ain't got faith, you ain't got anything."

Our question on how someone gets to heaven added to the confusion. James's initial response sounded hopeful: "You have to accept Jesus as your Savior." But then he digressed into a series of works: "You must obey the Bible. You have to be sincere. You have to follow Jesus' teaching. You have to basically be a good person."

Is James a Christian who simply does not know how to articulate his faith in Christ? Or is he lost but does know how to express some Christian verbiage? If James's interview was an isolated incident, we might conclude that James was a confused Christian. But after our multiple interviews, we were more likely to conclude that these U1s do not grasp the gospel as a free gift and continue to depend on a works salvation.

> After our multiple interviews, we were more likely to conclude that these U1s do not grasp the gospel as a free gift and continue to depend on a works salvation.

The implications of the U1s' confusion are numerous. For the relatively few churches that do have some regular plan of direct evangelism, is it possible that the members are walking away from the homes of U1s with a false assurance of salvation? Do Christians in the marketplace hear the "right" words and then stop sharing their faith with the U1s?

The confusion abounds. The gospel is simply not clear to these U1s. They have some of the concepts right, but they mix them with a form of works salvation. The U1s need to hear from Christians who will present the gospel with clarity. They are so close, yet they are still an eternity away from heaven.

## If We Get Them to Come to Church . . .

By this point you are probably expecting me to talk about inviting the U1s to church. I will not disappoint you. Look again at the likelihood of a U1 coming to church if he or she is invited.

### Table 7.3

| If Invited to Church, Would You Attend? | |
| --- | --- |
| Response of the U1s | |
| Very likely | 52% |
| Somewhat likely | 45% |
| Not likely at all | 3% |

If their actions match their words, 97 percent of U1s will attend church if you invite them. And once they come to church, develop relationships with Christians, and hear the gospel, this group is highly likely to accept Christ as their Savior.

A good example of this issue took place in Deborah White's interview with Carla L. of Georgia. Carla is thirty years old and has a Southern Baptist background. She did not expand on that church background. She describes her attitude toward the church as "very friendly."

She is familiar with much religious terminology, so she tells us quickly that one must "accept Jesus" to go to heaven. But when we asked Carla specifically what one must do to become a Christian, her response does not have the same clarity as her previous comments: "To be a Christian you have to have an awareness of God. You must change your life. And you must become a good person." Again, we heard the strange mix of faith and works.

But Carla is more than happy to come to church if she is invited. Her response was that she is "very likely" to attend if invited. And then when we asked her if she would like to say anything else at the conclusion of our interview, she responded almost wistfully, "It's funny you asked me to be a part of this interview. When I received your telephone call, I was excited about talking to you. My husband and I have been talking about going to church. Maybe we will."

I suspect that if a Christian in Georgia does not invite Carla and her husband to church, they will not take the initiative on their own. But once they get to a Bible-based church, they will hear the gospel. Most of these U1s, it would seem, will respond readily. The tragedy is that so few Christians are inviting the unchurched to church.

Deborah White summarized the interview well. "Carla is definitely a U1," she concluded. "She grasps basic issues of God and Christ and is very receptive. She has tried church in the past, but somewhere along the way the church did not follow through. This girl has let some silly issues stop her from attending church and hearing the gospel. Now she simply needs someone to show her the way."

Well said. You just might be that someone God will use to show an unchurched person the way. How will you respond?

## To Reach the Most Reachable Group

It is ironic that the church in America is so ineffective in reaching such a receptive unchurched group as the U1s. Our research cited earlier indicates that for every eighty-five church members only one person is reached for Christ in a year. If we simply reached one-half of the U1s, our churches would see nearly 9 million new Christians blessing our congregations.

In the final chapter of this book, I will bring the various components of our study to a concluding strategy. But I do not want to leave this chapter on the U1s until I discuss some key issues in reaching the unchurched. Remember, we had the advantage in this study of being guided by new Christians whom we called the formerly unchurched. Their insights provided a significant help in forming this study, asking the questions, and formulating some conclusions.

When I wrote *Surprising Insights from the Unchurched* for our previous study, I indicated my motivation for such a book. Many good works have been written about the unchurched, but the American populace is no more Christian today than it was thirty years ago. So the formerly unchurched project proceeded with the thesis that it might be better to hear from new Christians on how they *were* reached than from non-Christians on how they *might* be reached.

Indeed, we did learn numerous invaluable lessons from the formerly unchurched. So we did not want to enter this project without getting guidance and insight from these new Christians. Who better to inform us of the unchurched world than those who had just left that world?

> Who better to inform us of the unchurched world than those who had just left that world?

The five basic issues discussed below were suggested to us by the formerly unchurched. The list is not exhaustive nor is it intended to be. We will give further details in the next chapter. For now, consider this information as you attempt to reach the U1s next door.

*Never Forget Prayer*

In my enthusiasm to report to you some of the sociological characteristics of all the unchurched in this study, I fear that I have understated the critical importance of theological issues. I will make those adjustments in the next chapter.

For now, we cannot overlook the testimonies of answered prayers we have heard from the formerly unchurched, those who have recently become Christians. Martina L. accepted Christ just eleven months ago. This Houston, Texas, native spoke with certainty as she told us the people and factors God used in her salvation.

"My mother has been praying for me to get saved for over twenty-five years," she said softly. "She didn't make a big deal of it to me, but I knew. You should've seen her at my baptism. Neither one of us could stop crying. Twenty-five years of praying, and she never gave up. She never stopped believing this day would come."

Gerald A., another formerly unchurched person, spoke poignantly about the power of prayer in his salvation. "I had no clue that three of my fraternity brothers from college made a decision when we left college to pray for my salvation every day. It's been seven years, and I told them that I got saved. They were blown away!" Gerald exclaimed. "Then I was blown away when I heard about them praying for me. Now I'm praying every day for two friends at work. I know prayer works."

### The Testimonies of Persistence

Many U1s will accept Christ as soon as they hear the gospel. Others will ponder the issues with care and conviction. But not all the U1s will respond on the spot. Unfortunately, some of the programmatic evangelism approaches do not consider that those who are not responding today just need a little more time. We should not abandon our efforts to reach them.

Margie H. of Vermont is a new Christian who heard the gospel from her coworker at the bank. "I guess I took the first step with Wanda," Margie told us. "It was obvious that she was a Christian. She read her Bible at work and always seemed to have a cheerful disposition. And that's not easy with the tyrant we have for a boss.

"God had been working in my life. I had never attended church, but I started thinking about it. First, my fiancé and I broke up. Then I couldn't stop watching Billy Graham on television. It was like everywhere I turned something about Jesus was being mentioned.

"I finally got up the courage to talk to Wanda. I basically asked her why she read the Bible. Deep inside I was hoping she would give me more information than I was asking. Boy did she!

"I guess she knew right away that I was a lost person seeking Jesus. She not only answered all my questions, she asked to take me to lunch the next day. And she was buying. I couldn't refuse.

"At lunch the next day, she shared with me in a real nice way how Jesus had saved her. I was hanging on to every word. Then she asked me if I would like to accept Christ. Right there in the restaurant! I tell you, I was so nervous that I had to leave the table. I thought I was going to be sick. I told her I had to leave.

"I couldn't sleep much that week. I was under conviction but scared to make a decision. I was also afraid that Wanda wouldn't talk to me anymore about Jesus. I mean, I did run out of the restaurant!"

Wanda patiently, lovingly, and persistently deepened the relationship with Margie. Three months later Margie accepted Christ. "What if she had given up on me?" Margie pondered. She did not, and Wanda is a lesson for us today in loving persistence in sharing our faith.

*Invite and Take*

As I have mentioned with methodical redundancy, inviting the unchurched to church is critical. As I have also indicated, inviting them and taking them into the church building is very important. The U1s in particular are eager to go to church, but many are fearful of walking into a placed that seems as strange as a church. Listen to Roy U., a formerly unchurched person from Iowa.

"A little over a year ago I was under so much conviction that I was just waiting for something to happen in my life or for somebody to help me. I had a deep void in my life, and I was hoping that someone could tell me about God. I wasn't even sure how Jesus fit into all of this."

Roy continued his story. "I was receptive to almost anyone helping me, so I surprised myself when Jimmy invited me to church and I turned him down. Jimmy is a neighbor of mine. We have sons on the same baseball team and have gotten to know each other pretty well.

"Here I was almost begging for someone to help me and I told Jimmy a flat 'no.' I went home that night and tried to figure out why I did what I did. I realized that I was scared to go into a church building by myself. It seems silly, doesn't it? A grown man afraid to go into a building. But I had only been to church a few times for special occasions, and I was just intimidated.

"Fortunately, Jimmy must have sensed something was wrong. Three weeks later he asked me to go with him and to have lunch with him after church. I was relieved. A few weeks later I accepted Jesus."

I wonder how many U1s are eager for someone to take them to church. How many U1s may just be a few steps away from accepting Christ? Invite them. Take them. Watch what God will do.

*The Bible and the U1s*

U1s are very desirous to learn about the Bible and are highly likely to respond positively to a Bible study invitation.

Mark B. is president of a service company in Arizona. He became a Christian about nine months prior to our interview. He told us: "I guess I have always been on the fast-paced life. But when I turned fifty years old, I began wondering if this is all there is to life. Get up. Work for twelve hours. Go home. Go to bed. Start over the next day.

"I knew there was more to life than the treadmill I was on. So when a friend, a businessman in another company, asked if I was interested in joining a Bible study, I jumped at it. We studied the gospel of John, and my eyes really began to open up to a world I had never known. The Bible study was six months long, but I accepted Christ after two months in the study."

Repeatedly we heard this common theme from the formerly unchurched. They are very close to becoming Christians. And God uses instruments like you and me to pray for them and to witness to them directly, lovingly, and persistently, even when they say no the first time. He also uses us to invite them to Bible studies. It is there where the Word of God does its convicting work to move a heart closer to the cross.

All of these testimonies have a central theme: We are not to be silent. We are not to be passive. We are to do something.

*A Final Word: Do Something*

I really have no idea how many people I have led to Christ. Likewise, I could not even guess how many people have become Christians under my preaching ministry. I have heard on occasion from some people that they have accepted Christ after hearing me do a radio or television interview, or even after reading one of my books. But then again, I have no idea how many that would be.

The reason I do not even care how many have been saved through my ministries is that I know the power for being Christ's witness is not my own. I know that I have saved no one. And, in those times that he has used me, I know that I am no more than his instrument. I thank God that he has given me the incredible privilege of telling others the good news of Jesus Christ.

But one thing I do know: I would not be witnessing to anyone today if Coach Joe Hendrickson had not shared Christ with me. I would not be writing books about the church and the unchurched. I would not be dean of the Southern Baptist Theological Seminary. I would not be consulting with churches and denominations. I would not be speaking around the world about his church.

You see, I recognize that in those times I have been privileged to be used of God, it has been all his strength for his glory. But I also know that every life that is touched and every soul that is saved under my ministry can be attributed to the courageous ministry of Joe Hendrickson. When no one else would tell me about Jesus, Coach Joe did.

If I have learned anything about evangelism, and if I have grasped any of the lessons taught to me by Joe Hendrickson and the unchurched, it is this one thing: We must do something. The Great Commission does not give us the option to be still or to be silent. We must go and tell.

You have now heard from five unchurched groups. They are truly the unchurched next door. And you just briefly heard from the formerly unchurched, a group of men and women who recently accepted

Christ. We now will hear a more complete story from the formerly unchurched. And what you will hear from these new Christians will only confirm what you have heard from the unchurched. The theme is predictable: We cannot remain silent. We cannot be still. We must do something. The eternal destiny of many remains in the balance.

## Chapter 8

# The Formerly Unchurched Offer Some Insights

I can tell you some crazy stories about what Christians do wrong and right to reach the unchurched.

*—Mark M.,*
*a formerly unchurched person*
*from Florida*

Mark M. is one of my favorite formerly unchurched persons. (Remember that a formerly unchurched person is someone who has accepted Christ in the past year and someone who has become active in a local church.) This lifelong Floridian rarely attended church during the first thirty-six years of his life. Through persistent and loving invitations to church by his fellow employee Chad, Mark finally agreed to go to church with him. He liked what he saw.

"I'm not sure what I expected," Mark said enthusiastically. "But it was so much better than I thought possible. I went with Chad the next two Sundays, and then I started going on my own." Mark would become a Christian in a little over a year.

While it is nothing less than miraculous anytime someone accepts Christ, Mark's story is especially compelling. Mark was a lifelong unchurched person. And he was a second-generation unchurched person as well. "My parents never went to church," Mark said. "I never really thought about attending; it just wasn't on my agenda."

We asked Mark why he finally attended a church.

"Because Chad invited me," he responded bluntly.

"Any other reasons?" we asked.

"Nope, just because I was invited."

"Had anyone ever invited you to church before?"

"Nope, no one."

"In all the thirty-six years of your life?"

"No one in all my life."

Here was a second-generation unchurched person who decided to go to church based on one person's invitation. And rarely have I seen any Christian with this level of zeal.

Mark participated in our previous research project on the formerly unchurched. Because he had been such a great subject for that project, I decided to call him to get his input for this project. I explained that I wanted to visit the world of the unchurched and determine different response levels to the gospel. He thought it was a great idea and gave me many suggestions on how to ask the questions.

A few months later, after our team was well into the current project, I called Mark again. I wanted him to hear my concept of what the team was now calling the Rainer scale. Mark responded with an outburst, "That's a great concept; it really explains what's going on in the world of the unchurched!"

Mark then explained to me that he had traveled across the entire Rainer scale. "When I was in college, some holy roller Christians started harassing me, and I let them have it. I realized then that I did not like Christians at all. I was what you call a U5."

But circumstances and time helped move Mark to a more receptive posture. "By the time Chad invited me to church, I guess I was a U3. I moved up to U2 then U1 after I started coming to church."

I could not have accomplished this project without the input of formerly unchurched persons such as Mark. They let me pester them and call them at all stages of this project. I asked them to brainstorm with me. I went back to them to get help in shaping the interview questions. I called them again when I wanted the perspective of a new Christian.

The formerly unchurched taught us many lessons about the unchurched.

And I asked them to look at my tentative conclusions and offer their input. The formerly unchurched were key in helping me understand the world they had recently left, the world of the unchurched.

Though the formerly unchurched have been instrumental in shaping much of what you have read thus far in this book, I wanted to devote a full chapter to them to let you hear their thoughts. We have heard from Mark and many other new Christians who were enthusiastic to help us understand better the world they just left.

## Resistance Is Not a Permanent No

Alicia G. of Oklahoma became a Christian at age forty-seven. She attended a Baptist church as a child but cannot remember attending since she was about ten years old. Alicia became a Christian when she was in a difficult and messy divorce. "Reba was the one who really showed she cared," Alicia told us. "I have a teenage daughter, and her dad's leaving was traumatic for both of us."

Prior to Alicia's divorce, Reba had invited her to church. "I wasn't very nice to her. She was always nice to me, so I felt kind of bad. But the next day she acted as if nothing had happened." Reba didn't mention church again until she heard that Alicia's husband Paul was leaving her.

"The reason I was such a jerk to Reba is that religion just scared me," said Alicia. "I'm not sure why. But it was like a trigger that was pulled anytime anyone, Reba included, mentioned God, church, or anything religious. I sure am glad she didn't give up on me."

Among the important lessons the formerly unchurched taught us about the unchurched is that a negative response should not be taken personally. Without exception, these new Christians told us that any negative responses they made when they were lost really had nothing to do with the Christian who was witnessing.

> Among the important lessons the formerly unchurched taught us about the unchurched is that a negative response should not be taken personally.

Jervis S. of California is a formerly unchurched who tells a similar story. Jervis looked at the Rainer scale and determined, "I was a U3 most of my life." He said he never really had any antagonistic feelings against Christians before he was saved. "I guess I didn't have many feelings at all."

Jervis married Lydia shortly before Jervis's thirtieth birthday. At the time of their marriage, neither of the two were Christians, but Lydia started attending church with her best friend, Gina. Lydia would accept Christ before the couple's first anniversary.

"I guess I was pretty nonchalant about Lydia. I mean, if religion was her thing, that was fine with me. I guess I was a U3 with my wife," Jervis laughed.

"Everything was fine as long as we could have our normal lives," Jervis said. "But I started noticing changes in my wife. I soon realized that things were not going to be the same.

"Wives who have husbands who are lost could learn lessons from my wife," Jervis said proudly. "She never nagged me. She didn't put me down. Just the opposite. She even became a better wife!"

Jervis watched carefully the new attitude of his wife. He saw her joy. And finally he decided on his own to go to church with her. In less than a year, Jervis became a Christian.

"I would later find out that my wife and a few other women were praying for me every day," the formerly unchurched Jervis told us. "Lydia also told me later that some older women in the church were mentoring her on how to be a godly wife when you are married to a lost man.

"I accepted Christ as the result of my wife's loving persistence," Jervis said. "She never gave up on me even when I acted totally uninterested. Thom, you tell the readers of your next book never to give up on lost people. You really don't know what's going on in their lives. That next witness or that next invitation to church may be the step God uses to bring those persons to Christ."

## Don't Dumb Down the Church!

A consistent theme among the nearly one hundred formerly unchurched we contacted to help us with this project was that doctrine really matters. Churches that attempt to reach unchurched people by compromising or diluting the teachings of Scripture are counterproductive.

Hank D. of Virginia became a Christian at age thirty-two. He found the watered-down teaching and preaching of many churches amusing at first, but then he changed his mind. "I was a true seeker," Hank told us. "I started looking around for a church just because I had this big empty place in my life that nothing was filling. No one invited me to a church. I just started doing it on my own."

Hank's experiences were often disappointing. "At first, I was kind of amused at the way churches dumbed down their preaching and teaching. And then it got disgusting. I'm not sure if they were trying to be seeker friendly or if they were just unprepared themselves."

In *Surprising Insights from the Unchurched,* the formerly unchurched were emphatic about churches having strong biblical teachings. They articulate this issue clearly since having become Christians, but they also insist that the issue was important before they became Christians. Cheryl S. of Maine said, "Even before I became a Christian I was really interested in what churches believed. I had enough common sense to know that they weren't all exactly alike. I wanted to find a church that would stick to their guns on their beliefs."

To the surprise of some, doctrine was the number one issue of importance to unchurched people seeking a church. Over 91 percent of the formerly unchurched said that doctrine was important, the highest ranking of all issues.

> Over 91 percent of the formerly unchurched said that doctrine was important, the highest ranking of all issues.

The formerly unchurched, however, were not just interested in the facts of doctrine; they were insistent that the churches should be uncompromising in their stand. These facts fly in the face of an increasingly pluralistic and theologically tolerant culture. It seems as if, when one takes the step from being firmly unchurched, a U5, to at least being an inquirer, a U2 or U1, attitudes change.

Seekers desire to discover truth and conviction among Christians about the reality of God, Jesus, and the entire supernatural realm. Jorge C. spoke rather bluntly about the issue: "I visited a few churches before I became a Christian. Man, some of them made me want to vomit. They didn't show any more conviction about their beliefs than I did. And I was lost and going to hell!"

The formerly unchurched were clear. They not only were interested in learning about doctrine, they were attracted to churches that were uncompromising in their beliefs.

Mandy L., a formerly unchurched woman from Montana, spoke softly but firmly. "When we were lost, we were looking for something that would not be like the world we were in. We were looking, even if we didn't realize it at the time, for the supernatural, for beliefs that transcend the unbelieving world around us. It was really sad to go to churches that thought they were being relevant when they were really just being worldly. I got out of those churches as quickly as I could."

## The Formerly Unchurched Speak about the Bible

Almost two years had passed since I spoke to Randy M. of Florida. I went back to Randy, a subject of the formerly unchurched research project, because of his candor and articulate responses. I shared with him the preliminary results of the unchurched next door project and told him that many formerly unchurched people had helped us shape and interpret this project. And I explained to him the concept of faith stages, or Rainer scale. He wholeheartedly agreed with our thoughts.

"Randy," I asked, "what would you tell Christians who wanted to reach out to their unchurched friends and neighbors?"

"That's a no-brainer," Randy quickly responded. "I am already doing it. Invite them to a Bible study. I remembered how much I wanted to learn about the Bible before I became a Christian. So after I accepted Christ, about six months after I became a Christian, I started a Bible study in my home."

> "It was really sad to go to churches that thought they were being relevant when they were really just being worldly. I got out of those churches as quickly as I could."

I was curious about how Randy invited people to this Bible study, so I asked him.

"I went to the easy ones first, mainly friends I have known for a bunch of years. I asked two coworkers that I felt comfortable with. But for my second Bible study, I went door to door on my street and gave them a flyer. I had six people in the first study and eight in the second when my neighbors showed up. It's been great!"

Randy then told me that of the fourteen in the first two Bible studies, four have already accepted Christ and become faithful attendees and members of the same church Randy attends. He has no doubt about the evangelistic potential of Bible studies. "I remember how I was," he said, recalling his pre-Christian life. "I really wanted to understand the Bible and probably would've gone to a Bible study if I had been invited to one."

I was curious if Randy thought the unchurched would attend a Bible study at a church as readily as attending one in someone's home. He paused for a moment before giving a thoughtful response. "Go back to the Rainer scale," he said. "I have invited people to my home Bible study and to my Sunday school class. Your scale makes perfect sense to the people I've invited. The U1s and the U2s will go to Bible studies in either place. The U3s and U4s will more than likely come to a home but not a church. Of course, the U5s won't go to any Bible study."

Such is the reason we asked the formerly unchurched to work with us throughout the project on the unchurched next door. They were able to tell us if our theories met the tests of reality. My one conversation with Randy alone was a major lesson in understanding the attraction of the unchurched to Bible studies.

Before our telephone conversation ended, Randy shared an insightful thought with me. "Thom, you say the name of your new book will be *The Unchurched Next Door*. That's a perfect title. I know you're talking in general terms about all the unchurched people around us. But I learned that my neighbors on the street where I live are perfect examples of typical unchurched people. And even though most of them did not know me well, they felt comfortable with me since we lived on the same street. Maybe 'the unchurched next door' makes a lot more sense than even you thought."

Invite the unchurched next door to a Bible study and see what God will do.

## "We'd Like to Get to Know You"

Very few writings on the unchurched have ignored the importance of relationships in reaching lost friends, neighbors, coworkers, relatives, and acquaintances. Indeed, in my previous book, the research team noted the critical importance of Christians connecting with non-Christians.

The formerly unchurched encouraged us to ask the unchurched specific questions regarding relationships. So, on their advice, we asked the unchurched who influenced their lives. We also asked them whether any Christians had been an influence in their lives. Then we asked specific questions about negative and positive influences. This input by the formerly unchurched enhanced the research project significantly.

These new Christians were particularly enthusiastic about the Rainer scale. "You know what I see on this scale more than anything?" Lenora T. of West Virginia asked. "I see where relationships make all the difference. I was what you call a U5 for the first forty years of my life. You know what moved me to be a U4 or a U3? Brenda. She was my coworker and she later became my best friend.

"I knew she was a Christian, but she didn't shove her beliefs down my throat. Instead, she was always there when I needed her. I remember one time when I asked why she always looked after me. She just said quietly, 'Because I'm a Christian.' For four years she just put me first. I was the one who finally asked her if I could go to church with her."

Lenora continued. "Once I started going to church, things moved pretty quickly. And when I accepted Christ, I told Brenda. You should've seen her. She smiled and hugged me, and then the tears came for both of us. She said she had prayed for me every day since we met. Can you believe that? Every day."

The pause on the other end of the telephone was lengthy by telephone standards. I thought I heard a soft sobbing sound. Then Lenora told me the news. "Brenda died of cancer last month. I met at the funeral I bet a dozen women that she had befriended, and every one of them said that Brenda was the reason they accepted Christ. Yeah, I really believe relationships are important."

Some of the formerly unchurched who helped us with this project expressed bewilderment that Christians do not more readily befriend the unchurched. Sam J. of Texas, after accepting Christ, went to his coworkers, whom he knew were Christians.

"I guess I wasn't too Christian acting for a new Christian," Sam told us. "But I went to the four of these dudes that I knew were Christians. They went to church and everything. But they didn't have much to do with me. So I confronted all of them at one time. I kind of got mad when I asked them why they never tried to get to know me better, when they knew I was lost. Not one of them said a word. So I walked away mad and got a parting word, 'Why didn't all of you just tell me to go to hell? That's what your actions said to me.'"

"Developing a relationship with a lost person is a high-commitment action," Lenora told us. "But how can we do nothing when we know that person is lost without Jesus? I hope I never get that disobedient."

"Developing a relationship with a lost person is a high-commitment action," Lenora told us. "But how can we do nothing when we know that person is lost without Jesus?"

## One Particular Relationship: Family Members

In our previous research project on the formerly unchurched, we heard not only about the importance of relationships, but also about the particular importance of family relationships in reaching the unchurched. When we asked if a relationship was a factor in their accepting Christ, a majority answered affirmatively. Perhaps the number who said yes was not as high as we would have anticipated, but it was nevertheless a strong response.

### Table 8.1

| Was a Relationship Important in Your Becoming a Christian? | |
| --- | --- |
| Yes | 57% |
| No | 38% |
| Uncertain | 5% |

But among the whole scope of potential relationships, the formerly unchurched were clear in their assessment that family relationships were the most critical. Note the persons of greatest influence as told to us by the formerly unchurched.

### Table 8.2

| What Person Was the Greatest Influence in Your Coming to the Church? | |
| --- | --- |
| Family members | 42% |
| No one | 25% |
| Other | 17% |
| Coworker | 8% |
| Neighbor | 6% |
| Merchant | 2% |

The formerly unchurched provided information that we in the church had only intuitively known. Christian family members are important connections to the unchurched world. Do you have a family member who is not a Christian? How are you intentionally reaching out to this relative?

The family issue becomes even more intriguing when we ask which family member was the most influential. Note the responses.

### Table 8.3

| If a Family Member Influenced You in Becoming a Christian, Which Person Was Most Influential? | |
| --- | --- |
| Wife | 35% |
| Child | 18% |
| Parents | 16% |
| Siblings | 5% |
| Parents-in-law | 2% |

The formerly unchurched first told us that wives were the most important in reaching the unchurched through relationships. More than one-third responded to the positive impact of this relationship. But husbands reaching wives was virtually a nonfactor.

Also note the influence of children in reaching their parents; nearly one out of five responded to this influence. Ten years ago the paradigm of youth ministry was "reach the parents to reach the children." Today the paradigm is "reach the children to reach the parents."

Of course the unchurched could not tell us the greatest influence on their becoming a Christian. After all, they were not Christians. But we did ask the unchurched to articulate what Christians had been influential in their lives. The responses are significantly different from those of the formerly unchurched.

## Table 8.4

| What Christians Have Been Influential in Your Lives? (Asked of the unchurched) | |
|---|---|
| Parent | 23% |
| None | 14% |
| Friend | 12% |
| Other family | 12% |
| Grandparent | 10% |
| Spouse | 2% |
| Other | 27% |

Obviously, the perspective of the new Christian is different from that of the non-Christian. More than one-third of the formerly unchurched said their wives were the biggest Christian influence in their lives. But a paltry 2 percent of the non-Christians gave a similar response. While children reaching parents was a huge issue for the formerly unchurched, the unchurched did not recognize the influence of their children at all. Such is the reason we asked the formerly unchurched to assist us in this research project. Researching the unchurched must include a healthy dose of caution, if not skepticism. An unregenerate person may not even realize that he or she has spiritual needs. We therefore depended on the insights of the formerly unchurched throughout this project. We concluded with little doubt that family members were critically important in reaching their lost relatives.

## That Moment of Crisis

In a previous chapter I mentioned the lessons we learned from September 11, 2001. God often uses moments of crisis to reach lost people. We saw an immediate increase in the interest in spiritual matters in the days following September 11, but we also saw that increase wane in just a matter of weeks. These times of crisis are significant opportunities for you to reach out to those who do not have a saving relationship with Jesus Christ.

The formerly unchurched agreed. The interviews we conducted of more than 350 of these new Christians gave us a plethora of evidence to verify this reality. Time and time again we heard the formerly unchurched tell us how a crisis moment made them more desirous to seek spiritual help.

But some of the formerly unchurched asked an indicting question of us long-time Christians: "Where were you in my moment of need?" Carla R., a formerly unchurched from Wyoming, had this to say: "When my husband was killed in an automobile accident, several Christians sent flowers or expressed their sympathies. Now, I don't want to sound ungrateful, but I really needed more than a token of sympathy. I had questions. I was hurting deeply and wondering how to make sense of all this. I needed a committed Christian just to sit down and listen to me."

> Times of crisis are significant opportunities for you to reach out to those who do not have a saving relationship with Jesus Christ.

Carla's story does have a good ending. She said that one Christian, "out of the over fifty I know," asked if she could come see her two weeks after her husband's tragic death. "Verna just said that she was hurting for me and wanted to know if she could come over and talk and listen. That's what she did more than anything. She listened. That was the beginning of my first major step to becoming a Christian," Carla noted. "One person who cared enough to listen."

Many of the formerly unchurched asked those of us who have been Christians for several years to become more aware of witnessing opportunities during moments of crisis. "It's a lesson I learned," said Carla. "I have had the opportunity to see seven people accept Christ after I became available for them in their time of need."

## Tell Them about Jesus

Here is a fascinating lesson from the formerly unchurched: One of the most effective ways to communicate the gospel to lost people is to tell them about Jesus. If my comments seem a bit sarcastic, it is because the formerly unchurched often helped us to see the obvious.

Mark W. is a formerly unchurched person who lives in a medium-sized town about sixty miles from St. Louis. He was one of several million unchurched who attended church the previous Easter Sunday. "I typically attended church on Easter," Mark told us. "There was no particular reason for my once-a-year church habit. No major crisis, no guilt trip. It was just something I did."

Mark gladly filled out the guest cards as requested in the service. He did not mind hearing from the pastor by letter and receiving information about the church. He was accustomed to the routine after this many years. He was surprised, however, when he received a telephone call from someone at the church requesting an opportunity to visit him. Mark agreed to receive two men from the church.

"These two men got right to the point," Mark commented. "They explained to me how I could become a Christian. I received Christ and have been in the church ever since."

The formerly unchurched in our study left little doubt as to the importance of direct personal evangelism in reaching the unchurched. Over one-half indicated that someone from the church they joined shared Christ with them. Another 12 percent told us that someone other than a member of the church they joined personally evangelized them.

Look at these numbers:

### Table 8.5

| Did Someone from the Church You Joined Share with You How to Become a Christian? (Asked of the formerly unchurched) | |
|---|---|
| Yes | 53% |
| Someone else did | 12% |
| No one did | 35% |

Only one-third of the formerly unchurched said that no one made an attempt to share Christ with them. While such factors as the building of relationships is very important in reaching the unchurched, we heard repeatedly that an evangelistic visit, even by a stranger from the church, had an eternal impact.

Have you become involved in personal evangelistic efforts through your church? Such an approach is certainly not the only way to reach the unchurched, but we have little doubt that God uses direct evangelism to reach many with the gospel.

## The Appearance of the Church

In *Surprising Insights from the Unchurched* I acknowledged my reticence to mention such seemingly mundane issues as the appearance of the church. Indeed, my concern was that more substantive issues become the foci for the church. After listening to new Christians for nearly two years, my views on the foundational issues being the most important have not changed. But my perspective on some of the more peripheral matters has adjusted.

Tina L. is a formerly unchurched single mom from Georgia. She and her former husband had moved there from Massachusetts because of his job transfer. In Georgia, Tina felt "like an alien in a strange land." After the divorce, she told us, "I felt so unbelievably alone. All my social relationships were built around my husband's friends at work. When he left me, I had no connections in this town. And I sure am different than the typical resident here. Some of the people can't understand my accent."

Tina had never attended church except for special occasions. But, in what she viewed as "an act of desperation," she decided to visit a Baptist church near her home. "You know I had to be desperate to visit a Baptist church in South Georgia, but I had to find something for Tara [her four-year-old daughter] and me."

The Sunday arrived, and Tina, with Tara in tow, went to the local Baptist church. "I couldn't believe how scared I was. I always thought I could handle any situation, but the idea of going to that Baptist church scared me to death."

To make the situation worse, a light rain started falling on the way to church. "I debated about going home, but I decided to push ahead.

I got there at 10:50 thinking I had plenty of time. I would learn quickly that church started at 10:45, but the sign outside did not give any times."

Despite her fear, the rain, and her tardiness, Tina got out of the car with determination. "I had to find some hope and people who cared somewhere. If I couldn't find it in a church, where could I?"

Tina was surprised to see the parking lot in deteriorating condition. She almost slipped on the grass growing in the cracks. And she was unable to find a parking place near the church. She still walked resolutely forward in the misty rain.

"I was already frustrated by the time I got to the door," Tina told us. "But when the front door was locked, I was livid." She finally found an open door that led to a maze of hallways with no directional signage. "We walked for a few minutes before someone gave me directions to the place to take Tara. But when I opened the door and saw one lady attempting to take care of twenty screaming preschoolers, I turned around and left. Never again, I told myself."

Tina's story does obviously have a happy ending. After all, she is a new Christian, one of the formerly unchurched we interviewed. But after her bad experience, Tina stayed away from church for several weeks. She eventually tried another church, a nondenominational church a little further from her home. At that church she heard the gospel and accepted Christ.

"The difference between the two churches was like day and night," Tina observed. "One church acted like they could care less about their facilities and ministries, and the other acted like they cared for people like me. The facilities and the preschool area are incredible in our church. Don't some of these other churches realize that they're telling people like me that God doesn't matter to them? Don't they realize that anything less than excellence for God is not good enough?"

We could cite dozens of stories similar to Tina's. I now understand better that seemingly mundane issues like facilities can have eternal impact. As you seek to become a better witness for Christ, observe how your church is doing in these areas. What do the facilities look like to an outsider? Are the children's and preschool areas clean and modern? Is signage clear and modern? Do guests have sufficient parking close to the church?

On the one hand, such issues may seem less than important. On the other hand, from the perspective of the unchurched, the issue may be of eternal importance.

## Praying for the Unchurched

The unchurched could not, of course, tell us about people who prayed for their salvation. They are not saved. But the formerly unchurched told us many such stories. One report comes from George G. of Arizona.

George learned a few weeks after his becoming a Christian that at least four people had prayed for him daily. "I wasn't surprised that Cindy [his wife] was praying for me. I knew she was worried about my spiritual state. She was the first one who told me after I accepted Christ."

Then George learned about others. "A friend of mine who lives over seven hundred miles away called me when he heard the news. He told me that he prayed for me twice a day. Can you believe that? Twice a day." George then heard about his mother-in-law praying for him every day. And then he got the word that someone from the church whom he did not know was praying for him as well.

"There may have been more than those four," George mused. "But it was still unbelievable that they cared for me that much. Why don't all Christians show that much concern for someone's eternity? I tell you one thing. I learned a whole lot about the power of prayer in salvation. And I've already started praying for some of my lost friends."

## Seeker Common Sense

For years the debate of seeker sensitivity and seeker targeting engendered controversy in many churches and denominations. The formerly unchurched really did not care to enter the debate. In fact, many of these new Christians thought that the conflict was much ado about nothing.

Janice T. is a relatively new Christian from New Mexico. She had never heard of the debate until after she became a Christian. She believes the issue is not one of seeker-sensitive or seeker-targeted services; she thinks the issue is simply common sense.

> Why don't all Christians show that much concern for someone's eternity?

"I am new to the church, so I really don't know a whole lot of what's going on. I hear some of the church members fussing about this and that," Janice commented. "The more I hear, the more I'm convinced that churches need to practice common sense. I mean, it's common sense to have a decent and clean building. It's common sense to be friendly to visitors. It's common sense to help everybody understand the songs that are being sung. And it's common sense not to make visitors feel uncomfortable."

Indeed, the comments that we heard from the formerly unchurched who had bad experiences at churches were typically related to commonsense issues: clean carpets, good signage, adequate guest parking, excellent preschool and children's areas, friendly greeters, easy-to-follow music, decent landscaping, and a lengthy list of other practical issues.

When I served as a pastor prior to becoming dean of Southern Seminary, I led our church to approach these commonsense issues from a different perspective. We would ask an unchurched woman to visit our church and give us a detailed and honest response. We would actually pay a respectable stipend for the woman to conduct this exercise. And we would find a different unchurched person every six months so that we could have a fresh perspective each time.

The assistance from the unchurched person would come in two phases. First, she would attend Sunday morning services and tell us of her experience. Did she find convenient parking? Were the greeters helpful and friendly? Could she find the way to her destination? Was signage adequate? What were her first impressions of the grounds and buildings? Were the rest rooms convenient and clean?

The next day, Monday, the unchurched woman would take a thorough tour of our facilities. She would have diagrams of all the rooms, and she would make notes for every single place she toured. At the end of the day, the woman would meet with our ministry staff, custodians, and lay leaders. Inevitably we would hear things that surprised us, even after six or seven consecutive reports in the recent past.

We always took the input of the formerly unchurched seriously. And most of the information they gave us was common sense. But we were often surprised to learn that we were not using common sense. Learn from the formerly unchurched and learn to become commonsensical in your church.

> Learn from the formerly unchurched and learn to become commonsensical in your church.

## Use the Formerly Unchurched in Evangelism

Jack R., a formerly unchurched man from upstate New York, has quite a network of lost friends. "The guys at work couldn't believe what happened to me. I really didn't think much about them until this Christian girl I'm dating said something almost off the cuff. She asked me if I had witnessed to any of my friends. I was kind of dumbstruck by her question."

But Jack decided that her question had real merit. "I went to one of our pastors and asked him to help me know how to witness to this bunch of guys I used to get drunk with. He began to teach me and mentor me. It was incredible. I led five friends to the Lord in less than six months."

The unchurched who accept Christ will likely have the most significant network of lost people in the church. If you are a longer-term Christian seeking to be obedient to the Great Commission, seek out these new Christians in your church. Ask them if you can work and pray with them to reach their lost friends, neighbors, and family members.

A number of the formerly unchurched who assisted us in this project reported very exciting information about the way God has used them to reach lost people. And in almost every case, the new Christian had teamed with a more mature Christian to be used of God to reach more people with the gospel.

## With Thanks to the Formerly Unchurched

This research project has been the result of hundreds of hours of work by one of the finest research teams ever assembled. The work they did will have eternal impact. My gratitude to these men and women is unending. I stand amazed at the work they accomplished.

But it has been my role to stay in touch with several new Christians, the formerly unchurched, to help us in this project. Before our team was ever assembled, I sought and received guidance from them to help shape our interview process.

During the research project, I would call some of these formerly unchurched to receive interpretation of our work to date. And as the project neared completion, I once again asked for their advice on some of the conclusions we were forming. This massive work would not have been the same without their tremendous help.

Nevertheless, I am concerned with more than a successful research project. At all phases of this work, my prayer has been to provide information to educate, inspire, and motivate Christians to reach out to lost men and women with whom they have contact. I hope that by this point you see that the unchurched are not always the profane, antagonistic people portrayed by stereotypes. They are the unchurched next door. They are your friends, family members, coworkers, and even casual acquaintances. And many of them are waiting for someone like you to share Christ with them.

Yet today it takes eighty-five church members a year to reach one person for Christ. Obviously, we in the American church are doing a poor job of reaching the unchurched next door. Thus far in this book we have attempted to show what God has used to reach lost men and women for Christ. Now we ask, "Why is the American church so unsuccessful in reaching the unchurched next door?" In the next chapter we will see ten reasons why we are not reaching them today.

## Chapter 9

# Ten Reasons We Have Not Reached the Unchurched

You're the first person who has ever asked me anything about God or Jesus.

*—Franklin B.,*
*U2 from Louisiana*

About two decades ago, I began a quest to gain a better understanding of the church. My interest was in the institutional church, but it was far more than that. I was interested in the people who are God's church. The field with which people identified me was called church growth, but my interest was more than church growth.

I am often amused when I hear myself identified as an expert in any area. If I am a perceived expert, it is because I have had the wonderful opportunity to listen to thousands of people over the past decade. They are the experts; I am little more than an interested reporter.

The information you are about to read is based largely on this particular research project, listening to the unchurched next door. But I also incorporate other research I have done over the past several years. After

the unchurched next door

nearly twenty years of researching, writing, and consulting, not to mention serving as pastor and interim pastor in a dozen churches, I have let the experts to whom I have listened help me shape several conclusions.

Please understand that, by the nature of this chapter, you are about to hear some negative assessments. We already know that American Christians are not effective in reaching their lost and unchurched friends and neighbors. We already know that it takes eighty-five church members in the United States a year to reach one person for Christ. Now we seek to find out why.

Though the information you are about to read is dismal, my ultimate assessment is not that pessimistic. I believe in the God of miracles. If my conclusions focused on human ability and goodness, I would have little hope. But my conclusions presume that the God of creation is on his throne. You will see more of that perspective in the concluding chapter.

For now let us focus on what is wrong. Let us look with stark honesty and candor at the ineffectiveness of most American believers when it comes to sharing their faith. And then let us, in God's power, reverse the dismal trend.

## Reason #1: Spiritual Lethargy

I was twenty-five years old before I ever witnessed to anyone. Jim had been on my mind for months. He had started attending church after his divorce, and it had become painfully evident to me that Jim was not a Christian.

I was a young banker seeking the fast track for my career. But God was getting my attention in a number of ways. Jim started visiting the church where I was a member, and then he started visiting my Sunday school class. And when I would return to my home after a Sunday at church, I could not get Jim off my mind.

This period in my life was one in which I was experiencing spiritual growth more rapidly than any other time. God was convicting me of a weak prayer life, showing me that I should give at least a tithe of my income to the church, and causing me to have an incredibly deep desire to learn his Word. And he was showing me that if I did not share my faith with others, I was nothing less than disobedient. That is when Jim started coming to mind. I knew what I had to do.

The problem was that I was unsure of how to witness. Nevertheless, I called Jim and asked him if I could visit him at home. He welcomed me gladly.

To this day, though it has been nearly a quarter of a century, I still remember the fear I had as I drove to his house. With sweaty palms and a racing heartbeat, I knocked on his door. At this point the only miracle I was seeking was for Jim not to come to the door. But he did.

Jim offered me a chair, but I could not sit down. I paced, tried to begin a conversation, and then paced again. Finally, Jim exclaimed, "Thom, what is the matter with you?" I froze. I stared right at my friend. And in an act of desperation, I cried out, "Jim, you don't want to go to hell do you?" *Oh great,* I thought. *I have really made an idiot of myself this time.*

But Jim looked at me with tear-filled eyes and whispered slowly, "No, I don't. Can you help me?" The next few moments were a blur. I shared the gospel, and Jim was ready. He received Christ as his Savior, and I went home that early evening as if I were floating on a cloud.

As I look back on those days, I realize that God was leading me to greater spiritual growth, the process we call sanctification. And part of that growth included becoming a regular witness for him. How can we expect to grow spiritually when we do not obey his direct command to make disciples (Matt. 28:19) and to be his witnesses (Acts 1:8)?

> Lack of spiritual growth inevitably leads to a diminished desire to share Christ with others.

One of the main reasons many Christians do not share their faith is simply explained by the word *disobedience.* Spiritual lethargy takes place when we fail to obey him. The problem for many Christians is that they are not growing spiritually, and lack of spiritual growth inevitably leads to a diminished desire to share Christ with others.

One of the joys of being involved in this and other research is hearing from new Christians who understand that they are believers today because God used the faithfulness of other Christians who witnessed to them. "Lance never gave up on me," Jonah Y., a formerly unchurched person from North Carolina, told us. "He kept showing Christ's love to me and telling me how Christ could give me hope. Now that I'm a Christian, I can see how witnessing is a part of his total obedience to the Lord. I plan to do likewise."

Many of the formerly unchurched understood clearly that if someone had not witnessed to them, they would not have heard the gospel. "It's simply a matter of obedience," Jonah concluded. In the battles of spiritual warfare, Satan is the victor when we remain silent in our witness.

## Reason #2: Growing Inclusivism

Please allow me a brief excursion to provide a theology lecture. My purpose is not to communicate this information as a mere learning exercise, but to issue some very serious warnings to believers.

Many years ago there was a growing belief in the false doctrine of *universalism*, which holds that all are saved; everyone will go to heaven. This doctrine waned in popularity in the post–World War II years, when the atrocities of Hitler and the Nazis became apparent. Very few wanted to believe that such evil people could actually go to heaven. Then universalism gained a slight momentum in America until September 11, 2001. But once again the evil actions of the terrorists left few believing that heaven is a place for everyone.

One of the faster-growing beliefs is *pluralism*, which holds that all religions lead to God and heaven for those who are faithful to their religious beliefs. The contemporary culture of America largely embraces this belief.

A variation of pluralism called *inclusivism* is a dangerous doctrine that is gaining momentum in many American seminaries, Christian colleges, and churches. This view affirms that Jesus is the only way of salvation but that he can be found in other "good" religions. This perspective sometimes views salvation through an "anonymous Christ." Explicit faith in Christ is not necessary. Jesus may save you without your knowledge of his work in your life.

I saw a practical example of this belief when I was consulting with a church in Georgia. One of the reasons for the consultation was the lack of growth in the church. I quickly saw that conversion growth in this church was almost nonexistent.

During my consultation, I visited a men's Sunday school class. The hot topic during the class was the recent death of one of the most prominent businessmen in the community. He was a moral beacon and the best example of ethics and integrity. He was also a Mormon.

The planned Sunday school lesson was quickly abandoned as a lively discussion ensued over the deceased man's eternal destiny. Now understand that the men in this class were not biblical neophytes. Indeed, I was impressed with their knowledge of Scripture. They therefore could not ignore such passages as John 14:6, where Jesus himself claims to be the only way of salvation.

The discussion was pleasant but intense. The men were trying to reconcile the exclusive claims of Christ with their knowledge that this man did not place his faith in the Christ of the Bible. They also mentioned on many occasions the moral standards of the man, the integrity of his business practices, and his many contributions to worthy causes.

Finally, the de facto leader of this class spoke. His words, as I best recall them, were as follows. "Men, we just cannot pretend that the Bible teaches any way of salvation other than Jesus." All heads nodded affirmatively. "But we know that our God is a God of love and mercy, and there is no way he would let [man's name] go to hell. We simply have to believe that Jesus saved him and took care of him even if he didn't accept Jesus the way that we do."

In our consultations, my team and I often distribute congregational surveys to the members. Several of the questions asked are issues of belief, including the way or ways of salvation. We are increasingly seeing more and more church members, even in evangelical churches, declare that Christ saves people outside of explicit faith in him.

Do you see the danger? First, the belief in inclusivism goes completely against the teachings of Christ and Scripture. The Bible teaches *exclusivism,* the belief that explicit faith in Christ is the only way of salvation. Second, the urgency to share the gospel is lost. Why should one go to the trouble of sharing Christ when that person can be saved without placing explicit faith in Christ? Why waste your time?

There is a subtle but growing belief among many Christians that somehow these "good" people will make it to heaven outside Christ. The unchurched next door will not hear the gospel from us if that belief persists and grows.

## Reason #3: The Growing Disbelief in Hell

Another theological and biblical issue that diminishes the urgency of evangelism is the denial of the reality of a literal hell. Again our congregational surveys show that more and more evangelical Christians are denying the existence of hell. The good news of Jesus Christ is that he saves sinners from an eternity in hell so that they might enjoy his eternal presence in heaven.

> Another theological and biblical issue that diminishes the urgency of evangelism is the denial of the reality of a literal hell.

An increasing number of Christians hold to a belief that those who do not place their faith in Christ will simply cease to exist at death — a view called annihilationism. For them, hell as taught in the Scriptures does not exist. Those who truly desire to reach the unchurched next door have a burden to see people in the eternity of heaven, but they also desire to see them escape the wrath of an eternal hell.

## Reason #4: Busyness

In our previous research on the formerly unchurched, we asked pastors of churches that were reaching the unchurched to keep a log of their time spent during a 168-hour week. In the span of one week, these pastors spent five hours sharing their faith with the un-churched. Another group of pas-tors, whose churches were not reaching the unchurched, spent zero hours sharing their faith.

Some Christians are too busy to share their faith.

The pastors of the latter group were not bad people involved in bad activities. To the contrary, every one of their activities was admirable: pastoral care, administra-tive duties, family time, counseling, and so on. But the pastors were so busy doing that which is good they failed to do that which is urgent.

I would assume that any reader of this book loves Christ and his church. I further would assume that most of the readers are very involved in their churches and communities and with their families. But often the good can replace the best. We can get so busy doing good things that sharing the greatest news ever can become sec-ondary or even nonexistent in our busy schedules.

Perhaps one of Satan's most effective strategies is to get us so busy that we fail to do that which is such a high biblical priority. We can be deluded into complacency about the lostness of humanity around us. The unchurched next door are waiting for you to tell them about Jesus. They need to be on your to-do list. What priority do you give to reaching the lost and unchurched?

## Reason #5: Fear of Rejection

Our research team interviewed a wide variety of unchurched per-sons, and some of our interviewers encountered some pretty hostile people. One was Leonard K. of Kansas. Leonard is definitely a U5 by our assessment — not only resistant to the gospel, but also antago-nistic in his attitude. We would learn later that Leonard did not want to participate in this interview, but a friend of a friend convinced him to help us. Profanity laced much of his conversation, but we will spare you that verbiage.

Leonard fits the stereotype that many people have of the unchurched. He had a seemingly very negative experience at church as a child. His mother was asked to leave the church after his father divorced her. "Those stupid so-called Christians practically threw my mom out of the church when she needed help the most. I swore I'd never go back to church, and I never have."

Leonard then began a verbal assault. "This Christian _____ is for losers. You are a loser too. You're trying to find ways to get people like me in the church, but the church is the worst thing for anyone. You should be minding your own businesses and leaving me alone."

Somehow we got to most of the questions on the interview form. The one that really seemed to make his blood boil asked, "What do you believe about Jesus Christ?" Leonard did not hesitate in his response: "I can't believe anybody believes that myth. It's easier to believe in the Easter bunny and Santa Claus together than believing the myth of Jesus.

"Look at the world around you. Look at the violence and the hate. Look what happened on 9-11. Look at the wars and the poverty. Look at this mess we're in. If Jesus was who some people think he is, he seems to have screwed up royally. He sure couldn't get things right here on earth. What a bunch of garbage."

Any attempt to thank Leonard for his time was an exercise in futility. "Look, I was just doing a friend a favor. I think you people and your beliefs are the main problems we have in this world. If people would just stop leaning on their religious crutch and try to solve life's problems themselves, the world would be a much better place. Look, I wish you would just stop wasting my time. I got a lot better things to do than just to speak to some religious nut."

Wow! Have a good day, Leonard.

Needless to say, that unchurched person did not embrace Christians and the beliefs we cherish. Indeed, the typical Christian in America would have taken this experience as a personal rejection and hesitated ever to witness again. Unfortunately, many Christians view such an encounter with the unchurched as normative and thus avoid such people because of the fear of rejection.

Two responses are in order. First, we must not receive the unchurched person's rejection of Christ as a personal rejection. Second, we must realize that very few unchurched people in America are antagonistic toward Christians. Let us review the Rainer scale again, with our estimated percentages of unchurched people for each category:

## Table 9.1

| | | |
|---|---|---|
| **U5** | Resistant and antagonistic | 5% |
| **U4** | Resistant | 21% |
| **U3** | Neutral | 36% |
| **U2** | Receptive | 27% |
| **U1** | Highly receptive | 11% |

Leonard clearly fits in the U5 category, the most resistant and antagonistic group toward the gospel and Christians. But the U5s account for only 5 percent of the total unchurched in America. For every one hundred unchurched with whom you share the gospel, only about five will express an antagonistic attitude.

But nearly four out of ten of the unchurched will be receptive to your concern for their eternity. And more than one out of three will simply be neutral to your attempts. Simply stated, fear of rejection is unfounded. The few with an antagonistic attitude are not rejecting you personally; their anger is merely a reflection of something in their past. And the overwhelming majority of the unchurched will never express the antagonism of the U5s.

> But the U5s account for only 5 percent of the total unchurched in America. For every one hundred unchurched with whom you share the gospel, only about five will express an antagonistic attitude.

Fear of rejection is an often-used excuse by Christians for their failure to witness, And it is just that: an excuse.

## Reason #6: A Desire to Be Tolerant

According to contemporary society and culture, intolerance is a great sin. And Christians, culture informs us, are especially intolerant, because their moral values say that some choices and some lifestyles are wrong. But the really intolerant Christian, we are told, is the one who insists that his or her way is the only way.

The message of the gospel, in some senses, is intolerant. It says that there is but one way of salvation. It says that only one select group of people will go to heaven. It says that this way is the only way, with no room for compromise.

The first of the Ten Commandments is intolerant. The one true God insists that there can be no other gods. He is a jealous God, and he leaves no room for other gods.

While most Christians will nod in affirmation at these statements, many followers of Christ find themselves in awkward positions in a culture that has determined that no absolutes exist. To defend exclusivity, or the one way of salvation, is deemed by many unchurched people to be the epitome of intolerance.

We have many records of interviews in which unchurched persons mentioned that intolerance of other religions is just not acceptable to them. And these interviews were in no way limited to the ravings of the U5s, such as those you just read from our friend Leonard.

Jackie P., for example, a U2 from Florida, was very cordial throughout the interview. She even expressed her appreciation to us for taking the time to talk to her, because she had "been thinking about spiritual matters lately." But at one point during the conversation, Jackie expressed her concern "about some fanatical Christians." For Jackie, a fanatic is a Christian "who insists that his beliefs are the only true beliefs. I mean, how intolerant can someone be, to think that they have a corner on truth?"

When confronted with the exclusive claims of Christ in such passages as John 14:6, Jackie hardly acknowledged the words of Jesus. Instead, she decided what Jesus is like. "Oh, Jesus is the last person who would suggest that other religions are bad, that they are not true. He was such a loving and open-minded person. I am sure that if he were walking on earth today, he would say Christianity is true, Judaism is true, Islam is true, and Buddhism is true. He certainly would not reject them as false religions, as some fanatics do."

In the postmodern culture of twenty-first-century America, Christians may as well accept that the criticisms of intolerance will continue. The greater concern is that many Christians are unwilling to take a narrow view because they do not want to be regarded as intolerant. But Jesus never wavered in his insistence that he is the only way. We simply cannot cave in to the demands of culture.

## Reason #7: Losing the Habit of Witnessing

Some Christians have been very active in sharing their faith with the lost and the unchurched. But, for myriad reasons, they get out of the habit, and it no longer becomes a priority. Witnessing, like prayer and Bible study, is a discipline.

> In the postmodern culture of twenty-first-century America, Christians may as well accept that the criticisms of intolerance will continue. The greater concern is that many Christians are unwilling to take a narrow view because they do not want to be regarded as intolerant.

As I write this chapter, my youngest son, Jess, is finishing his final year of high school football. His dad can proudly claim that Jess is the number one head-hunter on the team with over 120 tackles for the season. It has been a remarkable season for Jess's team. The football program at his school is only five years old, but the team has made it to the state playoffs for the past three years. This year they have progressed further than ever. They are in the quarterfinals. If they win the next two games, they will be in the finals for the state championship in Kentucky.

Rarely have I seen a team at this level with such incredible discipline. The players are faithful to their conditioning program. They work diligently to learn new plays each week. They discipline themselves with a weight program during the off season. And they spend hours viewing the tapes of their previous games and those of upcoming opponents. Such discipline seems rare in the high school athletic world. But a similar discipline for witnessing seems rarer in the Christian world. Witnessing is a habit to learn, to retain and, if lost, to regain.

## Reason #8: Lack of Accountability

I wish I were so obedient to God in all I do that I would need no level of accountability to anyone but him. Unfortunately, I cannot make that claim. In several aspects of my Christian walk, I need the gentle nudge of a Christian friend to keep my focus where it should be.

When I was a seminary student, I took a course in personal evangelism. In addition to exams and papers, we were required to share our faith every week and write a witnessing verbatim on our experience. If we failed to do so, we failed the course.

I grumbled at first, but this weekly accountability was a blessing to my life. Knowing that my professor would read my witnessing encounters each week, I made certain that I prayed for and sought opportunities. Never did a week go by that I did not have the opportunity to present the gospel to a lost and unchurched person.

On one occasion I went to downtown Louisville to witness to the downtrodden on the city streets. Immediately after I parked the car, three men started walking toward me with obvious ill intentions. While I debated running from them, one of the men saw that I had a Bible in my hand. He spoke to the other two men and said, "Don't touch this guy. He's a holy man." I then had the opportunity to share Christ with the three men.

In those days of seminary training, and in my years of research that would follow, I learned two important lessons. First, God typically honors our prayers for opportunities to witness. In fact, I cannot recall a time when I have asked for the chance to talk to a lost and unchurched person that God has not responded pretty quickly.

Second, I have also seen the power of accountability in sharing our faith. The academic exercise of submitting a witnessing verbatim each week kept the evangelistic priority at the forefront in my life. Some of the most effective evangelistic encounters of recent years have taken place when I met weekly with Dr. Ted Cabal, a faculty colleague at Southern Seminary. Each week we would take a few minutes to "report" to each other our witnessing experiences of the previous week.

Programmatic evangelism in local churches is sometimes denigrated because it is a "canned" approach to witnessing. But one of the strengths of many of these programs is that some inherent system of accountability is built into the program itself. Accountability is likely to engender more witnessing attempts to the unchurched. Attempting more evangelistic encounters creates a habit of witnessing that then increases our zeal for evangelism.

If you have found yourself evangelistically apathetic lately, you may do well to find someone to whom you can be accountable each week. It will not be long before the evangelistic fires will be burning again.

## Reason #9: Failure to Invite

If you thought you would hear no more about inviting the unchurched to church, you were wrong. The reality we have found in our research is that very few Christians invite the unchurched to church. A few will invite Christians looking for a church home to their churches. But most will invite no one at all. And only a minuscule minority will actually invite the unchurched.

Angela S. of California is a formerly unchurched person who accepted Christ seven months prior to our interview. Her story is indicative of the sentiments of many of the unchurched.

"I remember that I would go to bed on Saturday nights with the intention of waking up the next morning and going to church," the thirty-one-year-old woman told us. "I have never been married and have no one to be accountable to, but I thought I could surely get up and go to church on my own. After all, no one has to make me go to work during the week."

Sunday morning would come and the alarm would sound. Angela, however, would go back to sleep. "I just couldn't get up the willpower to go. It was worse than trying to stay on a diet."

But Angela was on a quest to discover meaning in her life. There were no major crises; it just seemed like life was less and less fulfilling. She had broken up with three boyfriends in the past five years. The job was financial security but offered no true fulfillment. And the days of going partying with her friends were old and boring.

Angela had warm childhood memories of attending church. "My parents did not take me to church much, but I always felt a warmth when I went. Some of my best childhood memories are the days I spent in vacation Bible school." Still she would not get up on Sundays to go to church.

"There is the one person at work," Angela said. "Everyone knows she is a Christian. She doesn't wear it on her sleeve, but she talks about her church and carries a Bible. And you could just tell that she is different from most of the people in my department."

Angela began to spend time with this Christian coworker, Vickie. "I was really hoping that she would invite me to church. I knew she had a family, but I still wanted to go to her church. I tell you, I hinted on several occasions about that, but she never picked up on the hint."

One day while Angela and Vickie were in a conversation, another coworker named Darlene joined them. As Darlene listened to Angela's questions, she spoke bluntly to Vickie. "Hey, Vickie, it sounds like Angela needs to visit your church. Have you ever invited her?"

Angela saw an immediate change in Vickie's facial expression. "I don't know if she was embarrassed or just suddenly became aware of the obvious, but she recovered quickly." "I, uh, no I haven't invited Angela to church," Vickie confessed. "I really have been negligent in that." She looked at Angela with total sincerity. "Angela, please forgive me. Would you consider coming to my church?"

Angela did not hesitate to respond. "Look Vickie, I know you have a husband and two kids who go to church with you each week, so I don't want to crowd in on your family. I would appreciate it if you would meet me at the church so I could know where to go."

The next Sunday Angela attended Vickie's nondenominational church. She had to get up that Sunday morning because someone was expecting her. And she no longer had the dread of trying to find her way in a building that intimidated her.

Five months later Angela accepted Christ and was baptized in the church. "Vickie and I are even closer friends today," Angela commented. "And we both learned an important lesson in this path I've taken to become a Christian. Sometimes there are people like me just waiting for an invitation to church. You've really got nothing to lose and a whole lot to gain."

Angela continued. "You know, Vickie was the most committed Christian I knew. But even she didn't invite me until Darlene opened her big and blessed mouth," Angela laughed. "I've got a lot to learn about what it means to follow Christ," she said. "But one thing I am doing already. I am inviting friends to go to church with me. Three other women are already coming to church since I invited them. It's really cool."

When is the last time you invited an unchurched person to church? When is the last time you offered to take a person to church or, at the very least, meet him or her at church? It is a simple gesture, yet so few Christians do it. People like Angela, however, know its eternal value.

## Reason #10: We Go to Churches That Do Not Reach the Unchurched

We reach only one person for Christ each year for every eighty-five church members in the United States. That is a frightening and terrible ratio. One of the key reasons we do not reach the unchurched is that most Christians in America are members of churches that do not reach the unchurched.

A well-intending Christian can be very active in his or her church and never be challenged to reach the lost. That church member could be at church every time the door opened and still not become involved in outreach to the unchurched.

> One of the key reasons we do not reach the unchurched is that most Christians in America are members of churches that do not reach the unchurched.

In my research for *Surprising Insights from the Unchurched,* I focused largely on the church's role in reaching the lost. I shared in the entire second half of the book the vital role of leadership in moving churches to a more evangelistic posture. But you may not be a pastor. You may not serve on the staff of a church. You may have picked up this book because you wanted to be more effective in reaching the unchurched yourself. You find yourself in a church that is busy with many activities but none that are specifically focused on reaching the lost and the unchurched. What do you do?

First, you need to realize that your pastor or minister is pulled in numerous directions. Most churches expect the pastor to prepare sermons, counsel the hurting, visit the sick and homebound, attend committee meetings, administer the church, resolve conflicts, perform weddings, bury the dead, stay in touch with the members, write the newsletter, cast the vision, prepare Bible studies, and maybe even take out the trash. And that is just a partial list.

Is it any wonder that pastors find themselves with little time for evangelism and outreach to the unchurched? The to-do list is just too long, and one of the most important ministries is neglected.

But you can pray for and encourage your pastor. And you can become a quiet but steady influence to elevate the biblical role of the pastor. Acts 6:4 clearly states that the role of the church leader is first prayer and ministry of the Word. The ministry to the widows in Acts 6 was assumed by others.

Become an advocate for the unleashing of the laity to do the work of ministry. Work positively to encourage church members that the bulk of ministry is theirs and not the sole domain of "hired hands." Deflect criticism aimed at the pastor when someone suggests that ministry is not being done. Help church members to see that pastors cannot be omnicompetent, omnipresent, and omniscient.

Second, be personally evangelistic even when your church is not. Be intentional about sharing your faith. Find someone to whom you can be accountable in your witnessing. Invite your friends, coworkers, relatives, and neighbors to church.

I have seen a few churches where one member with zeal to reach the lost and the unchurched has changed the direction of the entire church. Real evangelism is contagious. You can be the difference-maker God uses in your church.

From a statistical perspective, you are likely to be in a church that is not very effective in evangelism. But that cannot be an excuse for your failure to reach out to the lost and the unchurched. The person to whom you are ultimately accountable is God himself. Is he pleased with your obedience in sharing the good news of Christ to those around you?

> I have seen a few churches where one member with zeal to reach the lost and the unchurched has changed the direction of the entire church.

## Reasons but Not Excuses

You have just read ten of the more common reasons Christians fail to obey the Great Commission. The list is not exhaustive, but it is fairly thorough. In God's power, however, there should be no reason why we do not reach the unchurched. The ten items you have heard are thus reasons but not excuses.

In the final chapter we will see what can be done to reach the lost and unchurched in America. Specifically, we will see how we can reach them at each of their faith stages.

The evangelistic state of the American church is weak but not hopeless. We can see millions reached for Christ, but it will not be in our strength nor our power, but by the Spirit of God Almighty (Zech. 4:6). To that hope we now turn.

Let me remind you again why this issue is one of redundant importance. Simply stated, most of the unchurched will come to church if they are invited. Look again at the Rainer scale to see the unchurched who said they would come if invited.

### Table 9.2

|  | Very Likely | Somewhat Likely | Total |
|---|---|---|---|
| **U5** | 0% | 20% | 20% |
| **U4** | 17% | 45% | 62% |
| **U3** | 23% | 63% | 86% |
| **U2** | 46% | 51% | 97% |
| **U1** | 52% | 45% | 97% |

As the unchurched person moves to a higher level of receptivity, he or she is more likely to attend church if invited. While only one in five U5s indicate they will attend church if invited, a majority of the other unchurched groups will come. More than eight out of ten of all the unchurched said they would come if invited by a Christian.

> More than eight out of ten of all the unchurched said they would come if invited by a Christian.

But remember, most of the unchurched indicated in our interviews that they were uncomfortable entering a church building by themselves. They were much more likely to attend if someone walked with them into the building.

## Chapter 10

# Reaching the Unchurched at Their Faith Stages

---

Where was the church when I needed it?

*—Malcolm J.,*
*U4 from Hawaii*

---

Now that we have studied the data on the unchurched, it is time to suggest a course of action based on the plethora of information we have gathered from the experts themselves — the unchurched and the formerly unchurched. This data is neither comprehensive nor infallible, but I pray that God will use it in your life.

### Some Preliminary Comments

Before we look at specific strategies for reaching the unchurched at their faith stages, allow me to make some preliminary comments. First, please do not view the strategies in this chapter as human-centered. I provide them with the firm biblical conviction that a sovereign God sits on his throne, and he does not need human intervention to accomplish his will. That he uses us at all is but a measure of his grace.

Second, by now you should be clear that this research would never suggest that methodologies and programs replace the simple sharing of the gospel. Every person at every faith stage needs to hear the gospel.

Third, this book may have understated the power of prayer in reaching the lost and unchurched world. If so, I would like to make that adjustment now. One of my life verses of Scripture is Acts 4:31: "*And when they had prayed,* the place where they had gathered together was shaken, and they were all filled with the Holy Spirit and began to speak the word of God with boldness" (NASB, emphasis added). I have presumed throughout this book that you are praying for lost people by name and for opportunities to share your faith.

Finally, I want to remind you that the Rainer scale is a visual tool to depict various levels of receptivity to the gospel. Appendix A is a reproducible inventory for guiding Christians to understand better the faith stages of an unchurched person. Keep in mind that our research and the inventory are fallible tools. Just because we have indicated that someone is, for example, a U5 does not mean that the person cannot be reached with the gospel. Do not give our research and tools more authority than they were intended to have.

Still, the faith-stage concept can help you understand better the unchurched next door — the men and women in your neighborhoods, offices, shopping malls, and even in your home. I pray that the following strategies will be used by you to be a more effective witness to persons at all faith stages.

## Strategies to Reach the U5s

U5s are the toughest group. They are not only resistant to the gospel, they are antagonistic toward Christians and our beliefs. Although they account for only 5 percent of the 160 million unchurched people in the United States, 8 million is no small number. What have we learned about reaching this group?

*They are often dealing with other difficult issues.* Marvin W. is a U5 from the Cleveland area. Like any of our U5 interviews, our time with Marvin was spent listening to a continuous verbiage of anger and profanity. But our interview also explained some of the anger.

"I lost my mom when I was twelve years old," Marvin said with a blend of anger and sorrow. "What kind of God would leave a twelve-year-old kid without a mom? And my dad is worthless, a big drunk. And you think you've got answers for someone like me?"

To compound Marvin's deep wounds over the loss of his mother, the church apparently dropped the ball as well. "This preacher comes over to our house right after Mom dies. He tells me that God took Mom for a reason and that I'd better just accept that and get on with my life." Now we cannot be certain about how accurate Marvin's recollection is, but obviously the wounds are deep.

Marvin is one of several U5s who has deep anger over both a tragedy in life and a negative experience with a church. When a Christian tries to talk to him, that believer is often the recipient of Marvin's anger and wrath.

If you are active in sharing your faith, you will encounter a person like Marvin about one in twenty times that you share your faith. You cannot take the anger personally. You must be sympathetic to the hurt that is present, but you cannot let that detour your attempts to share the gospel.

Chris G. is a fairly new Christian from Oregon. Chris told us he became a Christian even though "I was a U5 just five years ago. Ned just wouldn't give up on me. He kept telling me about Jesus even when I cussed him out. Now when I meet people like the U5s you describe, I remember how I was and I don't let their ravings bother me. I just tell them about Jesus every chance I get."

Some of the formerly unchurched told us about people praying for them and their anger. Sometimes the most powerful way to deal with U5s' anger is to pray for them and for the reasons behind their anger.

*Most U5s will admit that they have not found happiness.* One of the simplest witnessing approaches to U5s is simply to ask them if they are really happy. The U5s are the most affluent and the most educated among our unchurched groups. They likely will have attempted to find happiness in material goods, in prestige, in positions, and in other earthly venues. And most of the U5s will admit that these attempts at happiness have been in vain.

> One of the simplest witnessing approaches to U5s is simply to ask them if they are really happy.

Stan G., a U5 from Texas, admitted to our interviewer that his apparent status of wealth and power in his company has done little to give him joy. "I don't care much for you holy rollers," he told us. "Y'all have this holier-than-thou attitude. You've got my wife snookered, but you can't fool me."

But in a rare moment of vulnerability, Stan said, "I've got to admit that my wife seems pretty happy. And with all the things I've got, you'd expect me to be happy too. But this junk doesn't do anything for me. Sometimes I just wish what you religious nuts believed was true so there would be hope for people like me."

Stan voiced those words in the interview when our researcher spontaneously asked if he was happy. Perhaps such inquiries will be of value when you talk to the antagonistic U5s.

*U5s may become more receptive after they have spent significant time with a Christian.* One of the benefits we had of having the formerly unchurched help us with this research project was their experiences with Christians before they became believers. Rachel R., for example, a new Christian from Kentucky, told us that the single most significant instrument God used to bring her to Christ was Meredith.

Meredith is a neighbor of Rachel's, and "she stuck with me for four years," Rachel told us. We already knew of Rachel's difficult past, including abuse by her father when she was a child. And we knew Rachel's story about how her abusive father was a respected elder in the church in the eyes of the church members. Rachel had already told us how "she hated anything associated with the church for years."

"But when I met Meredith," Rachel said, "I knew she was different. I cringed when I found out that she was real active in her church.

She invited me a few times, but she never was condescending like I remember the people in church where I grew up."

Rachel's testimony focuses on the faithful persistence of Meredith. "I began to see in Meredith the Jesus I never saw in other Christians. I saw that not all Christians were hypocrites like the people in my childhood church. Eventually I knew that I wanted what Meredith had."

> A true witnessing encounter with a U5 could be a long-term project.

A true witnessing encounter with a U5 could be a long-term project. And the relationship is not always pleasant. But U5s need the gospel, and God uses people like you to make sacrificial investments of time and energy to reach them.

*Apologetics can be effective in reaching U5s.* These unchurched persons are the most likely to be atheists and agnostics. Many of them have many questions and doubts about religious matters.

If you can get past the anger and antagonism in the U5s, it is not unusual to find that they can be very engaging on some deep spiritual issues. One of the researchers reported on his encounter with Dan J., a U5 from Alabama. "I had to recall some of my classes in apologetics and theology to talk to this guy. Dan had some real good questions and actually seemed willing to have a conversation as long as I took him seriously. But I wouldn't advise an unprepared Christian talking to Dan. He's sharp and would eat alive anyone who did not know what and why they believed."

> This postmodern culture will increasingly scoff at anyone who suggests there are absolutes.

God exhorts us through the apostle Peter to "prepare your minds for action" (1 Peter 1:13 NASB). Though we do not have the data to determine trends, I suspect the U5 population of America is growing. This postmodern culture will increasingly scoff at anyone who suggests there are absolutes.

We must be prepared to converse with these unchurched persons. Though formal theological training may not be an option for you, you can spend more time in God's Word. You can read works on apologetics and learn better to defend the faith. I have earlier noted books by C. S. Lewis, Lee Strobel, and Josh McDowell. We must prepare our minds for action, because we can be sure that the enemy is doing all he can to oppose us.

## Strategies to Reach the U4s

I indicated earlier that the U4s are significantly different from the U5s. Look at the noticeable shift in attitudes between the two groups.

### Table 10.1

|  | U5 | U4 |
|---|---|---|
| The Bible is truthful | 0% | 10% |
| Heaven exists | 13% | 54% |
| Hell exists | 20% | 51% |
| Christ is the Son of God | 7% | 34% |
| Very or somewhat likely to attend church if invited | 20% | 62% |

You can expect a much less antagonistic group when you witness to a U4. That is not to suggest that they will not be resistant to the gospel; it just means that the U4s are not belligerent in their attitudes toward Christians and the church. How then can we reach this second most resistant unchurched group?

*Discuss eternal issues.* Note the shift in attitudes toward the existence of heaven and hell. Over half of the U4s believe there is life beyond this one. The U5s, to the contrary, typically think eternal life is a superstitious myth.

The research team found that the U4s were both concerned and curious about life after death. Wayne D. of Connecticut is a clear example of this fascination with eternity. When we asked him his beliefs about heaven, he began to ramble.

"I've had these moments, you know, where I will just be sitting down doing nothing, when all of the sudden I'm wondering what will happen to me when I die." Wayne paused for a moment and then admitted, "It's a scary thought. I can't believe that there is just this one way to heaven like you Christians do, but I do wonder if everybody's going there. No, that can't be either, because there are some really evil people who don't belong in heaven."

We could have given you the long version of Wayne's ramblings, but the shorter version makes the point. The moment we began talking about heaven, Wayne was ready to talk. And although he told us clearly that he rejected the claims of the gospel, we did have an attentive ear when eternal destiny was the topic of discussion.

It seems as if many of the unchurched in America are concerned about where they will spend eternity. Certainly that was the case with many of the U4s we interviewed. If you encounter someone who appears resistant to the gospel, try turning the conversation to topics of heaven and hell. You just might have a willing and curious listener.

> It seems as if many of the unchurched in America are concerned about where they will spend eternity.

*U4s need clarification on Jesus.* On the surface, the number of U4s who affirm the existence of Jesus is encouraging. Going just one level deeper, however, shows much confusion about who Jesus really is. The following are some of the responses we received when we asked U4s to tell us who Jesus is.

> "A prophet."
> "A great teacher."
> "Someone sent from God to teach us."
> "A leader who became a model for all to follow."
> "The founder of the Christian religion."
> "A religious martyr who had many followers."
> "A great leader who fought religious tradition."

While none of the responses is incorrect; each is woefully incomplete. The U4s either could not or would not grasp the divinity of Christ. The person who witnesses to a U4 must be prepared to share much about the nature of Christ. Because U4s do not totally reject

Scripture, they might be receptive to seeing the passages of the Bible that deal with Christ as the Son of God and as God himself.

*U4s struggle with the idea that Jesus is the only way of salvation.* This issue is difficult for U4s. "It's like God messed up when you say things like that," June P. of Arizona told us. "Here God is with this great plan to save all humanity, and you say that he only makes one way for everyone to be saved. He has these other religions at his disposal, and he says, 'Nope, don't need you. You either. All of you religions are a waste of time. I just need one.' That just doesn't make any sense. Can't you see how stupid that sounds?"

> They want to believe in Jesus to some extent, but they cannot accept his exclusive claims.

June articulated more illustratively what many, if not most, of the U4s felt. To them the concept of one way of salvation is not tolerant nor does it make common sense. They want to believe in Jesus to some extent, but they cannot accept his exclusive claims.

One of the realities that you as a faithful witness of the gospel will confront is the growing rejection of Christ as the only way of salvation. Indeed, some of the unchurched will attempt to make you feel intolerant and unloving for holding to this cardinal truth. But the biblical reality is that if we compromise on this doctrine, we compromise on the gospel itself. In fact, we violate the first of the Ten Commandments because we put other gods on the shelf with the one true God.

The U4s may push on this issue. Stand firm. You have truth and the Holy Spirit on your side.

*Invite them to church.* Six out of ten U4s indicated that they would go to church if invited. There are approximately 160 million unchurched people in the United States, and we estimate that 33 million of those are U4s. So if 62 percent will go to church if we invite them, we calculate that almost 21 million U4s would welcome an invitation to church. Even if only half of these U4s would actually come, the number is significant.

As we have shown throughout this research, an invitation to church is one of the most powerful evangelistic tools at our disposal. Yet very few Christians invite anyone to church. And even fewer invite unchurched persons to church. Perhaps one of the most significant findings of this study is that churches and Christians must become more strategic in inviting lost and unchurched people to church.

## Strategies to Reach the U3s

If one group caused our researchers more frustration than others, it would be the U3s. Even the belligerent U5s were not as frustrating. We at least knew where they stood. But the U3s often left us scratching our heads. Nevertheless, we did find some potential areas to direct you in your witnessing endeavors with the U3s. The first is directly related to the message of the gospel.

> Perhaps one of the most significant findings of this study is that churches and Christians must become more strategic in inviting lost and unchurched people to church.

*The U3s need clarity in understanding the gospel.* Every Christian should be able to articulate a simple and effective presentation of the gospel. Such is the case particularly with the U3s. They seem to have some level of receptivity to hearing about the way to heaven, yet they are confused about the basic facts of the gospel.

The strategic approach to this issue is simple. You must become competent and confident in sharing the gospel. The U3s seem ambivalent to Christians and the church, but they do seem to desire to learn more about the true way of salvation.

*Invite them to church ... again.* More than 57 million persons — 86 percent of the U3s — who are lost without Christ would likely come to church if you invited them. The difference between this group and the U4s is that the U3s are not resistant to the gospel. Yet they are not necessarily receptive to the gospel either. But if they respond to your invitation to come to church, they are more likely to hear and respond to the gospel than the U4s or U5s.

*The U3s are the first of the unchurched groups to see the church as relevant.* The U4s and U5s simply do not see the value of the church. As one U4 commented, "It's okay for some people if it makes them feel better." But U3s are not resistant to the gospel or to the relevancy of the church. They are the first of the unchurched groups to which an appeal to the benefits of your church may be productive.

> U3s are not resistant to the gospel or to the relevancy of the church. They are the first of the unchurched groups to which an appeal to the benefits of your church may be productive.

Pamela U., one of the formerly unchurched who helped us in this project, said, "I wasn't particularly seeking anything. I guess by the information you showed me I would have been a U3." Pamela continued, "My attitude toward Christians and the church was just pretty neutral. I grew up in a nonreligious home and had never given much thought to church things. When other kids in the neighborhood went to church, I played outside. I never really thought much about it."

Pamela did not become receptive to the gospel immediately. She became attracted to the church. "I have a first cousin who is like a sister to me. Stacy started telling me about this church she had joined. Again, I didn't make much of it because Stacy had been a Christian for several years.

"But then her kids kept telling my kids how much fun they were having at this church. They told them about all the activities and camps and trips they took. The next thing I know, my kids are begging me to take them to church."

Pamela decided to take her children to church. "How do you say no when your children want to go to church?" she asked. "Well, I thought this would be another motherly sacrifice on my part. You know, let the kids have fun while you wait. I was really surprised when I found that I enjoyed the church too. Of course I began hearing the gospel every week, and I started befriending Christians. It took over a year, but I eventually accepted Christ."

One way to reach this seemingly ambivalent group is to introduce them to a church that has programs and ministries that will excite them and meet their needs. Or, as in the case of Pamela, the church first attracted her children. The U3s are not antichurch. You may find a point of connection for them and their families.

*The reality of hell is a concern for the U3s.* Seven out of ten of the U3s believe in the existence of hell, and many of them have a biblical understanding of hell. Needless to say, those who have a biblical understanding of hell want to avoid going there.

Interestingly, while some of the U3s may seem ambivalent to the gospel, you can notice a decided change in their level of interest when the topic turns to hell. We do not suggest that you approach a U3 and immediately declare that he or she is going to hell. Your cries of warning may be taken as a profane derision. But if you have a conversation with someone who is apathetic in your attempts to witness, perhaps a change in the approach would engender interest. A question concerning the destination of those who are not going to heaven may start a whole new level of conversation.

We noticed this phenomenon taking place in many of our U3 interviews. A look of near boredom covered their faces until we asked, "Do heaven and hell exist?" The question asked for a "yes" or "no" response, but the U3s often would add their own unsolicited comments. And if we did not get further comments, their body language indicated some discomfort with the question.

"Yeah, I believe there's a hell," Sean J., a U3 from Seattle responded. We said nothing else, but Sean decided to add further comments. "I try not to think about it too much because I haven't quite figured out who goes there. Now I'm sure of some hellbound people. You know, like Hitler, mass murderers, that idiot Bin Laden. But some people may be on the bubble."

Understand that our interviewer was saying nothing in this dialogue-turned-monologue.

"I guess I'm a little concerned about folks on the bubble. Take me, for example. I'm a fairly moral guy. I don't hurt other people. I don't think I would be on the bubble. What do you think?"

We think Sean moved from a U3 to U2 before the interview was over. We pray that he will soon move all the way to the cross.

## Strategies to Reach the U2s

We estimate the U.S. population of U2s to be 43 million. Most U2s are receptive to the gospel and will become Christians within a year with consistent and loving witness. What then is hindering the U2s from becoming Christians, or at least from becoming U1s, those most receptive to the gospel? Answering that question leads to our strategy to reach this group.

*Many U2s struggle with a works understanding of salvation.* U2s are true seekers. They know something is missing from their lives. Many of them have become regular Bible readers. Others have begun praying daily. A significant number are doing whatever it takes to please God so they can go to heaven. They think that salvation is by works.

> U2s are true seekers. They know something is missing from their lives.

Here is yet another case of why you need to be prepared to present the gospel clearly and cogently. The U2s are seeking, but many have not heard the truth of the grace of our Lord Jesus Christ. Your simple but clear sharing of the gospel may be the key factor in their accepting Christ or, at the very least, becoming even more receptive to the gospel.

*Invite them to church.* Of the U2s, 97 percent said they would come to church if they were invited. Ninety-seven percent. Enough said.

*Get family members to show Christ to them.* One of the major discoveries of our previous research project was that family members are the most influential in moving a person to become a Christian. Among family members, wives reaching husbands was the most common relationship connection.

When you think of sharing your faith, do you think of sharing Christ with lost family members? Have you ever sought training or biblical insights on how to be the most effective witness to a member of your family?

Often when we think of the unchurched, we think of people "out there." But some of our best opportunities to share Christ may be a lot closer. The unchurched next door may be a family member in the same house.

*Invite them to a Bible study.* The U2s desire to know about Christ. They want to be invited to church. And they strongly desire to learn about the Bible. From our interviews with the unchurched, and from the guidance we have received from the formerly unchurched, we are convinced that U2s will go to a Bible study if you invite them. They are unlikely to go, however, unless someone like you takes them to the Bible study. Their fear of going alone has kept them away to this point.

The type of Bible study does not seem to be a factor with the U2s. They will eagerly attend a study in your home, go to a neutral location, or go to your Sunday school class with you.

One of the reasons Sunday school has declined in many churches is the failure of church members to invite and accompany the unchurched to a Sunday school class.

> The problem is not that Sunday school is not working; the problem is that most churches are not working Sunday school.

Historically Sunday school was a highly intentional evangelistic tool in the church. Now it is rare for church members to invite the lost and unchurched to Sunday school. The problem is not that Sunday school is not working; the problem is that most churches are not working Sunday school.

One of the simplest yet most effective strategies for reaching U2s is to respond to their desire to study the Bible. Take them to a Bible study or Sunday school class. Watch God do a work through his Word.

## Strategies to Reach the U1s

U1s are the most receptive to the gospel and are waiting for someone to share the gospel with them. In fact, many became Christians during our interviews. They represent more than 17 million people in the United States alone. The strategy to reach them is about as simple as a strategy can be.

*Tell them about Jesus.* When a U1 hears the gospel, a common response is: "Where have you been? You have the news I have been seeking." Why then are we not reaching these highly receptive persons? By now you can anticipate the answer: The typical American Christian churchgoer does not share his or her faith.

> When a U1 hears the gospel, a common response is: "Where have you been? You have the news I have been seeking."

The American church is in decline not because the culture is more pagan, worldly, or postmodern. While these may be accurate descriptions of twenty-first-century American culture, culture is not to blame. The evidence is clear if not overwhelming: The silence of Christians is our own downfall. We must share our faith. We cannot be silent. Millions are waiting to hear from us.

*Invite them to church.* In the unlikely event that a U1 does not respond to the gospel immediately, he or she will come to church. Ninety-seven percent of the U1s told us that themselves. We simply have no excuse. We must be obedient to a command given nearly two thousand years ago. Failure to share the Good News is not merely a ministry that has not been accomplished; it is nothing less than sinful disobedience.

## They Are the Unchurched Next Door

The book of Haggai, the only two-chapter book in the Bible, takes place in the years following the Babylonian exile of the Jews. When the Persians become the dominant power, they allow the Jews to return to their homeland of Jerusalem. The Jews have a mandate from God to rebuild the temple and are given resources by the benevolent Persians to do so. The foundation of the house of God is laid, but then the work comes to a halt.

Haggai is God's spokesman. Through him the Jews hear from God for the first time since the exile. God's words through the prophet are indicting: "'You look for much, but behold, it comes to little; when you bring it home, I blow it away. Why?' declares the LORD of hosts. 'Because of My house which lies desolate, while each of you runs to his own house'" (Hag. 1:9 NASB).

God's people had been commanded to build the temple. Instead, they chose to focus on their own comforts and desires. As a consequence God removed his blessings from the people.

We have been given the Great Commission to make disciples, to share the gospel, and to build God's house. But significant numbers of American Christians are not being obedient. For many reasons we remain still and silent. And none of those reasons is acceptable to God.

Two years ago I assembled a research team to do another project. The purpose behind the project was not to provide good experiences for my students and coworkers. Nor was the primary purpose to write a book. While I am grateful for those two benefits, neither was my purpose. Rather, my desire was to understand unchurched people as much as possible so that you and I could be more effective witnesses to them. I wanted you to hear directly from these men and women so we could understand them better.

You have heard throughout this book from the formerly unchurched. The insights and guidance of these new Christians have been invaluable in helping us understand more clearly the world they just left. I will use the words of Emily N., a new Christian who was one of our formerly unchurched, to conclude this book.

"Just a few months ago, I was not a Christian. I wasn't having a major crisis in my life and I wasn't particularly interested in finding a church to go to. But I did know that something was missing in my life. For all of my forty-three years, I guess, this emptiness was somehow always present.

"I didn't go to church growing up, so I didn't think much about going there to help me fill the hole in life. And for forty-three years no one ever mentioned church to me. Not until Celeste came along."

Celeste was an acquaintance Emily had met through their sons' basketball team. "Our boys' team had umpteen practices and games, so you really got to know the parents who were there pretty well. I found myself wanting to spend time with Celeste. We started becoming pretty good friends.

"I knew Celeste was different. In fact, I knew she had that peace that I didn't have. We had known each other for just three weeks when Celeste started telling me about her faith. She invited me to church. No, she came by my house and picked me up. Two months later I accepted Christ.

"You need to understand that I went from totally unchurched, no church background, no knowledge of church to becoming a Christian in just a matter of weeks."

One person made a difference. One person cared.

"What I'm still trying to figure out, with the millions of Christians in America, is how come it took forty-three years for someone to share about Christ with me? Where were all the other Christians?"

They are the unchurched next door. They are your friends, your neighbors, your classmates, your coworkers, your merchants, your acquaintances, and your family members. They need Christ. And they are waiting to hear from you.

# Appendix A:
# Faith Stages Inventory

This inventory is to be used by Christians who are attempting to share their faith with others. The Christian is to give his or her best guess to each of the following characteristics of the unchurched person. The inventory can then be used as a guide to learn more about a particular unchurched individual.

You may reproduce and distribute this survey freely.
(Circle the number corresponding to your answer.)

**The unchurched person I know ...**

| <u>Somewhat/Yes = 2</u> | <u>Don't Know = 1</u> | | <u>No = 0</u> | |
|---|---|---|---|---|
| 1. is willing to talk about religious matters. | 2 | 1 | 0 |
| 2. shows no anger at the church or Christians. | 2 | 1 | 0 |
| 3. asks sincere questions about the Bible. | 2 | 1 | 0 |
| 4. indicates a desire to go to church. | 2 | 1 | 0 |
| 5. has a positive attitude toward the church. | 2 | 1 | 0 |
| 6. seems concerned about where he/she will spend eternity. | 2 | 1 | 0 |
| 7. has a positive attitude about pastors. | 2 | 1 | 0 |
| 8. has visited a church in the past six months. | 2 | 1 | 0 |
| 9. recalls positive experiences with the church. | 2 | 1 | 0 |
| 10. has family members who are Christians. | 2 | 1 | 0 |
| 11. likes to attend special events at churches. | 2 | 1 | 0 |

12. prays at least once a week.                                2  1  0
13. reads the Bible at least once a week.                      2  1  0
14. is interested in attending a Bible study.                  2  1  0
15. has parents who attended church regularly.                 2  1  0
16. believes the Bible is totally true.                        2  1  0
17. believes that Jesus is the unique Son of God.              2  1  0
18. earns less than $100,000 per year.                         2  1  0
19. does not have a master's or doctoral degree.               2  1  0
20. is under 50 years old.                                     2  1  0

Now add all the numbers you circled. Put that total here: _____.

Now you can see where the number you derived places the person on the Rainer scale.

| U5 | Antagonistic, resistant | 0–9 |
|----|------------------------|------|
| U4 | Resistant | 10–18 |
| U3 | Neutral, noncommittal | 19–27 |
| U2 | Receptive | 28–34 |
| U1 | Highly receptive | 35–40 |

# Appendix B:
# Research Design and Statistical Review

A uthor's note: We asked Professor Jon Rainbow to assist in the
design of our survey instrument for this project and the previous
project published as *Surprising Insights from the Unchurched*. The
information below reflects his assessments of both projects.

## Methodology

This research design/project follows the criteria for qualitative
design. The assumptions regarding this design are closely related to the
structure and intent of the qualitative approach. This study is an excellent example of research assumptions that require a design that is concerned with process rather than outcomes or products. Thus, the
primary research interest is meaning and interpretation — how people
make sense out of their experiences.

This researcher uses primary instruments for data collection and
interpretation, and this researcher is more than adequately equipped to
function in that role, as these data are rich in descriptive analysis and
inductive interpretation. The design has three sources of comparative
data for clarification of the research assumptions. Also, the data are
accurately documented and interpreted within the best characteristics of
the qualitative approach. This study is representative of the qualitative
research guidelines found in R. C. Bogdan and S. K. Biklin, *Qualitative
Research for Educators: An Introduction to Theory and Methods*
(Boston: Allyn & Bacon, 1992); and C. Marshall and G. B. Rossman,
*Designing Qualitative Research* (Newburg Park, Calif.: Sage, 1989).

## Population and Sample

The parameters of the data collection are identified, and the purposeful sample is specified. The number of subjects more than adequately provides for the content accuracy of the results. The amount of data available for analysis gives confidence in the summary of the findings. Sample size is not critical for qualitative research design; however, the number of subjects used in this study is more than sufficient for the design requirements. The use of triangulation as data collection and a group comparison tactic improves the validity considerably (S. Mathison, "Why Triangulate?" *Educational Research* 17, 2 [1989]: 13–17).

## Survey Instrument

The rationale for this study justifies the survey method. The only alternative for extracting data is the survey interview approach. At the time of this research, no other research instrument existed. The comprehensive interview generated the data necessary to explore the research assumptions. The researcher describes carefully his survey process in hope that the next design for this topic can move to a combined qualitative and quantitative approach. Obviously, no cause-and-effect conclusions are inferred from this study. No generalization is attempted or implied (A. Fink, *How to Ask Survey Questions* [Thousand Oaks, Calif.: Sage, 1995]; R. Sapsford, *Survey Research* [Thousand Oaks, Calif.: Sage, 1999]).

## Statistics

The data collected from this type of study can only be interpreted with descriptive statistical analyses. Some researchers feel only inferential analyses are worth pursuing; contrary to that position, these descriptive results are rich with meaning and interpretation findings. These research assumptions can only be approached with the explanations rendered in this study. The foci of findings are accurately and thoroughly presented. The amount of material is exhaustive, and this researcher has selected the results and presented those that most directly relate to the reading audience. However, several additional paths of explanation remain to be explored from the data. Some researchers underrate the effective use of descriptive statistics, but study demonstrates this analysis at its best productivity. The main purpose of the analyses is to reduce the whole collection of data to simple and more understandable terms without distorting or losing too much of the valuable information collected. Dr. Rainer has done extremely well in this respect (H. M. Blalock Jr., *Social Statistics*, 2d ed. [New York: McGraw-Hill, 1979]).

## Reviewer's Note

The need for research in this area is critical, and those like Dr. Rainer who begin to explore topics such as the one in this study begin a process of discovery that will prove productive in future research. I lend my affirmation of the helpful work accomplished in this study.

*—Jon Rainbow*
*Research and Statistics*
*Consultant*

# Appendix C:
# Faith Stages Survey Instrument

This appendix contains the interview instrument used by the research team. The interviewers were instructed to ask all the questions on the instrument, but they also had the freedom to carry the conversation in other directions. We are able to tabulate data from the objective questions. Many of the subjective responses are included in the book.

Name: _____

Phone number: _____

State in which interviewee lives: _____

Sex:   ❏ Male   ❏ Female

1. How would you describe the city where you live?
   a. Open country/rural area
   b. Town (500–2,499 people)
   c. Small city (2,500–9,999 people)
   d. Medium city/downtown (10,000–49,999 people)
   e. Medium city/suburbs (10,000–49,999 people)
   f. Large city/downtown or inner city (50,000+ people)
   g. Large city/suburbs (50,000+ people)

2. To insure a diverse representation of backgrounds, would you identify your ethnic group?
   a. Anglo
   b. African American
   c. Hispanic
   d. Asian American
   e. Other

3. Do you mind sharing with us your age?
   a. Under 18
   b. 19–35
   c. 36–50
   d. 51–65
   e. 66+

4. What is your highest level of education?
   a. High school
   b. Some college
   c. Undergraduate degree
   d. Master's level studies or degree
   e. Doctoral level studies or degree

5. What is your annual income?
   a. Below $20,000
   b. $20,000–$49,999
   c. $50,000–$99,999
   d. Above $100,000

## Faith Stages Questions

1. What is your religious background, if any?

2. Would you describe your attitude toward the church as antagonistic, resistant, neutral, friendly, or very friendly?

3. How many times in a year (if any) do you attend a religious service?
   a. 1–2 times per year
   b. Fewer than 5 times per year
   c. I go for special activities/ministries
   d. Never go

4. Why do you think many people do not attend church today?

5. What, in your opinion, do churches need to do to attract more people?

6. What programs or ministries would you like to see a church offer?

7. What is your view of the typical Christian? (multiple choice)

   Committed? Hypocritical? Narrow-minded? Loving? Generous? Friendly? Snobby? Unapproachable? Open-minded? Preachy? Other?

8. Do you pray to God on a regular basis? How often? To you, who is God?

9. What source (if any) do you go to for spiritual guidance? Bible? Website? Self-help books? Other?

   How often?
   a. Once a day
   b. Once a week
   c. Once a month
   d. Once a year
   e. When I'm looking for special inspiration/help for a specific problem
   f. Never

10. Do you believe the Bible is truthful/applicable in all areas of life?
    a. Totally truthful/God's Word
    b. Truthful/applicable in some areas
    c. It is myth
    d. Don't know

11. What is your view of the typical pastor/preacher/minister?

12. If you decided to attend a church regularly, what would be your preferred day and time?
    a. Weekday — day
    b. Weekday (except Friday) — evening
    c. Friday — evening
    d. Saturday — day
    e. Saturday — evening
    f. Sunday — day
    g. Sunday — evening

13. Do heaven and hell exist?
    a. Heaven: _____ yes
    b. Heaven: _____ no
    c. Hell: _____ yes
    d. Hell: _____ no

14. If heaven exists, how do you believe someone gets there?

15. What do you believe about Jesus Christ?

16. What is your biggest "turnoff" by Christians?

17. What is your biggest "turnoff" by churches?

18. What is your view of the religious/spiritual climate in our nation?
    a. Tolerant of all religions
    b. Too much Christian influence
    c. Certain religions are favored
    d. Certain religions receive prejudice
    e. Never think about it

19. What do you think is the future of organized religion in America?

20. What person or persons has/have been the greatest influence in your life? What is their relationship to you?

21. Have any Christians been influential in your life? Who?

22. Has a Christian ever shared with you how to become a Christian? Who? What did they say?

23. If different from your answer to the previous question, what do you believe it takes to become a Christian?

24. Have you ever attended a concert or speaking event, or Easter or Christmas presentation in a church? What did you think of it? Did it affect you in any way?

25. Have you ever had a negative experience in a church or with a Christian? If so, what?

26. Have you ever had a positive experience in a church or with a Christian? If so, what?

27. Have you ever attended a Sunday school class or some other church small group?
    a. As a child only
    b. Occasionally throughout my life
    c. Never

28. If you have attended, who invited you?
    a. Family member
    b. Friend/acquaintance
    c. I went at my own initiative

29. If you attended church as a child, did you enjoy going?
    a. Yes
    b. No
    c. Sometimes

30. If a Christian friend or family member invited you to a church function now, how likely would you be to attend?
    a. Very likely
    b. Somewhat likely
    c. Not likely at all

31. Would you be uncomfortable in a traditional church building?
    a. Yes
    b. No

32. Do you think that most churches are corrupt and are only after your money?
    a. Yes
    b. No

33. What else would you like to share?

**Interviewer's Summary:**

# Appendix D
# Faith Stages Survey Responses

| Questions | U1 | U2 | U3 | U4 | U5 | Total |
|---|---|---|---|---|---|---|
| Interviewed: | | | | | | |
| | 11% | 27% | 36% | 21% | 5% | 100% |
| Demographic Info: | | | | | | |
| Male | 35% | 38% | 54% | 60% | 47% | 48% |
| Female | 65% | 62% | 46% | 40% | 53% | 52% |
| City: | | | | | | |
| Open country/rural | 10% | 5% | 7% | 7% | 7% | 7% |
| Town | 20% | 9% | 2% | 7% | 14% | 8% |
| Small City | 7% | 10% | 9% | 10% | 14% | 9% |
| Medium City/Downtown | 7% | 7% | 10% | 5% | 7% | 8% |
| Medium City/Suburbs | 10% | 20% | 18% | 12% | 7% | 16% |
| Large City/Downtown | 10% | 7% | 6% | 17% | 7% | 10% |
| Large City/Suburbs | 36% | 40% | 48% | 42% | 43% | 42% |
| Ethnic Group: | | | | | | |
| Anglo | 87% | 83% | 76% | 81% | 80% | 80% |
| African-American | 6% | 10% | 11% | 3% | 13% | 9% |
| Hispanic | 3% | 3% | 2% | 7% | | 3% |
| Asian American | | 4% | 2% | 2% | 7% | 2% |
| Other | 3% | | 8% | 7% | | 5% |
| Age: | | | | | | |
| Under 18 | | 3% | 2% | | 7% | 2% |
| 19–35 | 48% | 56% | 55% | 48% | 40% | 52% |
| 36–50 | 35% | 26% | 23% | 27% | 13% | 26% |
| 51–65 | 6% | 11% | 16% | 20% | 40% | 16% |
| 66+ | 10% | 4% | 4% | 5% | | 4% |

| Highest Education: | | | | | | |
|---|---|---|---|---|---|---|
| High School | 29% | 77% | 23% | 22% | 20% | 24% |
| Some College | 35% | 40% | 42% | 42% | 20% | 40% |
| Undergraduate Deg | 29% | 20% | 24% | 19% | 20% | 22% |
| Master's Studies/Deg | 6% | 13% | 9% | 8% | 13% | 10% |
| Doctoral Studies/Deg | | | 2% | 8% | 26% | 4% |
| Income: | | | | | | |
| Below $20,000 | 16% | 23% | 24% | 27% | 13% | 23% |
| $20,000–$49,999 | 55% | 52% | 42% | 42% | 33% | 45% |
| $50,000–$99,999 | 19% | 21% | 25% | 24% | 33% | 24% |
| Above $100,000 | 10% | 4% | 6% | 7% | 13% | 7% |
| No answer | | | 3% | | 7% | 1% |
| Faith Stages | | | | | | |
| Religion: | | | | | | |
| Catholic | 19% | 28% | 23% | 27% | 21% | 24% |
| Baptist | 42% | 27% | 26% | 25% | 36% | 29% |
| Other Evangelical | 35% | 35% | 29% | 28% | 13% | 31% |
| Sect/World Relgion | | 4% | 12% | 7% | | 7% |
| Don't Remembr/Know | 3% | 3% | 1% | 2% | 7% | 2% |
| None | | 3% | 9% | 10% | 21% | 7% |
| Attitude to church: | | | | | | |
| Antagonistic | | | 3% | 18% | 29% | 5% |
| Resistant | 6% | 8% | 11% | 18% | 29% | 11% |
| Neutral | 23% | 31% | 44% | 40% | 42% | 36% |
| Friendly | 45% | 51% | 35% | 22% | | 37% |
| Very Friendly | 26% | 10% | 7% | 2% | | 11% |
| Attending church: | | | | | | |
| 1–2 times per year | 29% | 25% | 24% | 31% | | 24% |
| Less than 5 times | 42% | 35% | 25% | 12% | 7% | 26% |
| Special activities/mins | 16% | 17% | 20% | 19% | 13% | 18% |
| Never | 10% | 18% | 27% | 35% | 80% | 27% |
| More | 3% | 5% | 4% | 3% | | 4% |

| Why people don't attd: | | | | | | |
|---|---|---|---|---|---|---|
| Lazy | 23% | 15% | 6% | 8% | 15% | 11% |
| Too busy | 42% | 32% | 38% | 29% | 8% | 34% |
| Not relevant | 3% | 10% | 14% | 19% | 31% | 13% |
| Hypocritical/holier than thou | 6% | 5% | 11% | 10% | 8% | 10% |
| Other | 26% | 37% | 30% | 34% | 38% | 32% |
| **Pray:** | | | | | | |
| Yes | 27/90% | 59/75% | 66/63% | 26/46% | 2/13% | 64% |
| No | 3/10% | 20/25% | 38/37% | 31/54% | 13/87% | 36% |
| Daily | 71% | 63% | 51% | 63% | 50% | 60% |
| Weekly | 11% | 13% | 13% | 3% | 50% | 12% |
| Monthly | 4% | 6% | 4% | 10% | | 5% |
| Other | 14% | 18% | 32% | 23% | | 23% |
| God: Creator | 43% | 32% | 26% | 16% | 50% | 27% |
| Lord/Savior | 7% | 3% | 5% | 4% | | 5% |
| Higher Being/Spirit | 18% | 22% | 33% | 30% | 25% | 37% |
| Father | 7% | 15% | 4% | 7% | | 8% |
| N/A or Other/Does not exist | 25% | 27% | 31% | 43% | 25% | 32% |
| **Source for Sp. Guid.:** | | | | | | |
| Bible | 36% | 36% | 28% | 10% | | 29% |
| Website | 7% | 3% | | | | 2% |
| Self-help books | 14% | 6% | 10% | 10% | 14% | 9% |
| Other | 43% | 55% | 62% | 80% | 86% | 60% |
| Of other, family/friend | 83% | 60% | 59% | 50% | 67% | 60% |
| | | | | | | |
| Daily | 15% | 14% | 8% | 17% | | 13% |
| Weekly | 12% | 15% | 9% | 9% | 17% | 12% |
| Monthly | 9% | 24% | 14% | 4% | 8% | 15% |
| Year | | 1% | 2% | 4% | 8% | 3% |
| Special Inspiration | 52% | 34% | 43% | 31% | 17% | 37% |
| Never | 12% | 12% | 21% | 35% | 50% | 20% |

| View of Bible: | | | | | | |
|---|---|---|---|---|---|---|
| Totally truthful/God's Word | 55% | 42% | 24% | 10% | | 30% |
| Truthful/applicable some areas | 33% | 41% | 55% | 51% | 40% | 46% |
| Myth | | 2% | 1% | 14% | 33% | 5% |
| Don't know | 12% | 15% | 20% | 25% | 26% | 19% |
| View of Typical Clergy: | | | | | | |
| Positive | 68% | 65% | 73% | 54% | 53% | 65% |
| Negative | 13% | 21% | 19% | 31% | 40% | 22% |
| No opinion/Don't know | 6% | 5% | 3% | 12% | 7% | 6% |
| Good and Bad | 13% | 9% | 5% | 3% | | 7% |
| Preferred Day/Time: | | | | | | |
| Weekday–Day | 3% | 7% | 5% | 3% | 7% | 5% |
| Weekday–Evening | 6% | 9% | 17% | 17% | 26% | 14% |
| Friday–Evening | | | | 2% | | 0.30% |
| Saturday-Day | | 4% | 5% | 3% | | 4% |
| Saturday–Evening | 16% | 4% | 8% | 7% | | 7% |
| Sunday–Day | 68% | 63% | 56% | 46% | 26% | 56% |
| Sunday–Evening | 6% | 13% | 8% | 8% | 7% | 9% |
| Other/Not going* | | | 1% | 13% | 33% | 4% |
| Heaven Exist? | | | | | | |
| Yes | 100% | 95% | 83% | 54% | 13% | 79% |
| No | | | 9% | 34% | 67% | 13% |
| Don't know/Other | | 5% | 8% | 12% | 20% | 7% |
| Hell Exist? | | | | | | |
| Yes | 94% | 82% | 70% | 51% | 20% | 70% |
| No | 6% | 6% | 21% | 41% | 67% | 21% |
| Don't know/Other | | 11% | 9% | 8% | 13% | 8% |
| In hell now (Yes/no also) | | 1% | 2% | 14% | 26% | 5% |
| To get to heaven: | | | | | | |
| Belief in Christ (ortho) | 48% | 38% | 17% | 19% | 7% | 29% |
| Good person/works | 29% | 46% | 66% | 37% | 13% | 46% |
| Other | 23% | 12% | 13% | 30% | 67% | 19% |
| Don't know | | 4% | 4% | 14% | 13% | 6% |

| Jesus Christ: | | | | | | |
|---|---|---|---|---|---|---|
| Son of God (orthodox) | 84% | 80% | 54% | 34% | 7% | 59% |
| Good person/teacher | 3% | 16% | 25% | 44% | 53% | 25% |
| Other/Don't know | 13% | 3% | 21% | 22% | 40% | 16% |
| **Turnoff by Christians:** | | | | | | |
| Hypocrisy | 35% | 33% | 27% | 22% | 13% | 29% |
| Think they're better | 23% | 15% | 14% | 15% | 26% | 16% |
| Pushy/Preachy | 16% | 11% | 24% | 15% | 20% | 17% |
| Other | 23% | 35% | 22% | 32% | 33% | 28% |
| None | 3% | 6% | 13% | 15% | 7% | 10% |
| **Turnoff by Churches:** | | | | | | |
| Irrelevance | 6% | 5% | 2% | | 7% | 3% |
| Boring | 3% | 9% | 7% | 5% | | 6% |
| Other | 68% | 66% | 64% | 73% | 80% | 68% |
| None/No opinion | 23% | 20% | 27% | 21% | 13% | 23% |
| **Religion climate today:** | | | | | | |
| Tolerant | 55% | 39% | 34% | 31% | 7% | 36% |
| Too much Xn influence | | 8% | 3% | 9% | 13% | 6% |
| Certain rel. favored | 32% | 21% | 28% | 27% | 33% | 26% |
| Certain rel. prejudice | 3% | 13% | 14% | 13% | 7% | 12% |
| Never think about it | 10% | 14% | 20% | 20% | 33% | 17% |
| Other | | 4% | 1% | | 7% | 2% |
| **Future of org. rel.:** | | | | | | |
| Get better | 35% | 44% | 30% | 32% | 13% | 34% |
| Decline | 26% | 14% | 27% | 22% | 47% | 23% |
| Stay the same | 23% | 28% | 29% | 31% | 26% | 28% |
| Don't know/No answer | 16% | 14% | 13% | 15% | 13% | 14% |
| **Person of Influence:** | | | | | | |
| Parent | 40% | 51% | 49% | 55% | 37% | 50% |
| Grandparent | 21% | 9% | 13% | 8% | 13% | 11% |
| Spouse | 5% | 5% | 6% | 8% | 6% | 6% |
| Friend | 5% | 6% | 7% | 8% | | 6% |
| Other family | 7% | 13% | 8% | 8% | 25% | 9% |
| Other | 22% | 14% | 17% | 12% | 13% | 15% |
| None/Don't know | 3% | 3% | | 1% | 6% | 1% |

| Christians influential: | | | | | | |
|---|---|---|---|---|---|---|
| Parent | 17% | 25% | 22% | 26% | 7% | 23% |
| Grandparent | 17% | 12% | 11% | 1% | 13% | 10% |
| Spouse | 3% | | 2% | 1% | | 2% |
| Friend | 14% | 9% | 13% | 19% | | 12% |
| Other family | 14% | 13% | 16% | 7% | | 12% |
| None | | 9% | 12% | 24% | 47% | 14% |
| Other | 34% | 32% | 24% | 21% | 33% | 27% |
| How to become a Xn: | | | | | | |
| Yes | 77% | 82% | 71% | 72% | 73% | 76% |
| No | 23% | 18% | 29% | 28% | 27% | 24% |
| Who: | | | | | | |
| Parent | | 9% | 8% | 4% | | 6% |
| Grandparent | 6% | 3% | | 4% | | 2% |
| Friend | 23% | 21% | 28% | 29% | 27% | 26% |
| Other family | 6% | 27% | 9% | 7% | | 11% |
| Other | 65% | 39% | 55% | 56% | 73% | 55% |
| Neg exp w/church/Xn | | | | | | |
| Yes | 61% | 68% | 64% | 61% | 69% | 64% |
| No | 39% | 32% | 36% | 39% | 31% | 36% |
| Pos exp w/church/Xn | | | | | | |
| Yes | 97% | 86% | 79% | 70% | 69% | 81% |
| No | 3% | 14% | 21% | 30% | 31% | 19% |
| Attended S.S./sm grp | | | | | | |
| As a child only | 58% | 60% | 69% | 59% | 57% | 62% |
| Occasionally | 39% | 38% | 22% | 20% | 29% | 29% |
| Never | 3% | 2% | 9% | 20% | 14% | 9% |
| Who invited you? | | | | | | |
| Family | 72% | 67% | 59% | 58% | 66% | 63% |
| Friend/Acquaintance | 24% | 17% | 19% | 12% | 7% | 17% |
| Own initiative | 3% | 8% | 9% | 8% | 7% | 8% |
| All of the above | | 8% | | | | 2% |
| No answer/Not applicable | | | 13% | 22% | 20% | 10% |

| As child, enjoy? | | | | | | |
|---|---|---|---|---|---|---|
| Yes | 61% | 54% | 48% | 33% | 33% | 48% |
| No | 19% | 15% | 18% | 22% | 33% | 19% |
| Sometimes | 19% | 30% | 30% | 34% | 33% | 30% |
| Not applicable | | | 3% | 10% | | 3% |
| If invited, attend? | | | | | | |
| Very likely | 52% | 46% | 23% | 17% | | 31% |
| Somewhat likely | 45% | 51% | 63% | 45% | 20% | 51% |
| Not likely at all | 3% | 3% | 14% | 38% | 80% | 18% |
| Uncomfortable in trad. building: | | | | | | |
| Yes | 10% | 20% | 10% | 25% | 53% | 18% |
| No | 90% | 80% | 90% | 75% | 47% | 82% |
| Churches corrupt: | | | | | | |
| Yes | 4% | 4% | 9% | 16% | 20% | 9% |
| No | 96% | 72% | 77% | 64% | 60% | 74% |
| Some* | | 24% | 14% | 20% | 20% | 17% |

*Option not offered during interview

# Notes

## Introduction: Why Justin Is Not Like Jane Is Not Like Jack

1. See James Engel and Hugo Wilbert Norton, *What's Gone Wrong with the Harvest? A Communication Strategy for the Church and World Evangelization* (Grand Rapids: Zondervan, 1975).
2. See D. James Kennedy and Tom Stebbins, *Evangelism Explosion: Equipping Churches for Friendship, Evangelism, Discipleship, and Healthy Growth,* 4th ed. (Wheaton, Ill.: Tyndale House, 1996).
3. See Thom S. Rainer, *The Bridger Generation* (Nashville: Broadman and Holman, 1997).
4. See Thom S. Rainer, *Surprising Insights from the Unchurched* (Grand Rapids: Zondervan, 2001).

## Chapter 1: The Unchurched Next Door

1. *Our Unitarian Universalist Faith: Frequently Asked Questions,* a pamphlet written by Alice Blair Wesley, explains the belief that Jesus was "a God-filled human being, not a supernatural being." Unitarians also assert that "among Unitarian Universalists, instead of salvation, you will hear of our yearning for and our experience of personal growth, increased wisdom, strength of character, and gifts of insight, understanding, inner and outer peace, courage, patience, and compassion." See this document online at *http://www.uua.org/aboutuu/uufaq.html*

## Chapter 3: "Religion Is Okay for the Weak-Minded"

1. Lee Strobel, *The Case for Christ: A Journalist's Personal Investigation of the Evidence for Jesus* (Grand Rapids: Zondervan, 1998), and *The Case for Faith: A Journalist Investigates the Toughest Objections to Christianity* (Grand Rapids: Zondervan, 2000).

# Name and Subject Index

We want to hear from you. Please send your comments about this book to us in care of zreview@zondervan.com. Thank you.

GRAND RAPIDS, MICHIGAN 49530 USA

WWW.ZONDERVAN.COM